Jeff,
Thanks for your friendship
and contribution to the FGBC.
Todd Scoles

Restoring the Household:

The Quest of the Grace Brethren Church

Todd S. Scoles

D1452073

BMH Books
Winona Lake, Indiana
www.bmhbooks.com

Restoring the Household:
   The Quest of the Grace Brethren Church

Copyright © 2008 by Todd Scoles

Published by BMH Books
P.O. Box 544, Winona Lake, IN 46590 USA
www.bmhbooks.com

ISBN 978-0-88469-092-4
RELIGION / Christian Church / History

Unless otherwise noted, Scripture references are taken from the New American Standard Bible®, Copyright © 1960, 1962, 1963, 1968, 1971, 1972, 1973, 1975, 1977, 1995 by The Lockman Foundation. Used by permission. (www.Lockman.org)

Printed in the United States of America

Acknowledgments

The process of turning an unformed collection of thoughts and ideas into an ordered unit of bound and printed pages always requires the cooperation and skills of a number of talented people. In most cases, some of them are at least partly motivated by the expectation of sharing in the profits of the final product. However, no such hopes were attached to the shaping of this project. A history of a relatively small association of churches does not bring material rewards to its contributors, but it does earn them my sincere and humble gratitude.

Thank you to Terry White at BMH Books for encouraging a project because it could benefit others and to Jesse Deloe for his thorough editorial work that made the finished product better than the raw materials. Thank you to Terry Hofecker and the people of Northwest Chapel who provided the opportunity and means for the studies that laid the foundation for the project. Thank you to Dale Stoffer for pointing me to rich stores of material while advising my doctoral research. Thank you to Jim Custer for allowing me to articulate, test, and refine my thoughts in many hours of discussions and friendship. Thank you to several good friends who saw value in the project and contributed the funds to make it possible.

Thank you to my wife, Linda, for patiently letting me cover the dining room table with my scattered fragments and sources and for believing that I could gather them into something that would make sense. It's just one more gift of kindness from the woman who has taught me what the Spirit's fruit looks like in human form.

Table of Contents

Table of Figures

*Figure 1: An early Brethren baptism as depicted in
Peter Nead's* **Theological Writings** *(1850)*

Introduction

In the first week of August 1708, eight religious dissidents gathered on the banks of the Eder River near Schwarzenau, the "Black Meadow," in the county of Wittgenstein, Germany, to be baptized. The group read from Luke 14:25-33 about counting the cost before committing to follow Jesus, because they knew their simple act of faith would likely bring persecution from the authorities of the Reformed Church. Several members of the group, including their leader Alexander Mack, had been baptized as infants into the official church of the region, but they had come to believe they had never joined the true church "since they had not received the baptism that they believed was the only Christian baptism."[1]

Mack's son, writing more than sixty years later, drew from his father's papers to describe the event in which "all eight were baptized in an early morning hour."[2] Four witnesses to another Brethren baptism just three years later testified that the candidate was dipped "three consecutive times under the water with these words: 'I baptize you in the name of God the Father, the Son, and the Holy Spirit.'"[3] Departing from the accepted practice of the Reformed Church,

Mack and his companions, through a process of study and prayer had sought for "the old paths" and "the good way" and had concluded that trine immersion was the form of baptism taught by Jesus and practiced by the first Christians.[4]

The eight radicals had carefully considered the reasons for the action they took that day. In an open letter circulated later the same summer they declared, "We have left all sects because of the misuses concerning infant baptism, communion, and church system, and unanimously profess that these are rather man's statutes and commandments, and therefore do not baptize our children, and testify that we were not really baptized."[5] They chose one of their members to baptize the others, but they did not record the person's name. When they entered the water, none of them "had ever seen the ordinance performed in the manner in which they expected to receive it this morning,"[6] but their hope as expressed in their letter of explanation was, "If we then begin in the footsteps of the Lord Jesus to live according to His commandment, then we can also hold communion together according to the commandment of Christ and His apostles in the fear of the Lord."[7] Renewed ordinances were needed for a renewed church, and "the personal decision for Christ and His body through baptism symbolized powerfully their concerns about the coercion of the state, religious freedom and the doctrine of the church as voluntary *Gemeinschaft*."[8]

The founding of the Brethren movement in 1708 did not spring from a desire to be innovative or progressive. The Brethren "considered the New Testament ordinances *in their original form* a visible sign by which Christ's true church could be recognized" (emphasis original).[9] Since these ordinances of baptism and communion required a community of believers and since the existing churches were hostile to the Brethren understanding of them, "full obedience to Christ therefore necessitated the establishment of a *Gemeinde* in order to practice those ordinances instituted by Christ."[10] As Alexander Mack wrote five years later in his pamphlet *Basic Questions*, "If the early ordinance of baptism had ceased to exist, then, of course, the church of Christ would also have ceased to exist. Even if there had been souls here and there who lamented the great apostasy, they could not have been called a church."[11] The eight who gathered at the banks of the Eder did not believe they were leaving one church to found a new church. They believed they were re-founding the true church.

They were not the first. They were a further expression of a movement of believers that has existed in every period of the history of the church, often outside the mainstream powers, associations, and records that form the more familiar story of the development of Christianity. The movement could not be labeled under any single organizational or ethnological title since its members could be found in many such groupings, doubtlessly influenced by the beliefs and practices of those associations, but remaining distinctive through a commitment to "act upon the New Testament and to follow the example of the New Testament churches."[12] Sometimes the members of this movement identified themselves closely with the beliefs and structures of one of the predominant churches of their time and accepted names such as Catholic or Protestant, Reformed or Lutheran. Sometimes they joined with others who explored and adopted models that could be called Anabaptist or Pietist. Sometimes, they felt compelled by their study of the New Testament to separate from any of the recognizable groups of their location. At other times, they were expelled forcefully and regarded as heretics.

Called by some the Pilgrim Church, the movement resisted the common tendency to make the present expression of the church, in any period of its history or any location of its operation, the determinative model for all times and all settings. Occasionally, groups within the movement tried to establish an order from which there could be no departure, but consistently there were individuals who committed themselves "in their meetings, order, and testimony to make the Scriptures their guide and to act upon them as the Word of God, counting them as sufficient for all their needs in all their circumstances."[13] This meant that "no theological tradition – Anabaptist, Radical

Pietist, or Reformed – was above scrutiny by Scripture."[14] The movement certainly learned and adopted doctrines and perspectives from each of those traditions, but it tried to sift and mix them under the higher authority of the Bible.

Church history has been written largely from the perspectives of the groups that held the material resources and societal acceptance to debate, record, and distribute their beliefs, practices, and structures. In essence, they were the ones who had the freedom and money to support scholars and to publish and preserve their works. At the same time, those groups, often using the power of the state, could suppress other points of view and silence their voices. In this way, "The victorious party was also able to destroy much of the literature of the brethren, and, writing their history, to represent them as holding doctrines which they repudiated, and to give them names to which an odious significance was attached."[15] It should be remembered that the "heretics" of church history were not always wrong. Sometimes they just happened to be a relatively powerless minority, and so their stories were told by those who hated them. The true measure of orthodoxy has always been obedience to the revealed instructions of God rather than conformity to the dictates of a human institution (Acts 5:29).

The belief that "the true church should always seek to restore its faith and life according to the apostolic standard" has sometimes been called *restitution*.[16] Henry Holsinger, in his history written more than a century ago, claimed of the Brethren church, "all her sacred peculiar doctrines may be traced all along the historical highway from Christ and His apostles down to the organization at Schwarzenau."[17] This conviction fostered the Brethren value of looking backward through history to the New Testament for the patterns to be applied to a body or community of believers. It inspired them to strive to understand and apply the model of the primitive or original church in doctrine, in corporate expression as the household of Christ, and in personal devotion to Jesus as Lord. It led Alexander Mack and his associates to search beyond the new traditions that the Reformation had laid upon the previous traditions of the Roman Church. Instead, they studied the external witness of the Scriptures and listened for the internal witness of the Holy Spirit. Mack valued a "direct calling and impelling by the Spirit of God" which "consists in the fact that the person is made inwardly exceedingly certain of it by the Spirit of God, and is not concerned whether men believe it or not."[18] For the early Brethren, this calling outweighed the voices of rulers backed by the strength of the state or councils authorized by declarations of the organized church.

Donald Durnbaugh, a prominent historian of the Brethren movement, wrote about the importance of a perspective on the past in order to set a course for the future.

> History is to the group what memory is to the individual. No sensible person ignores his past experiences when an important decision must be made. He may decide to act differently than he did in the past because of changed circumstances, but his judgment is tempered by past successes and failures. Similarly, for a group to act intelligently it must be informed of its heritage. It must understand how it came to be what it is, in fact, today.[19]

It is easy to dismiss the past without pausing to understand it. Models and methods will and should adjust and evolve. Circumstances and environments emerge, influence, and are replaced regularly. Important people and initiatives shape new perspectives that eventually become old in their turn. The constant changes make it difficult to trace a clear path from a rich heritage to a rich future. However, Durnbaugh's point is that our heritage has formed our present, and we should not ignore it when projecting our next steps. We must recognize the values and principles that have become part of our fiber and character. We can choose to change them or set them aside, but we should do so intentionally and not ignorantly.

In the case of the Grace Brethren movement, this historical perspective should not be limited to events and developments since the division of 1939 or even to the time of Alexander Mack. The Brethren movement is a relatively recent manifestation of a line of people who have studied the Scriptures for their models and practices since the founding of the New Testament church. At times, they were part of the dominant churches because they found freedom to pursue their faith within that framework. At other times, they did not join but watched from a distance and learned, adopting certain features that seemed to fit the commands of the New Testament. Occasionally, however, they made the decision to separate in order to follow what they deemed to be obedience to Christ. That was the position claimed by Alexander Mack and his companions in 1708. If the Brethren developed new doctrines and symbols simply to distinguish themselves from other groups, then their practices were mere traditions and policies, but if they returned to an observance of the church as intended by Jesus, then they were transcending sectarian concerns to fulfill discipleship.

I have been involved in the Fellowship of Grace Brethren Churches (FGBC) for more than 30 years, the last 20 as a licensed or ordained elder. Many of the friendships and associations that I have forged in those years are deep and abiding. People within the Fellowship have taught me, challenged me, listened to me, and cared for me in ways I cannot repay. The idea for this book did not come out of a detached curiosity or a critical distance. The FGBC is my close family within the universal body of Christ. We are a group of people who sincerely want to know and follow Jesus, but I believe we have suffered from a sort of identity crisis. We are a relatively small segment of the evangelical community, and we sometimes wish for a more prominent role within that movement. We tend to look for examples of success in size and activity, then adopt or adapt the models of ministry we find without really considering whether or not those models fit our distinctive beliefs and heritage. We try to apply denominational strategies to a fellowship of autonomous churches or we take structures that require a strong, central leader and wedge them into our system that jealously guards shared leadership. Our commitment to finding our practices in the Bible slows us in quickly rolling out innovations. Our sense of equality within the body makes us suspicious of dynamic, autocratic leaders as we initially give them an audience but resist their calls to action. Our instincts toward separation make us reluctant to join too closely with the styles and authority structures of other groups, and our understanding of discipleship creates discontentment with events and rallies that stir a lot of energy but then move on to the next venue. These limitations and characteristics frustrate us at times, but if they are tied to biblical values, we have to accept them as traits of our identity.

Our distinctive beliefs and practices do not make us Brethren, but they are expressions of convictions and values that identify us as the offspring of a distinctive stream within church history; one that interweaves with the more recognizable channels of the Reformation, Anabaptism, Pietism, fundamentalism, and evangelicalism, sometimes seeming to merge with those currents for a while and sometimes following a different course. As traced in this book, certain consistent values can be found that mark the Brethren movement. We have, once in a while, drifted from them, but we have never lost them completely, and they continue to shape our identity and our mission. These are the true "distinctives" of the Brethren movement with their origins in the principles and commands of the New Testament, rediscovered and applied to contemporary settings.

SECTION I

Brethren Roots

CHAPTER 1

Beginnings
of the Church

Before his ascension into heaven, Jesus instructed His followers to wait in Jerusalem for the coming of the Holy Spirit that would signal the inauguration of a new phase in God's dealings with His people (Acts 1:4-8). Jesus told them that the effect and continuing work of the Spirit would be to empower them to be His representatives to all the earth. When the event happened on the day of Pentecost, the Holy Spirit came with the sound of rushing wind, and the fire appeared as individual flames upon those gathered in the upper room (Acts 2:1-4).

The Spirit made it possible for the disciples to be witnesses to people of many nations that very day by enabling them to speak in different languages. Then, when roughly three thousand responded to Peter's declaration of Jesus as the Messiah, the water baptism that Jesus had instituted in Matthew 28:19 was practiced for perhaps the first time (Acts 2:41). It called for the repentance that had been the central piece of John's baptism (Luke 3:3-6) and the clear identification as a follower of Jesus that Christ Himself had added later.[20]

Peter's Jewish audience would have understood the call to repentance that echoed the cry of John the Baptist, but two new features now were added to the rite of water baptism: it was done in the name of, or under the authority of Jesus, and it was connected to the gift of the Holy Spirit.[21] It was a call for "a public, radical testimony of conversion, not a private, noncommittal request for salvation with no conditions."[22] It took place at a time when the city of Jerusalem was "immensely swollen" with Jewish pilgrims,[23] and it took place, most likely, near the temple mount among the "immersion pools that worshippers used to purify themselves ritually."[24] The testimony of the three thousand could be watched, not only by fellow believers who would rejoice at each successive immersion, but also by Pharisees, Roman soldiers, and others who might have more sinister responses. From the beginning, baptism was a public expression of commitment to a discipleship that could lead to imprisonment, exile, and even death. It made believers accountable to their friends and recognizable to their foes.

On that day, the church was born, an expression of faith distinct from all other religious systems and philosophies, any alternate means of obtaining righteousness, and the priority of any previous associations. It had no property, no legal status, and no manual of procedures and practices. Jesus had given the apostles instructions to make people into His disciples by baptizing them and teaching them to observe all that He had commanded (Matthew 28:19-20). The twelve were the recognized leaders, but the flock they led had very little idea of what to do next. What might it have been like the morning after Pentecost when three thousand people looked back on the experiences of the previous day and wondered, "Now what?" In answer, they adopted six practices, recorded in Acts 2:37-42, that would ground them in the essential truths and habits necessary for their growth and for the unity and health of the church.

1. *Evangelism.* They proclaimed the truth that had so recently changed their lives, calling others to repentance from sin and identification with the salvation accomplished by Jesus and with the church as the group of people who had received it. Given the clear and public

nature of their commitment, there were undoubtedly many opportunities to offer an explanation for their willingness to adopt a new identity.

2. *Baptism.* They submitted to an initial act of obedience to Christ that publicly identified them with the Triune God, with the salvation He provided, with His church, and with the call to live as disciples of Jesus. Salvation was accomplished by repentance and conversion through the work of the Spirit, but water baptism was the visible act of commitment through which other believers could recognize those who had identified themselves as followers of Jesus. The idea of a Christian who had never been baptized was unknown in the New Testament.[25]

3. *Apostles' teaching.* They listened to the eyewitness accounts of those who had been with Jesus as they rehearsed the events they had seen and the words they had heard. Later, these memories were recorded in the Gospels, and further structure and interpretation was given to the church through the inspired epistles of the New Testament.

4. *Fellowship.* They had entered a new organism called the church, and they now shared a bond closer than any previous relationships. At the outset, since many of them chose to remain in Jerusalem away from their homes and usual means of income, this included pooling their material resources to make sure no member of the body suffered from physical need. Fellowship was not a social occasion. It was a mutual responsibility.

5. *Breaking of bread.* This phrase "became a kind of shorthand way of speaking of the Lord's Supper" in the early church.[26] They observed the elements of the communion ordinance that Jesus had given. It served as a teaching tool to illustrate and remember the basic truths of their new faith and as a memorial of His work that had made their salvation and fellowship possible. It was a daily occurrence in whatever home believers

gathered and "a principal reason" for the gathering of the church.[27]

6. *Prayer.* They communicated with the Head of the church for needs of provision, protection, and direction while offering Him praise and devotion as He had instructed His disciples to do.

The first two of the six practices were steps that led to participation in the church. A person had to respond in faith to the proclamation of the gospel and the call to repentance and had to identify with the followers of Christ through baptism to be counted as a member of the body. The last four practices were natural and logical habits to adopt for people who had begun to travel the path of discipleship. Indeed, they may have been the essential four elements for a gathering of the members.[28] Even today, these six practices are accepted universally as biblical requirements for the life of a local Grace Brethren church. At the core of our various methods and programs and strategies is the recognition that we must find ways to promote and preserve these habits, and our definition of them in large part influences the methods and programs and strategies that we adopt. They are critical to our model of a church that is obedient to the instructions of the Lord of the church.

It was a similar commitment to faithfully observe these elements that led Alexander Mack and his companions to the waters of the Eder in 1708. They gathered at a time when the free observance of each of the six activities described above was viewed as an act of heresy by the national churches and as an act of treason by the state officials of the German Rhineland. The recognized state churches, backed by the armed might of the local governments, claimed the exclusive right to these spiritual practices so they could be conducted only in authorized locations at authorized times by authorized officials. Within the Roman Catholic, Lutheran, and Reformed churches of the day, the requirements for membership had been diluted from a voluntary expression of faith followed by the evidence of an obedient life to rituals performed upon unknowing infants or possibly unbelieving people as obligations of citizenship. Mack and the early Brethren found it necessary to leave behind all associations with the state church system and begin a new community of faith. Since Mack wanted the new movement to avoid the mistakes of these other groups, "its conditions of membership, its rites, its ministry and its method of organization must be different."[29]

It is important to notice that the Brethren movement was primarily a rejection of the Reformed and Lutheran churches that dominated central Germany in the early eighteenth century. For many in the twenty-first century, a Christian is either Catholic or Protestant, based on a popular view of church history that sees the Protestant Reformation as the defining moment in the formation of two competing systems. By this model, the roots of the Brethren movement are a simplistic derivation of the Protestant break with Rome in the sixteenth century as reflected below in *Figure 2*.

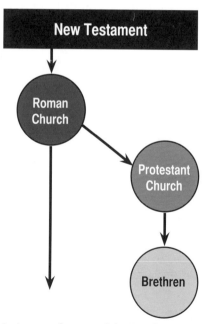

Figure 2: Assumed roots of the Brethren movement according to the simplified Roman/Protestant model of church history

However, the convictions that directed Alexander Mack were only partially influenced by the Reformation. Indeed, the state churches that grew out of the Reformation were bitterly opposed to the early Brethren. E. H. Broadbent, a church historian from the early 1900s, observed that the Roman and Reformed churches have produced volumes of documents and records because they were the dominant faiths that had the resources to commission and preserve such writings. They also were effective at suppressing and destroying the works of groups that did not conform to the official positions of the state churches.

It is often thought that when the Reformation was established, Europe was divided into Protestants (whether Lutheran or Swiss) on the one hand, and Roman Catholics on the other. The large numbers of Christians are overlooked who did not belong to either party, but who, most of them, met as independent churches, not relying, as the others did, on the support of the civil power, but endeavoring to carry out the principles of Scripture as in the New Testament times. They were so numerous that both the State Church parties feared they might come to threaten their own power and even existence.[30]

The Brethren were certainly shaped by the doctrines and church models of other groups, the Roman and the Reformed churches among them, but they also drank deeply from the fountains of Anabaptism and Radical Pietism. Even this does not tell the full story, for, although Alexander Mack and the Brethren were in part products of history, they consistently looked to the New Testament to try to determine which influences fit the commands of Christ. Thus, a truer picture of the roots of the Brethren movement is seen in *Figure 3*.

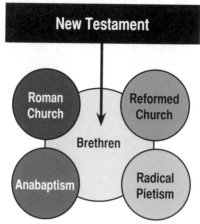

*Figure 3: A better representation of Brethren
roots, reflecting historical influences adopted
or rejected based on New Testament principles*

The six practices listed in Acts 2:37-42 provided the framework for the people of God as they organized and moved ahead with the mission Jesus had given to His church. The centuries between that beginning and the founding of the Brethren movement in 1708 is the story of how the church maintained and altered, communicated and denied, and forgot and rediscovered those lessons and intentions through long years of social, political, and geographical changes. While a detailed chronicle of the events and people who shaped the church is far beyond the scope of this book, it is possible to highlight some of the factors that contributed to the Brethren understanding in distinct periods of history. The early Brethren observed the outcomes of each of these historic expressions of the church and made decisions to adopt aspects of them that seemed to be in keeping with the direction of the New Testament while rejecting other aspects they deemed to be corrupted or merely cultural. As Martin Brumbaugh observed in his landmark history of the Brethren, "They were debtors to all and followers of none."[31] They may not have chosen correctly at all times, but consistently they sought to protect and preserve what they believed to be the model and pattern of the New Testament church.

CHAPTER 2

From Persecution to Persecuting

The apostles were central figures in the establishment and early development of the community of believers. Their recollections of the words and activities of Jesus were the formational teaching of the church while the ordinances of baptism and communion provided ways for the members to rehearse and identify with the foundational truths that marked Christ's followers. Soon, the earthly life of Jesus was set in writing by the apostles or their close associates in the Gospels, so eyewitness accounts were available to the local churches even when one of the twelve was not present. Later, the apostles gave further structure and interpretation to the church through the inspired epistles. As these writings were being composed, copied, and collected, the church was especially vulnerable to the influences of other philosophies and interpretations that could produce a syncretism that took bits and pieces from various systems. People who claimed to have spiritual knowledge could gain a hearing through dramatic eloquence or a promise of hidden secrets. This was the essence of Gnosticism, "a variety of movements, each one offering some way of enlightenment prescribed by... a philosopher who possessed the *gnosis* or knowledge of the way of life."[32]

The apostles, most notably Paul and John, addressed these errors many times in their epistles, and church leaders who knew the apostles, such as Clement, Ignatius, and Polycarp, continued to battle against Gnostic teachers into the second century. Once the apostles and their immediate successors were gone, however, the churches felt a growing need to standardize their beliefs in order to preserve them from the corrupting influences of Gnosticism, mystery religions, Judaism, and competing interpretations of Scripture. This concern provoked the Christian community to ask three questions.

1. *Who is fit to lead the church?* The New Testament had provided for the passing of the apostles by instructing that elders be selected for each local church based on standards of character and faithfulness.[33] However, what gave them greater authority than those who claimed special revelation from angels or God? And when they were confronted with issues that affected more than a single local church, who could declare for the churches what was truth and what was error?

2. *What is the canon or measure of Scripture?* The New Testament writings had been accepted as the inspired communication of God to the church. But now, with an accumulating proliferation of written literature, some of which asserted their own divine origins, how could the church know which were authentic and which were spurious? And what level of credibility and authority should be given to a document written by a recognized leader?

3. *What is the essence of the faith?* The gospel spread across geographical and cultural boundaries as Jesus had intended, but the distance and diversity made it harder to be certain that the integrity of the message was maintained from location to location. Was the message of salvation preached in Corinth the same as the one understood in Jerusalem, or had it been accommodated to the Greek philosophies of that pagan center? What would be the test for the church to distinguish true believers from those who followed other philosophies?

By some, the three questions were answered with concepts that would be defined and developed slowly but eventually would shake the church from its biblical foundations. Initially, the answers seemed to make sense and to bring order to the confusion of conflicting statements, documents, and beliefs. The question of leadership was answered with the idea of apostolic succession in which the logical choice to replace a departing leader was a person who had worked closely with that leader. The question of Scripture could be resolved by the consensus of a group of leaders meeting in a council. The question of the faith could be settled by the formulation of a creed or "symbol of faith"[34] that would summarize the essential elements of belief and membership. However, since these answers were founded in systems of human organization and authority, they would prove to be susceptible to ambition, abuse, and misunderstanding once the church gained access to wealth and power. In the end, these means "to preserve unity of doctrine affected the Church even more than the heresies themselves, for it was largely due to them that the Episcopal power and control grew up along with the clerical system."[35]

The early church faced hostility first from the established Jewish religious system and later from the authorities of Rome. By the time the apostolic age closed at the end of the first century, the Roman government had declared that it was illegal to be a Christian. Christian gatherings were seen as acts of defiance since an imperial edict had forbidden unauthorized meetings. Persecutions of the church over the next 200 years were not constant, but the threat of suppression was almost always present. This tension greatly influenced the believers' view of their relation to the state. They were a persecuted minority with little hope of participating in the decisions and policies of government. The sword of the state more often hunted them than defended them. Property and the resources to build centers of worship were scarce, and those constructed could become targets of the next round of persecutions. Self-identification with the message and people of Jesus promised a share in the reproach, poverty, and vulnerability of that group as "the lists of martyrs grew longer and longer, and there seemed to be no end in sight."[36] Indeed, to the Christians, the logical end of "this extraordinary warfare between the mighty world-empire of Rome and these unresisting churches" seemed destined to be "the complete extinction of the Church."[37]

Then, "the last great imperial persecution of the Christians under Diocletian and Galerius, which was aimed at the entire uprooting of the new religion,"[38] ended with an *Edict of Toleration* in 311. The *Edict*, possibly a concession by Galerius that a painful illness that afflicted him was a judgment from God,[39] recognized that the willingness of Christians to die for their faith made the policy of continued persecution to protect the pagan religion of Rome ineffective. It was better to let Christians practice their religion than to force them to abandon the outward display of all religion.

> Finally, when our law had been promulgated to the effect that they should conform to the institutes of antiquity, many were subdued by the fear of danger, many even suffered death. And yet since most of them persevered in their determination, and we saw that they neither paid the reverence and awe due to the gods nor worshipped the God of the Christians, in view of our most mild clemency and the constant habit by which we are accustomed to grant indulgence to all, we thought that we ought to grant our most prompt indulgence also to these, so that they may again be Christians and may hold their conventicles, provided they do nothing contrary to good order.[40]

Although persecutions against Christians would continue for a short time in the western empire under Maxentius, the *Edict* began an amazing period of seventy years that would see Christianity rise from the persecuted to the persecutor in the Roman Empire.

Figure 4: Constantine's vision: "In this sign conquer"

The very next year, Constantine secured his imperial throne by defeating his rival Maxentius at the Milvian Bridge. The emperor claimed to be guided by a dream of a cross that appeared in the sky with the words, "In this sign conquer."[41] Christianity was thus elvated to a favored status and was appealed to as a basis for political power. Conquest, not salvation or compassion, was the new mission of Constantine's Christianity. He made his choice official in 313 with the *Edict of Milan* which granted the Christian faith imperial protection.

Therefore, your Worship should know that it has pleased us to remove all conditions whatsoever, which were in the prescripts formerly given to you officially, concerning the Christians and now any one of these who wishes to observe Christian religion may do so freely and openly, without molestation.[42]

The *Edict* included provisions that allowed the people of the empire to "follow whatever religion they chose"[43] and that "the persecution of Christians would stop, and that their churches, cemeteries, and other properties would be returned to them."[44] There has been much debate over whether Constantine acted from "motives of policy, of piety, or of superstition,"[45] but unquestionably he openly favored Christianity as "he allowed Christian ministers to enjoy the same exemption from taxes as the pagan priests; he abolished executions by crucifixion; he called a halt to the battles of gladiators as a punishment for crimes; and in 321 he made Sunday a public holiday."[46]

The transition from persecution to power was made complete and official on February 27, 380, when the emperor Theodosius issued the following *Proclamation*.

It is Our Will that all the peoples we rule shall practice that religion which the divine Peter the Apostle transmitted to the Romans. We shall believe in the single Deity of the Father, the Son, and the Holy Spirit, under the concept of equal majesty and of the Holy Trinity. We command that those persons who follow this rule shall embrace the name of Catholic Christians. The rest, however, whom We adjudge demented and insane, shall sustain the infamy of heretical dogmas, their meeting places shall not receive the name of churches, and they shall be smitten first by divine vengeance and secondly by the retribution of Our own initiative, which We shall assume in accordance with divine judgment.[47]

In that single proclamation, the state assumed guardianship of the Christian faith with the rights to determine correct doctrine, to organize an official church that would include all loyal citizens of the state, and to inflict punishment on any who deviated from the doctrine or organization approved by the state. The Roman Empire became the Christian empire with an implicit connection between the will of its political rulers and the will of God. The spread of the empire was no longer just a worldly quest for power. It was now sanctioned by God as the means of taking His grace to heathen tribes whether they wanted it or not.

*Figure 5: Augustine
of Hippo (354-430)*

Soon after this, Augustine of Hippo (354-430) argued that the Roman Church alone could dispense truth and salvation. The church that Jesus wanted to build was not a loose community of believing individuals according to Augustine. It was an institution that would partner with the state to establish His rule over the earth.

> The Catholic Church is the work of Divine Providence, achieved through the prophecies of the prophets,

through the Incarnation and the teaching of Christ, through the journeys of the Apostles, through the suffering, the crosses, the blood and the death of the martyrs, through the admirable lives of the saints. When, then, we see so much help on God's part, so much progress and so much fruit, shall we hesitate to bury ourselves in the bosom of that Church? For starting from the Apostolic Chair down through successions of bishops, even unto the open confessing of all mankind, it has possessed the crown of teaching and authority.[48]

Since, in Augustine's view, the organized Church of Rome held this vital role, it was imperative to preserve it and the empire that supported it against all enemies, political or spiritual. Thus, when Augustine read in Luke 14:23, "Go out . . . and compel them to come in," he concluded that the sword of the state should be used rightly to compel people by fear and pain if necessary to come to the teaching that would save their souls.[49] Speaking of his own salvation, Augustine said, "I would not believe the gospel, if I were not compelled by the authority of the universal church."[50]

The alliance between the Church and the state brought new freedom and influence to the followers of Christ, but it also presented profound and unexpected challenges to them in their observance of the six basic practices of the church. The government treated church leaders as "civil servants and demanded unconditional obedience to official pronouncements, even when they interfered with purely church matters."[51] Church councils convened by the emperor at Laodicea in 363 and at Carthage in 392 decided to drop the love feast altogether and celebrate the bread and cup alone.[52] Christian worship adopted incense, clerical garments, gestures of respect to the emperor, and lavish processionals as it was "influenced by imperial protocol."[53] Cathedrals or basilicas were constructed according to an architectural plan that emphasized the elevated role of the clergy as the agents who handled the sacraments. These buildings "inevitably tended toward more liturgical services of formality," and simple practices of feetwashing and a love feast were deemed "incongruous in this new church splendor and consequently faded from the practice of the Church."[54] It could be said that the full observance of the Lord's Supper was discontinued, in part, because the buildings left no place for it.[55]

Figure 6: Depiction of Leo I in the forefront with Peter behind holding the keys of the kingdom

As the Roman Church shared and copied the material and organizational trappings of the Roman Empire, it was only a matter of time before the leader of the Church would establish a basis for authority to match and even challenge that of the emperor. Leo I, in 441, on the anniversary of his ascension to the bishopric of Rome, delivered a sermon that formed the foundation for what would become known as the Petrine Doctrine. He claimed the primacy of the Bishop of Rome over all other servants of the Church and further argued that the papacy was invested with apostolic authority through direct spiritual succession from the apostle Peter.

The dispensation of Truth therefore abides, and the blessed Peter persevering in the strength of the Rock, which he has received, has not abandoned the helm of the Church, which he undertook. For he was ordained before the rest in such a way that from his being called the Rock, from his being pronounced the Foundation, from his being constituted the Doorkeeper of the kingdom of heaven, from his being set as the Umpire to bind and to loose, whose judgments shall retain their validity in heaven, from all these mystical titles we might know the nature of his association with Christ. And still to-day he more fully and effectually performs what is entrusted to him, and carries out every part of his duty and charge in Him and with Him, through Whom he has been glorified. And so if anything is rightly done and rightly decreed by us, if anything is won from the mercy of GOD by our daily supplications, it is of his work and merits whose power lives and whose authority prevails in his See.[56]

Leo went on to state that the authority of his office was perpetual since "as that remains which Peter believed in Christ, so that remains which Christ instituted in Peter."[57]

The relationship of power between the Roman Church and the Roman Empire was further forged by the Emperor Justinian who understood the role of the pious ruler to be "the maintenance of the Christian faith in its purity and the protection of the Holy Catholic and Apostolic Church from any disturbance."[58] His *Codex Justinian* was a compilation and standardization of Roman laws from the time of Hadrian (A.D. 117-138) to its publication in A.D. 529. Its opening section was titled "Concerning the most exalted Trinity and the Catholic Faith and providing that no one shall dare to publicly oppose them."[59] The *Codex* quoted from and expanded upon the earlier *Proclamation of Theodosius*, positioning the state as the divinely appointed protector of the institutional church and the earthly purveyor and enforcer of Christian doctrine. If the church was essential to the purposes of God in the world, then the state was equally necessary to seeing those purposes accomplished successfully.

In this system, the momentum – first developed in the battle against Gnosticism – toward centralized power in the clergy and a uniform statement of doctrine established by authorized leaders was encouraged and strengthened by the secular government. Identification with the body of Christ was assumed as a facet of citizenship in the state, obedience to the Church was deemed essential to achieve salvation, and a relationship of personal faith and discipleship to Jesus was defined by conformity to political and institutional goals and expectations. The ordinances, which had been given to believers as tools to express an identity with the salvation and people of God above any other human association, became tools to enforce loyalty to the political nation and to the authority of the institutional church. Any who refused to practice them as such were threatened with physical punishment and spiritual banishment from all hope of eternal life. In addition, since the ordinances could be administered only by authorized clergy, they could also be withheld from anyone who challenged the system.

The effects of this nationalizing of the church can be summarized in the four key doctrines that became pillars of the Roman Church.

1. *Sacramentalism:* Certain rites of the Church are channels of God's grace, and so are necessary to gain salvation. These sacraments are accessible only in an authorized place and through an authorized agent. According to Augustine, the sacraments are ex opera operato ("by virtue of the work done"). This means that the faith of both the celebrant and the recipient have no bearing on the efficacy of the rite. An unbelieving priest could give communion to an unbelieving parishioner, and the grace of God for salvation would still be exchanged!

2. *Sacerdotalism:* Only those authorized by apostolic succession or appointment are empowered by God to administer the sacraments effectually. The people are wholly dependent on the clergy to receive the grace of God.

3. *Sectarianism:* The Roman Church is the only true church and the only purveyor of truth. It is intended to last as

a perpetual, universal institution. It must be preserved and protected if the kingdom of God is to prevail upon the earth.

4. *State Church:* The state is meant to be the sword of the church, and the church is meant to be the conscience of the state. The church and the state dispense salvation and citizenship and mark the people as their spiritual and national possessions.

Infant baptism removed any element of personal identification with Christ, salvation, or His body. Instead, these commitments were assumed as a result of the rite having been administered before a conscious choice was possible. In like manner, the bread and the cup, through the doctrine of transubstantiation, became the repeated sacrifice necessary to maintain the hope of eternal life. Since the body and blood of Christ were too holy for common hands, participation was reduced to the reception of the wafer from the hands of those who alone were permitted to truly commune with God behind the altar. For anyone else, direct communication or fellowship with God was impossible.

The nationalization of the church also eliminated much of the cost of identification with the message and people of Christ. As Shelley observed, "Prior to Constantine's conversion, the church consisted of convinced believers," but with the favor and coercion of the government "many came who were politically ambitious, religiously disinterested, and still half-rooted in paganism."[60] There were now social, political, and commercial advantages to being associated with Christianity, and the government made it known that it wanted all to participate as a sign of loyalty, so the church was flooded with new adherents. Baptism and communion were affected profoundly by this influx because the ordinances were seen as both the visible means of identification and participation as well as the sacramental means of salvation. They had once marked "the gulf dividing the Church from the world," but in the state church they were used "to bridge it, infant baptism and the general administration of the Lord's

Supper doing away with the necessity for personal faith."[61] The "identities of True Christians could not be determined," and "'believer' came to mean 'all the baptized.'"[62]

From the beginning, Constantine had hoped that the church would become the "cement of the Empire," a rallying point of unity among a diverse population. However, some groups of believers viewed these changes as "a great apostasy" and withdrew to a monastic life in the desert while others stayed and voiced their disapproval.[63] These dissenters soon found that the leaders of the church now had the power of the state to enforce their decisions, and so the formerly persecuted minority became the persecuting majority. The state, in the interest of unity, began to force theological agreement on Christians. Councils were called by the state to settle religious questions, and the decisions and creeds they produced were declared the orthodox positions for all Christians with legal penalties for dissent. To those who watched the alliance of political and ecclesiastical purposes with mistrust, even if the decision of a Council was right, "the way of reaching it by the combined efforts of the Emperor and the bishops and enforcing it by the power of the State, showed the departure of the Catholic church from Scripture."[64] Among these was a young priest who would soon put his desire for change into writing and shatter the monopoly of the Roman Church on the Christian world.

CHAPTER 3

A Reformation of Theology

T he document that Martin Luther nailed to the doors of Wittenberg Cathedral on October 31, 1517, was not intended to spark a rebellion against the existing structure of the Roman Church. Luther's tone was certainly direct and his statements were confrontational, but his *Disputation of Doctor Martin Luther on the Power and Efficacy of Indulgences* stated in a set of 95 theses was an attempt to force dialogue and debate that could lead to reform. The door of the cathedral was the accepted place to post notices of public forums, and the preface of Luther's document expressed his motive.

Figure 7: Martin Luther (1483-1546)

Out of love for the truth and the desire to bring it to light, the following propositions will be discussed at Wittenberg, under the presidency of the Reverend Father Martin Luther, Master of Arts and Sacred Theology, and Lecturer in Ordinary on the same at that place. Wherefore, he requests that those who are unable to be present and debate orally with us, may do so by letter.[65]

Although the Protestant Reformation has been characterized by many as a renunciation of the Roman church, it would be more accurate to view it as a "'modification of Catholicism' in which Catholic problems remain, but different solutions are given."[66] The early reformers recognized the desperate need for change, but they hoped that it could come through a "furtherance of scholarship and education" that would produce "a return to the sources of Christianity – both biblical and patristic."[67] The problems they proposed to solve were, without doubt, profound, and the solutions they offered were great improvements on the legalism and corruption that had gripped the Roman system. Luther focused on several core questions and proposed answers that challenged the monopoly claimed by the church on the dissemination of truth and grace. His main points could be summarized as follows.

Question: How is a person saved?
Answer: "Not by works but by faith alone."

Question: Where does religious authority lie?
Answer: "Not in the visible institution called the Roman church but in the Word of God found in the Bible."

Question: What is the church?
Answer: "The whole community of Christian believers, since all are priests before God."

Question: What is the essence of Christian living?
Answer: "Serving God in any useful calling, whether ordained or lay." [68]

Luther wanted to purge the church of any doctrine or practice "that contradicted Scripture," while others, most notably Ulrich Zwingli, went a step further and insisted, "only that which had scriptural foundation should be believed and practiced."[69] The approach of Luther was more tolerant of church traditions and offices not supported by the New Testament as long as they did not violate a clear teaching of the Bible. He wanted to preserve and strengthen the good stones by rooting out and removing those that were crumbling. Zwingli was more inclined to push for a massive deconstruction of the existing system so that it could be rebuilt on a purer foundation. Both, however, wished initially to bring about change within the existing structure of the Roman Church.

Figure 8: Ulrich Zwingli (1484-1531)

Rome proved to be violently uncooperative in such efforts. Within a year of the posting of his call to debate, Luther was summoned to three interviews with a papal legate who demanded that he retract his errors and give absolute submission to the Pope. Luther at first hoped for leniency and a chance to explain his position more clearly to Leo X, but as he studied more deeply the New Testament and early church history, he found "no trace of popery and its extraordinary claims in the first centuries before the Council of Nicea" and gradually came to believe that the church was beyond hope of reform.[70] On June 15, 1520, the Pope issued *Exsurge Domine*, a statement of condemnation against the efforts of the reformers and an excommunication of Luther in which he was pictured as a dangerous animal to be hunted.

> Arise, O Lord, and judge your own cause. Remember your reproaches to those who are filled with foolishness all through the day. Listen to our prayers, for foxes have arisen seeking to destroy the vineyard whose winepress you alone have trod. When you were about

to ascend to your Father, you committed the care, rule, and administration of the vineyard, and image of the triumphant church, to Peter, as the head and your vicar and his successors. The wild boar from the forest seeks to destroy it and every wild beast feeds upon it.[71]

In October, after first seeing a copy of the Pope's order of excommunication, Luther composed a letter to Leo X that indicated that any reconciliation was impossible.

The Church of Rome, formerly the most holy of all churches, has become the most lawless den of thieves, the most shameless of all brothels, the very kingdom of sin, death, and hell; so that not even Antichrist, if he were to come, could devise any addition to its wickedness.[72]

Luther formally received *Exsurge Domine* on November 4 and burned it a few weeks later.

A dialogue about differences of doctrine and practice was no longer even a remote possibility, and the reformers increasingly turned to princes and political leaders for protection from the wrath of the Roman Church and became increasingly militant in their calls for an enforced program of change. Luther had written an *Address to the German Nobility* in the summer of 1520 in which he called upon the secular authorities to bring about a reformation of the church through legal pressures. He did not advocate military action, but he challenged those who possessed military resources that "it is enough that the Pope should be so mad and foolish, but it is too much that we should sanction and approve it."[73] Once he defiantly burned the papal bull of excommunication on December 10, the Church of Rome became his enemy and certain German princes openly vowed their willingness to fight for his cause. Then, in 1524, the peasants of Germany reacted against the oppressive rule of the nobles. Luther at first supported their claims for justice, but when they used the teachings of the reformers as justification for rebellion, he urged the German princes to crush them, saying, "With threefold horrible sins against God and men have these peasants loaded themselves, for which they have deserved a manifold death of body and soul."[74] Thus, the growing ties between the reformation and the state were strengthened, and the state was once again given the role of protecting the faith.

The desire, in the initial phase of the Reformation, to reform the Roman Church rather than to separate from it led to a modified continuation of many of its practices. While the reformers rejected the sacerdotal system of the priesthood altogether, they were less certain in their departure from the sacramental system of the Roman Church. Of the seven mysteries observed in the Roman system the reformers retained only baptism and communion as valid sacraments because these two were instituted by Christ and were "a physical sign of the promise of the gospel."[75] They agreed that the sacraments should be placed within a community of believing Christians, rather than in the hands of an exclusive priesthood. But the community of believers became a state church, and infant baptism continued to be seen as a means of enrolling the national population into the national religion. Communion continued to be held as necessary to appropriate the forgiveness of sins by faith, and so it was offered to everyone regardless of personal faith. Both sacraments could be obtained only within the established church system.

Meanwhile, the desire, after Luther's break with Rome, to replace the Roman church rather than to separate from it led to a new nationalization of the churches. Luther identified "two governments among the children of Adam, – the reign of God under Christ, and the reign of the world under the civil magistrate, each with its own laws and rights,"[76] yet he also "maintained the principle of the union of Church and State, and accepted the sword of the State as the proper means of converting or punishing those who dissented from the new ecclesiastical authority."[77] The distinction between the Church and the State, which Luther, Zwingli, and John Calvin found in the New Testament, was "difficult to apply to concrete situations,"[78] and "the very men who claimed and exercised the right of protest in essentials . . . denied the same right to others, who differed with them in nonessentials."[79] The reformers, in an ironic twist, appealed to the *Proclamation of Theodosius* to justify a new state suppression of religious dissent. Luther "frequently expressed his regret for the lost liberty of the Christian man and independence of the Christian congregations that had once been his aim," but "once the new Church was put under the power of the State it could not be altered."[80]

The name "Protestant" was first applied to the reformers at the Second Diet of Speiers in 1529, when Lutheran princes protested a requirement to return to the Catholic faith. In 1530, Emperor Charles V, an avid defender of the Roman faith, returned to Germany after an absence of nine years. He was determined to end the Lutheran heresy in his territories and called for an explanation of Luther's beliefs at Augsburg. The resulting *Augsburg Confession*, written by Philip Melanchthon and approved by Luther, was signed by most of the Protestant rulers of Germany. When Charles demanded that the signatories return to the Roman faith, they refused, so the emperor declared that they must recant by April of the following year or suffer the consequences.

The Protestant princes formed the Schmalkald League, a military confederation of civil states for a religious purpose, to defend their territories from the expected advance of the emperor's armies. After some hesitation, Luther agreed that the church should use force to resist the force of the emperor. When the fighting was concluded temporarily in 1555 by the *Peace of Augsburg*, Lutheranism was established as the state church in much of Germany and Scandinavia by the concept of *cuius region, eius religio* or "whose rule, his religion." A pattern was set in which the only accepted and authorized belief of a region was determined by the faith of its ruler.

By this time, the central tenets of the Reformation had been compromised to the demands of a partnership between the church and the state. The concept of *sola scriptura* meant that only

Scripture can give authoritative instruction to the people of God. Luther had debated at Leipzig in 1519 that "Neither the church nor the pope can establish articles of faith. These must come from Scripture."[81] But the *Augsburg Confession* and other creedal statements would soon become the tests of orthodoxy. *Sola fidei* meant that faith alone is the basis for salvation, and Luther had stated, "Good works do not make a man good, but a good man does good works."[82] However, in the state churches, infant baptism and open communion provided the assurance of forgiveness and eternal life without the need for personal faith. The reformers argued for the *priesthood of all believers,* but the sacraments of baptism and communion were

Figure 9: The execution of Michael Servetus at Geneva, October 27, 1553

considered valid only within the prescribed boundaries of the authorized church.

The new state churches of the Reformation guarded and enforced their power and authority against dissenters with a jealousy as fierce as the Roman Church had exercised against them. Again, under the guise of religious authority enforced by the state, the persecuted became in turn the persecutors. Zwingli achieved a combination of ecclesiastical and political control in Zurich before his premature death in battle in 1531. John Calvin became the virtual spiritual and civil dictator of Geneva, and used his authority in 1553 to entice Michael Servetus to the city under the promise of safety. Then he had Servetus arrested, tried, and burned at the stake as a heretic. Calvin defended his actions saying, "Whoever shall maintain that wrong is done to heretics and blasphemers in punishing them makes himself an accomplce to their crime and guilty as they are."[83]

Outside of the recognized branches of the Reformation and outside of the Roman Church remained groups of believers who thought the compromise between church and state was a continuation of the betrayal of primitive Christianity that first took place when Constantine converted the Roman Empire. They applauded the reformers' commitment to the authority of Scripture, justification by faith, and the priesthood of every believer, but they felt the Reformation erred by retaining its close link to the civil government. These representatives of the Pilgrim Church learned and borrowed from the reformers, but they did not identify themselves with the Reformation. They were the people who, according to one Brethren historian, attempted to practice "a Biblicistic faith in the midst of an unfinished reformation."[84] To the extent that the Reformation urged or accomplished the return of the church to its New Testament foundations, these groups adopted and repeated the arguments of the reformers, but they rarely joined themselves to the churches of the Reformation. As Gillin noted in his dissertation on the early Brethren, for too long had "the government oppressed them" and "the ascendant religions persecuted them," so that any doctrines that had helped produce the oppressions and persecutions "must in the eyes of the persecuted be wrong."[85]

CHAPTER 4:

The Anabaptist Church Model

On January 21, 1525, a small group of believers in Zurich "arose from prayer to take one of the most decisive actions in Christian history"[86] and "clearly the most revolutionary act of the Reformation."[87] The City Council of Zurich had demanded that all parents have their infants baptized. On that very night, George Blaurock and Conrad Grebel baptized one another and then baptized their band of companions before sharing together the Lord's Supper,[88] essentially renouncing their association with the Reformed Church.

As David Plaster states, they were among the "radicals of the Reformation," because "rather than wanting simply to reform the existing Roman Catholic Church, they wanted to begin an entirely new church based solely on what was taught in the New Testament."[89] Their act earned them the title of Anabaptists or rebaptizers, but it was a misnomer because they "did not hold that one should be rebaptized, but rather that infant baptism was not valid, and therefore the first real baptism takes place when one receives the rite after having made a public confession of faith."[90] Schaff noted that denying the effectualness of infant baptism "virtually unbaptized and unchristianized the entire Christian world,"[91] and Estep observed that "no other event so completely symbolized the break with Rome."[92]

Although baptism gave the Anabaptists their name, the central issue for the movement was "the establishment of a pure church of converts in opposition to the mixed church of the world."[93] In this church, baptism and the Lord's Supper were the "visible ceremonies" that identified and distinguished the church from the general population.[94] The founders of the movement had been involved in the reform efforts of Ulrich Zwingli, but they came to disagree over the nature of the church, specifically the question of whether a government has the right to decide matters that relate to the church. The alliance between the church and the state that had been formed after the conversion of Constantine and renewed in the Reformation had produced a confused distinction between the true church and the rest of society that had not been corrected in the creeds of Luther and Zwingli which some saw as far too conservative. The Anabaptists recognized that "while one belongs to a society by the mere fact of being born into it, and through no decision on one's own part, one cannot belong to the true church without a personal decision to that effect."[95] Infant baptism, therefore, had to be rejected as a "human institution invented in the kingdom of antichrist,"[96] a "coercion of conscience"[97] that assumed a person became a believer simply by being born into a supposedly Christian society. The goal was a new church after the apostolic model "made up only of those confessing Christ as Lord followed by believers' baptism, instead of everyone born in a given parish."[98]

The spread of this church brought the ordinance practices of the movement into direct conflict with both the state and the authorized church. Since church and state were considered indivisible, "any deviation from the established churches was considered a crime of treason."[99] In this system, the priestly monopoly on the administering of the sacraments was the key to bringing the "nation under a domination in matters of faith and conscience, which, when working in unison with the State, or civil government, make free churches impossible, and religion a matter of nationality."[100] In contrast, the Anabaptists promoted "religious liberty: the right to worship with others of like faith without state support and without state persecution."[101] Therefore, a "voluntary act of the witting person, freely choosing a life of discipleship" through baptism,[102] or a "love meal aimed at demonstrating a loving fellowship sharing material and spiritual support along with mutual discipline"[103] became acts of treason that threatened to destroy the assumed right of a united, territorial church. Broadbent noted that these independent activities exceeded the limits that a national church could permit.

> It can take in unbelievers, and condone much wickedness, and can even allow its clergy to express disbelief in the Scriptures; but, if it has the power to prevent it, it will not tolerate those who baptize believers, or who take the Lord's Supper among themselves as disciples of Christ, because these things strike at the foundations of its character as a national church.[104]

The national church of the sixteenth century defended itself with all its combined secular and religious power. Eberli Bolt, "burned at the stake in Schwyz, Switzerland, at the hands of Roman Catholic authorities on May 29, 1525" was the first to die for his Anabaptist faith.[105] One historian estimates that from that time until the Treaty of Westphalia largely ended executions if not persecutions of dissenters in 1648, "between four and five thousand Anabaptists were executed by fire, water, and sword."[106] Others place the number much higher, with Gonzalez surmising it was "probably more than those who died

*Figure 10: The drowning of an Anabaptist woman as depicted in **The Martyrs Mirror***

during the three centuries of persecution before the time of Constantine."[107] The stories of many of them were recorded in *The Bloody Theater or Martyrs Mirror of the Defenseless Christians Who Baptized Only Upon Confession of Faith, and Who Suffered and Died for the Testimony of Jesus, Their Savior, From the Time of Christ to the Year A.D. 1660*, a massive volume still reprinted among the descendants of the Anabaptists. Since the crime was being baptized as a believer after previously receiving infant baptism, the favored method of punishment was drowning. As the Zurich Council declared in 1526, "He who dips, shall be dipped."

If Martin Luther, Ulrich Zwingli, and John Calvin are remembered as the faces of the Reformation, a good representative of the Anabaptists would be Dirk Willems. Unlike the famous reformers, Willems never achieved a position of power, and he most certainly never sought state or military support for his beliefs. Willems was arrested and imprisoned in the Netherlands as an Anabaptist in 1569. He was able to escape his jail in the local palace by lowering himself from a window

with a rope of knotted rags. As a guard pursued him, Willems ran toward safety across a frozen pond. His pursuer, weighted by his armor, broke through the ice and began to drown. Willems turned back and rescued the man, who promptly took him in custody back

Figure 11: Dirk Willems rescues his pursuer in 1569

to the palace. Not long afterwards, Dirk Willems was burned at the stake.[108] This attitude, perhaps more than any other trait, distinguished the Anabaptist movement from the Roan and Reformed churches. The Anabaptists would not organize themselves into a new state church for protection or retaliation against the violence of their antagonists. Their model of the church demanded that they face death rather than combine the body of Christ with weapons of force.

In 1527, Michael Sattler, who would die at the stake three months later, and a group of Anabaptist leaders composed the *Schleitheim Confession of Faith* in which they affirmed, among other statements, that baptism should be administered only to believers.

> Baptism shall be given to all those who have learned repentance and amendment of life, and who believe truly that their sins are taken away by Christ, and to all those who walk in the resurrection of Jesus Christ, and wish to be buried with Him in death, so that they may be resurrected with Him and to all those who with this significance request it of us and demand it for themselves. This excludes all infant baptism, the highest and chief abomination of the Pope.[109]

The *Confession* then cited baptism as a requirement for participation in the celebration of communion.

> All those who wish to break one bread in remembrance of the broken body of Christ, and all who wish to drink of one drink as a remembrance of the shed blood of Christ, shall be united beforehand by baptism in one body of Christ which is the church of God and whose Head is Christ. For as Paul points out, we cannot at the same time drink the cup of the Lord and the cup of the devil.[110]

The state and the state churches received strong condemnation in the *Confession*, although it should be remembered that these institutions were killing Anabaptists at the time. There could be no accord between them.

From this we should learn that everything which is not united with our God and Christ cannot be other than an abomination which we should shun and flee from. By this is meant all Catholic and Protestant works and church services, meetings and church attendance, drinking houses, civic affairs, the oaths sworn in unbelief and other things of that kind, which are highly regarded by the world and yet are carried on in flat contradiction to the command of God, in accordance with all the unrighteousness which is in the world.[111]

In spite of the violence they suffered at the hands of their enemies, the Anabaptists viewed the use of weapons, either in aggression or in defense, as incompatible with the true church.

Therefore there will also unquestionably fall from us the unchristian, devilish weapons of force – such as sword, armor and the like, and all their use for friends or against one's enemies – by virtue of the Word of Christ. Resist not evil.[112]

More than a century later, the same refusal to take up weapons was reaffirmed by a Dutch Mennonite conference held in Dordrecht, Holland.

From this we understand that therefore, and according to His example, we must not inflict pain, harm, or sorrow upon any one, but seek the highest welfare and salvation of all men, and even, if necessity require it, flee for the Lord's sake from one city or country into another, and suffer the spoiling of our goods; that we must not harm any one, and, when we are smitten, rather turn the other cheek also, than take revenge or retaliate.[113]

This call to non-resistance in the face of severe persecution was an enduring tenet of the Anabaptist movement, and it was sorely tested by local and imperial authorities. In 1526, less than a year after Blaurock, Grebel, and their companions defied the Reformed Church of Zurich, the Zurich Council made "rebaptism and attendance at Anabaptist meetings punishable by death."[114] A decree of the imperial Diet of Speiers in 1529 that "every Anabaptist and rebaptized person of either sex be put to death by sword, or fire, or otherwise"[115] accelerated the program of extermination by requiring all Christian courts to condemn any who held to the beliefs of the Anabaptist heresy. When Melanchthon and the Lutheran princes presented their *Augsburg Confession* to Charles V in 1530, they were careful to distinguish themselves from the Anabaptists, condemning them by name in five of the document's articles.[116] In 1535, Charles V issued an edict in which he promised rewards to those who reported Anabaptist activities to the authorities and warned of consequences for those who failed to do so.

> And in order to better detect these Anabaptists, their adherents and accomplices, we expressly command all subjects, to make known and report them to the officer of the place where they reside or shall be found; and if anyone shall know of persons of this sect, and do not report them to the officer of the place, he shall be punished as a favorer, adherent, or abettor of the sect of the Anabaptists; but he who shall report or make them known, shall have, if the accused is convicted, one third of their confiscated property.[117]

The Anabaptists had many enemies, and it was not safe to befriend them, or even to remain neutral toward them, in the Christian world.

Even so, Anabaptist groups continued to form and teach their beliefs about a pure church of confessing believers under the authority of the New Testament and not any civil or ecclesiastical government. To them, as stated in *The Martyrs Mirror*, the true church was "all believing, regenerated persons, gathered and purified by the Holy Spirit" and so, infant baptism was "nothing less than a contemning and trampling under foot of the true baptism of Christ."[118] They believed the church was subject to the secular authorities in secular matters as reflected in the *Dordrecht Confession.*

> We believe and confess that God has ordained power and authority, and set them to punish the evil, and protect the good, to govern the world, and maintain countries and cities, with their subjects, in good order and regulation; and that we, therefore, may not despise, revile, or resist the same, but must acknowledge and honor them as the ministers of God, and be subject and obedient unto them, yea, ready for all good works, especially in that which is not contrary to the law, will, and commandment of God; also faithfully pay custom, tribute, and taxes, and to render unto them their dues, even also as the Son of God taught and practiced, and commanded His disciples to do.[119]

At the same time, the spiritual care of the people of God belonged exclusively to the church and its appointed elders and pastors. The *Schleitheim Confession* of 1527 stated that such a leader held the position solely by being "one who out-and-out has a good report of those who are outside the faith," and that the elder should be supported by "the church which has chosen him"[120] so that the system of accountability remained local, free from the political and ecclesiastical hierarchy of the state government and the state church.

> This office shall be to read, to admonish and teach, to warn, to discipline, to ban in the church, to lead out in prayer for the advancement of the brethren and sisters, to lift up the bread when it is to be broken, and in all things to see to the care of the body of Christ, in order

that it may be built up and developed, and the mouth of the landerer be stopped.[121]

The commitment to a separation of church and state and to the principle of nonresistance was both reinforced and undercut by events in the Anabaptist haven of Munster in 1534-1535. After the uprising of German peasants was crushed ten years earlier, many fled to Anabaptist groups to escape the oppression of the Lutheran princes. Some among these refugees harbored lingering resentments and hopes of retaliation, and they were ripe for the call to action that came when

Figure 12: Jan of Leyden, "King David" of Munster

Anabaptist radicals in Munster expelled the Catholic population, along with the bishop, from the city. The Catholic Church raised an army to support the bishop, but the Anabaptists took up arms and defended themselves from the siege. Jan of Leyden, a former innkeeper, assumed the title "King David," enforced Old Testament law on the city, claimed supernatural visions from God, and even instituted polygamy.[122] The city finally fell to the bishop's forces, and the episode ended with the execution of the "king" and many of his followers. The immediate result was a renewed devotion to nonresistance by Anabaptists, most notably Menno Simons,[123] wanting to distance themselves from the radicals. However, "for centuries thereafter Europeans upon hearing 'Anabaptist' thought of the Munster rebellion."[124]

If the Reformation provided a corrective model of theology, the Anabaptist movement put the theology into practice and proposed a biblical model of the church with five main principles.

1. *A pure church of believers.* Membership in the church had to be distinct and separate from membership in the

state. Luther had identified "two governments among the children of Adam," but the Anabaptists maintained that separation in practice. A Mennonite *Confession of Faith*, written around 1600 by Pieter Jansz Twisck, affirmed that baptism could be granted "only upon faith, repentance, and reformation," and that the infant baptism performed in the state churches "we regard as a human institution, invented in the kingdom of antichrist, which ought justly to be rooted out and rejected."[125]

2. *The ordinances as symbols and affirmations.* The Anabaptists recognized baptism and communion as closely related observances that identified true followers of Christ. According to Twisck's *Confession*, only those who had "received upon faith the Christian baptism here spoken of" could be allowed "into the Christian communion," and participation was the sign "by which we submit and obligate ourselves to actually observe all the commandments and ordinances of God."[126] In general, Anabaptists closely linked the love feast with the bread and cup, and they treated feetwashing as a required part of the communion rite.[127] In many ways, the Anabaptists restored the biblical intentions and lessons of the ordinances, making them once again expressions of identification and faith, while the constant threat of persecution restored to them their sobering cost. At the same time, they could mistakenly reduce the ordinances to signs of separation from the doctrines and practices of the state churches.

3. *The authority of Scripture alone.* The Anabaptist understanding of *sola scriptura* could be summarized in a statement prepared for the Bern disputation of 1538 in which the Old Testament, the law, and the prophets are subjugated to the testimony, gospel, and message of Christ.

> We believe in and consider ourselves under the authority of the Old Testament, in so far as it is

a testimony of Christ; in so far as Jesus did not abolish it; and in so far as it serves the purpose of Christian living. We believe in and consider ourselves under the authority of the Law in so far as it does not contradict the new law, which is the Gospel of Jesus Christ. We believe in and consider ourselves under the authority of the prophets in so far as they proclaim Christ.[128]

Twisck's *Confession* also emphasized the preeminence given to the New Testament, saying, "To this new law of Jesus Christ all decrees, councils and ordinances made contrary to it by men in the world, must give place; but all Christians must necessarily, as far as the faith is concerned, regulate and conduct themselves only in accordance with this blessed Gospel of Christ."[129] The primacy of Scripture placed boundaries around the authority of any clerical position or creed. All Christians, including spiritual leaders, were accountable to the Bible.

1. *Separation of church and state.* The *Schleitheim Confession* observed, "The government magistracy is according to the flesh, but the Christian's is according to the Spirit."[130] The Anabaptists recognized and respected the proper place of human government as an agent of God to protect the innocent and to punish the wicked, but they reserved the right to organize and discipline Christians to the church. The desire to be free of governmental intrusion was natural given the suffering they experienced at the hands of civil authorities, but, unlike the Reformation churches, the Anabaptists declined, as a matter of doctrine, to take advantage of opportunities to use the resources of the state to advance their cause. Theirs was a separation of principle and not just circumstance. Even if given the chance to take the reigns of secular power, the Anabaptists believed they should refuse, for, "They wished to make Christ king, but He fled and did not view it as the arrangement of His

Father. Thus, we shall do as He did, and follow Him, and so shall we not walk in darkness."[131]

2. *A commitment to nonresistance.* Actually, the Anabaptist concept encompassed an avoidance of three uses of force: for resistance, for retaliation, and for coercion. They would not take up weapons to protect their lives or their property, to take revenge for a wrong inflicted upon them, or to force others to believe against their consciences. As the *Dordrecht Confession* stated, "The Lord Christ has forbidden and set aside to His disciples and followers all revenge and retaliation, and commanded them to render to no one evil for evil, or cursing for cursing, but to put the sword into the sheath."[132]

Unlike the churches of the Reformation, which began out of the Roman Church and soon established their own similar structures of clerical and political power, the Anabaptist movement attracted "communities of men and women who had freely and personally chosen to follow Jesus" without demanding a "single body of doctrine" or a "unifying organization."[133] The Bible, studied and applied within these communities, was the authority, not the pronouncements of politically motivated councils or creeds. Believers could embrace the lessons of Anabaptism without giving themselves to a system that claimed to supersede the New Testament. Like any movement, however, time and circumstance brought tendencies to drift from original intentions and to make principles into systemized procedures. In their search for a pure church, the Anabaptists could often become legalistic, and "in the interests of sheer survival, they lost their evangelistic zeal."[134] Anabaptism significantly advanced the work of reformation and renewal in the hard realities of nations dominated by state churches, but it did not complete the work. That work is continual, depending on each new generation of believers to read and study the Scriptures and to obey them within their unique context.

CHAPTER 5

The Pietist Christian Life

When the Treaty of Westphalia calmed the open warfare between competing state churches in 1648, the Protestant countries of Europe were "exhausted economically and suffering from the moral degradation of a generation brought up in conditions of violence and disorder," and their churches "were more occupied with a rigid orthodoxy than with a godly manner of life."[135] The spiritual mood that prevailed was that "God requires of believers nothing more than correct doctrine and a decent life."[136] Yet there

Figure 13: Johann Arndt (1555-1621)

were some who saw the need for something more than a good theology of the mind. In 1606, Johann Arndt, a German Lutheran pastor, published *True Christianity*, which contained "proposals for the reform of life (*reformatio vitae*), intended to follow up and to complete Luther's reform of doctrine (*reformatio doctrinae*)."[137] Arndt described the Christianity he hoped to present and practice.

True Christianity consists, not in words or in external show, but in living faith, from which arise righteous fruits, and all manner of Christian virtues, as from Christ himself. Since faith is hidden from human eyes and is invisible, it must be manifested by its fruits, inasmuch as faith creates from Christ all that is good, righteous, and holy.[138]

The foundation of Pietism can be seen in the desire for a renewal within the existing churches that stressed the need for regeneration, "not a theological doctrine but the indispensable experience of the Christian."[139] It was hoped that this would bring the true fulfillment of the Reformation. The main concern was that "true Christian faith should issue in pure Christian living."[140]

The two men who catalyzed the movement, Philip Jacob Spener (1635-1705) and August Francke (1663-1727), were Lutheran like Arndt, but Pietism was "the first truly inter-confessional movement of the modern world,"[141] in that it drew together like-minded people from Catholic, Reformed, and Anabaptist traditions to a common purpose of spiritual renewal. Spener focused on the Lutheran concept of the priesthood of all believers, suggesting that there should be a more intense life of devotion and study among the laity. He did not want to "found a sect," feeling that he did not have "the energy and force of a Reformer, but rather an ability to tolerate differences."[142]

In 1675, Spener published a book that outlined the Pietistic formula for renewal. Its full title was *Pia Desideria or Heartfelt Desire for a God-pleasing Reform of the True Evangelical Church, Together with Several Simple Christian Proposals Looking Toward this End*. Spener's six proposals were based on Reformed doctrine but sought to apply them to the individual life of the believer and to the corporate life of the church outside the narrow structure of the church institution.

1. *More Scripture*. Spener aimed for every Christian to be able to read and study the Bible under the direction of the Holy Spirit. Sermons, while valuable, were not enough

to feed the flock because they could not hope to address all the themes that God intended for His people.

> If we put together all the passages of the Bible which in the course of many years are read to a congregation in one place, they will comprise only a very small part of the Scriptures which have been given to us. The remainder is not heard by the congregation at all, or is heard only insofar as one or another verse is quoted or alluded to in sermons, without, however, offering any understanding of the entire context, which is nevertheless of the greatest importance.[143]

Spener encouraged reading of the Scriptures in family, private, and small group study outside of the normal gatherings of the congregation.

2. *More lay participation.* The sacerdotal system of the Roman Church had reduced the average person to a mere spectator, dependent on the schedule and presence of the clergy for spiritual instruction. Spener saw the laity as a great untapped resource for the church.

> Indeed, it was by a special trick of the cursed devil that things were brought to such a pass in the papacy that all these spiritual functions were assigned solely to the clergy . . . and the rest of the Christians were excluded from them, as if it were not proper for laymen diligently to study in the Word of the Lord, much less to instruct, admonish, chastise, and comfort their neighbors, or to do privately what pertains to the ministry publicly, inasmuch as all these things were supposed to belong only to the office of the minister.[144]

Spener wanted a true priesthood of all believers in which the laity was freed from the spiritual monopoly of the ecclesiastical hierarchy and free to serve others in the body with the abilities and resources God had given.

3. *More practice of the faith.* The state churches placed great emphasis on orthodoxy, a strict conformity to approved doctrine, but Spener wanted doctrine to produce habits and patterns of righteousness in life, especially the practice of love that fulfills the law. He proposed that this could be best accomplished in close relationships of mutual accountability.

Figure 14: Philip Jacob Spener (1635-1705)

For this purpose, as well as for the sake of Christian growth in general, it may be useful if those who have earnestly resolved to walk in the way of the Lord would enter into a confidential relationship with their confessor or some other judicious and enlightened Christian and would regularly report to him how they live, what opportunities they have had to practice Christian love, and how they have employed or neglected them.[145]

In this way, the people of God could grow in faith and service through counsel and instruction from the clergy but also from one another.

4. *More grace in disputes.* The practice of Christian love should include those within the faith according to Spener, but it should be extended also to those who are outside the faith either because of unbelief or through having fallen into error. It was necessary to contend with

them for the truth, but it should be done in a manner that displayed love.

> While we should indicate to them that we take no pleasure in their unbelief or false belief or practice and propagation of these, but rather are vigorously opposed to them, yet in other things which pertain to human life we should demonstrate that we consider these people to be our neighbors, . . . regard them as our brothers according to the right of common creation and the divine love that is extended to all, . . . and therefore are so disposed in our hearts toward them as the command to love all others as we love ourselves demands.[146]

The goal of these "disputes" should be the reconciliation or restoration of the opponent to God and not the personal glory of winning an argument.

5. *More training in piety.* Even though Spener advocated more freedom and involvement for the laity, he knew that the clergy would continue to set the tone for the spiritual life of the church. However, universities and seminaries had become notorious for mixing study in spiritual academics with decadent lifestyles among the students. Spener realized, "Since ministers must bear the greatest burden in all these things which pertain to a reform of the church, and since their shortcomings do correspondingly great harm, it is of the utmost importance that the office of the ministry be occupied by men who, above all, are themselves true Christians."[147] Therefore, "students should unceasingly have it impressed upon them that holy life is not of less consequence than diligence and study, indeed that study without piety is worthless."[148] Spener proposed that students be required to bring testimonials of their character to gain admittance into

the universities and that professors evaluate the students' lives as well as their studies.

6. *More practical sermons.* Spener believed that public speaking was intended to deliver a message of benefit to an audience. It should not be used as a platform to draw attention to the speaker's eloquence or intellectual prowess.

> Many preachers are more concerned to have the introduction shape up well and the transitions be effective, to have an outline that is artful and yet sufficiently concealed, and to have all the parts handled precisely according to the rules of oratory and suitably embellished, than they are concerned that the materials be chosen and by God's grace be developed in such a way that the hearers may profit from the sermon in life and death.[149]

The success of a sermon was not to be found in the applause of the audience but in the application of the audience as the hearers understood and lived the principles of Scripture delivered from the speaker.

In 1702, one friend wrote to another on the subject of Pietism and described Spener's work, saying, "He endeavored to kindle in the hearts of men the beautiful fire of piety, which had seemed nearly extinguished, showing them through his good life and his shining virtues the way to true happiness."[150] One of his most effective methods was the formation of *collegia pietatis* or study groups in piety. These put into practice the suggestions Spener listed in *Pia Desideria*. They were not meant to replace the church, but because they often met outside the prescribed schedules and locations of the state church and because their members were often critical of the scholastic orthodoxy of the Lutheran system, they soon drew unfriendly attention from the ecclesiastical and political authorities. In addition, Pietism contained a strong individualistic emphasis that encouraged the belief that personal experience outweighed any creed, tradition, or statement of clerical leaders. Such an independent spirit inevitably led to conflict with the clergy who believed they were spiritual superintendents of the people.

When conflict did come, the state church reacted with characteristic force as it defended the state against supposed rebellion and the church against assumed schism. The author of the letter related the sufferings of the Pietists to his friend.

> I shall tell you only that many of them have been sent to prison for their belief, many of them have been exiled and deprived of their business and condemned by their friends, not for having committed punishable crimes, by the severity of the laws, nor for having incited seditions against the magistrate, but for having found occasion to speak to our clergy and trying to oppose ungodliness, which reigns in all the orders of society, and for having (according to the dictates of their conscience) deserted our temples, or rather the false pastors or the false prophets, and for having obeyed the commandments of God. I know some even who say that they never doubt that they will die for this belief, and who are preparing every day for it with an admirable fortitude.[151]

Given this intensely hostile response to an attempt to renew the church from within, the Pietists increasingly lost hope that their efforts could change the existing system. Some quietly withdrew from involvement in the Lutheran Church to follow their own beliefs. Others maintained visible membership in the state church while secretly attending Pietistic gatherings. Still others, however, felt that something more drastic was needed.

Within the Pietist movement, there were people who definitely wanted to break from the existing churches and to organize according to what they believed were New Testament principles. These separatists, also known as Radical Pietists, "maintained that the contemporary churches had fallen away from apostolic Christianity and had failed to preserve it against the ravages of time and enemies."[152] They even began referring to the established churches as "Babel" to emphasize that they had grown wicked and deserved God's judgment.[153] Among them were Gottfried Arnold (1666-1714) and Ernst Christoph Hochmann (1670-1721), who, of all the Radical Pietists, were the most influential in the life and thought of the early Brethren. Arnold's history, *The First Love, That is the True Portrayal of the First Christians*, published in 1696, interpreted church history as a record of decline and proposed a church model based on primitive practices found in the New Testament. This book helped the Brethren find their "supposed spiritual forebears in the persecuted sects of the Middle Ages"[154] and their model for the church in the practices of the apostolic church.

Meanwhile, as a traveling evangelist, Hochmann preached sharply against the immorality and the ineffectual clergy of the Roman, Lutheran, and Reformed churches and "awakened" many who would form the first Brethren congregations.[155] Alexander Mack, Jr., the son of the founder of the Brethren, writing in 1799, acknowledged the debt the Brethren owed to Pietism.

> It pleased the good God in His mercy at the very beginning of this present century and age to support His saving grace, which appears to all men, through some voices calling for repentance and awakening. ...Here and there private meetings (in which the newly-awakened souls sought their edification) were established alongside of the usual church organizations.[156]

Hochmann himself was not interested in establishing a new church, probably because of his belief that the existing church as Babel must be replaced by God's kingdom with "spiritual priests who were able to recognize the need of the hour through divine inspiration and could therefore lead God's spiritual church.[157]

He was concerned that the ordinances be reserved for "the chosen disciples of Christ, who by the renunciation of all worldly things, follow Christ in deed and truth."[158] Many Radical Pietists "rejected the need for the outward observance of both baptism and communion, advocating instead spiritual baptism and spiritual communion with Christ,"[159] but others saw the ordinances as pure expressions of the apostolic church and of real conversion. Baptism was "the one outward sign which everyone could identify and with which one could be identified."[160] Arnold had earlier refuted infant baptism and had declared that believer's baptism was necessary for participation in the Lord's Supper that was itself the gathering for the fellowship of believers only. This Pietistic focus on personal transformation and continuing discipleship would encourage the early Brethren to practice the biblical purposes and forms of the ordinances. When they could not find freedom to observe them within the structures of the national churches, they would apply them in the context of an Anabaptist church model outside the recognized assemblies.

The theology of the Reformation and the pure church concept of Anabaptism supplied two important pieces to the framework upon which the Brethren movement would be built. The Pietistic renewal added a pattern for the Christian life with special attention to four key assumptions.

1. *The Christian life begins with an experience of regeneration.* This was a sharp departure from the orthodox view in which a person was encouraged to continue in the grace received at baptism as an infant. The Pietists believed there must come "a moment of complete passivity in a person which gives room to the omnipotent working of God."[161] Without this life-changing experience of God's grace a person remained unable to discern spiritual truth.

2. *The Christian life holds certain personal responsibilities.* The Pietists accepted Luther's doctrine of *sola fidei* as the basis for salvation, but they also emphasized the necessity of growth in obedience and good works. Spener weighed the balance when he wrote,

> We gladly acknowledge that we must be saved
> only and alone through faith and that our works
> or godly life contribute neither much nor little to
> our salvation, for as a fruit of our faith our works
> are connected with the gratitude which we owe
> to God, who has already given us who believe
> the gift of righteousness and salvation.[162]

Mack and the early Brethren would apply this principle to the church as the setting in which believers should practice their good works according to the commands given in the Scriptures.[163]

3. *The Christian life is a process of salvation.* If regeneration was the necessary beginning of the Christian life and works of righteousness its expected fruit, then the whole of the Christian life is a process of being saved from sinfulness and punishment to perfection and eternal life. Hochmann believed complete sanctification was possible in this earthly life, saying, "I may be sanctified through Jesus Christ, not only justly but perfectly, so that no more sin may remain in me, when I shall have come to complete manhood in Christ."[164] Although salvation is granted "justly" at the time of regeneration, the process of working it out "perfectly" is the required evidence.

4. *The Christian life is empowered by the Holy Spirit.* While the Pietists agreed with the Protestant commitment to *sola scriptura*, they believed the Bible was "a devotional resource more than a source of doctrine, a guide to life rather than just the source of belief and faith."[165] A *testimonium spiritus internum* or internal testimony of the Spirit was needed to make the dead writing alive in the believer.[166] Francke wrote, "God, in his infinite mercy to his children, imparts to them the internal operation of his Spirit, at other seasons than when engaged in reading his Word."[167] Thus, the interpretation and application

of Scripture could be more subjective than a careful adherence to orthodoxy.

Church history is a complex study with seemingly independent tributaries separated by chronology and geography from time to time intertwining to form blended streams that branch into diminishing pools or join to form important rivers. It is difficult to separate the waters that have mingled and mixed when attempting to trace the sources of any present flow. Stoffer has said, "Three basic elements were alloyed in shaping the mind of the early Brethren: Reformed thought, Pietism, and Anabaptism. Of these, Pietism and Anabaptism were the most significant."[168]

The Protestant Reformation attempted to change the Roman Church from within, and, when it encountered violent resistance, set up its own national churches to rival that of Rome. The Anabaptist movement offered a separate model of the church that rejected the Roman and Reformed models. Pietism, however, did not focus on a model for the church but on a model for the Christian life. It did not concern itself primarily with doctrine but with how doctrine could be made real in everyday thought and habit and deed. Those who would later begin the Brethren movement were mostly Reformed in their church associations. Durnbaugh recognized that the early Brethren were most directly influenced to change by radical Pietism, then they accepted the church model of Anabaptism.[169] In other words, Pietism was the impetus that moved them to question their place in the national churches and to consider the possibility of a primitive church.

Brethren Foundations

CHAPTER 6

Under the Providence of God

The Brethren movement was born into the hostile environment of the state churches' reaction to the Anabaptists and Pietists. The initial wars between the Catholic and Protestant rulers were settled in 1555 by the *Peace of Augsburg* which provided for the recognition, rights, and protection of the "Estates espousing the Augsburg Confession" and the "Estates and Princes who cling to the old religion,"[170] meaning the Lutheran and Catholic faiths, respectively. The principle of *cuius region, eius religio*, or "whose rule, his religion," established the basis for dividing the political and religious territories of Europe. However, the document did not extend its provisions to any outside of these two churches, stating specifically, "All such as do not belong to the two above named religions shall not be included in the present peace but be totally excluded from it."[171]

Likewise, when the *Treaty of Westphalia* ended the Thirty Years War in 1648, it promised "free Exercise of their Religion, as well in public Churches at the appointed Hours, as in private in their own Houses, or in others chosen for this purpose by their Ministers, or by those of their Neighbors, preaching the Word of God."[172] These rights, granted to Catholic and Lutheran states, were now extended to include those of the Reformed faith.

It has been found expedient to confirm and ratify it by this present Treaty, in the same manner as the above said Agreement has been made with the said Crown of Swedeland; also with those called Reformed, in the same manner, as if the words of the above said Instrument were reported here verbatim.[173]

Anabaptists again were left outside the provisions of the *Treaty*, and since each of the three authorized systems demanded the national church practices of infant baptism and open communion, those who believed in a pure church model found that the *Treaty* "had the effect not of producing religious liberty but of uniting the Catholic, Reformed, and Lutheran churches into a new persecuting force."[174]

The Radical Pietists, with their strong denunciations of "Babel," also became targets of the legal churches and the political systems that supported them. Ernst Hochmann and others were arrested in the Palatinate region of Germany after the Elector had issued an edict in 1706 against the heresy of Pietism. He called it a "gracious decree," but its terms were hardly gracious.

Those who commit this evil and do not respond either to kindly or severe warnings to abandon these wicked intentions and maintain this especially stubbornly are to be arrested at once without special authorization. They are to be put in prison, and as many of them as there are must be locked to wheelbarrows and kept on public work on the fortifications or at other common labor. They are to be separated from one another in various places, and put on a bread-and-water diet. You are to publish this present gracious decree of ours in the entire city so that everyone can conduct himself accordingly and know how to avoid trouble.[175]

Gillin compared the conditions surrounding those who resisted the national churches with the first Christians in

Jerusalem, saying, "It was the poor that were involved in the movement. They had little hope for better things in this world."[176]

The realities of the aftermath of the Thirty Years War, however, made pockets of religious toleration desirable even within the restrictions of the *Treaty of Westphalia*. Germany, in particular the Palatinate area of southern Germany, had been devastated and now was composed of 300 independent states with a variety of Catholic and Protestant princes.[177] The county of Wittgenstein officially was a Reformed territory, but Henry Albert, Count of Sayn-Wittgenstein-Hohenstein, granted toleration to those who would settle in his lands that had been depopulated during the War. Henry Albert justified his action through a loophole in the *Treaty* that invested the multitude of local rulers with "territorial" as well as "ecclesiastical" rights that "never can or ought to be molested therein by any whomsoever upon any manner of pretence."[178] Since *cuius region, eius religio* gave him the authority to dictate the religion of his lands and subjects, he assumed the right to declare a religion of toleration.

Into this haven of freedom came Alexander Mack (1679-1735) in late 1706, fleeing the restrictive Reformed officials of the Palatinate. Mack had been baptized into the Reformed Church as an infant in Schriesheim, but he had grown increasingly dissatisfied and in 1705 joined a group of Pietists who had separated from the state church. Mack had been introduced to Ernst Hochmann and had hosted him briefly. After relocating to Schwarzenau in Wittgenstein he traveled and taught with Hochmann in the spring and summer of 1707.[179] Mack agreed with Hochmann and the Radical Pietists except on issues of church organization and practice. The Radicals wanted only an invisible church led by the Holy Spirit, but Mack was "coming to believe that the New Testament supported the institution of an organized church along with the practice of such rites as baptism, the Lord's Supper, and discipline."[180]

Mack and a small group of like-minded associates believed there should be no coercion in the choice of religion, and so they rejected the religion imposed by the state and the infant baptism that accompanied it. This refusal alerted them to the awkward position they had adopted, for although they were convinced that baptism was a necessary act of initiation into the church, they had "no adult baptism to take its place," and this caused some of them to be "worried about the state of their salvation."[181] A pair of visitors, Anabaptists from among the Collegiants or Polish Brethren, to the area in 1708 urged the Pietists in and around Schwarzenau to be baptized, and the ensuing discussions revealed to Mack and his companions "quite by accident" that they all shared this common concern.[182] They wrote for advice to Hochmann who replied with encouragement that they be sure of their repentance and faith and avoid forming another sect. He also warned them of the expected reaction by the established church authorities.

> From such actions at the present time will inevitably follow nothing but the cross and misery, as the anti-Christ will still rage against the members of Jesus Christ. One must, therefore, first carefully count the cost, if one will follow after the Lord Jesus in all the trials which will certainly follow from this.[183]

The group continued their discussions with Bible study and prayer. Then, in the summer of 1708, they issued a tract or open letter to the Pietists of the Palatinate in which they declared their intentions

> Under the providence of God, in Christ Jesus the beloved, I announce and make known to the brethren beloved in God the wonderful divine ordinance which has revealed itself among brethren through their manifest confession about the true baptism.[184]

They invited others to join them in preparation for their step of obedience.

So then, if some more brethren wish to begin this high act of baptism with us out of brotherly unity according to the teachings of Christ and the apostles, we announce in humbleness that we are interceding together in prayer and fasting with God. We will choose him whom the Lord gives as the baptizer as God will reveal to us. If we then begin in the footsteps of the Lord Jesus to live according to His commandment, then we can also hold communion together according to the commandment of Christ and His apostles in the fear of the Lord.[185]

In the first week of August 1708, eight of them gathered at the Eder River and were baptized, bringing together the various pieces of church history that they had accepted as consistent with Scripture. Their Anabaptist leanings had led them to reject infant baptism, but their Reformed heritage did not allow them to give up the ordinance entirely as unimportant in a physical form. Their Pietistic beliefs guided them to study the New Testament and the early church for an answer and influenced their conclusion that "baptism was a gate and the only way through which an individual could become a member of the congregation for which they were all longing."[186]

CHAPTER 7

A Network of Influences

Henry Holsinger, who was in the forefront of a dramatic reassessment of the Brethren movement in the late 1800s, wrote, "It is not essential to an orthodox denomination that her organization should date back to the apostolic age. It is only essential that she be established on the truth."[187] That the Brethren did not appear as a sect in the records of church history until 1708 does not make them any less or more biblical than earlier or later groups of Christians. It is not necessary to validate the movement by reconstructing direct links, generation by generation, between the first century church and the baptisms at Schwarzenau.

There were many interruptions and deviations in the intervening centuries, but there were also many individuals and churches who, like Alexander Mack and the Brethren, searched the New Testament and diligently sought to apply its directives to their lives and contexts. Holsinger believed that "conscientious readers of God's Word, uninfluenced by fear or favor, with an intelligent understanding of the language in which they read the Bible, would declare the same doctrine, and practice the same ordinances in substantially the same manner."[188]

In chapter one of this book, we introduced a model, reproduced below in *Figure 15*, for the roots of the Brethren movement. The four outer circles represent the major organizations and philosophies that shaped the Christian world of 1708, not only for Mack and the Brethren, but for all who claimed the designation Christian in Germany at that time. Various people responded to these influencing forces in different ways, embracing some, adapting some, and rejecting some. The positioning of the Brethren circle in the center of the figure is not intended to argue that the Brethren balanced these influences equally, but the Brethren could not escape the cultural and historical realities of their environment. They looked to the New Testament for direction, but they interpreted and applied what they read within the framework of those realities.

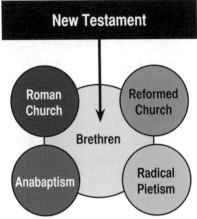

Figure 15: Model of Brethren roots and influences

Now, having examined the development and characteristics of these influences in their historical settings, we may identify the elements that each of them contributed to the organization and foundational beliefs of Brethrenism. In broad terms, the model could be summarized by *Figure 16.*

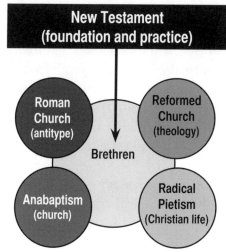

*Figure 16: Contributions of the historical
influences to the Brethren*

More specifically, the contributions of each could be listed as seen in *Figure 17*.

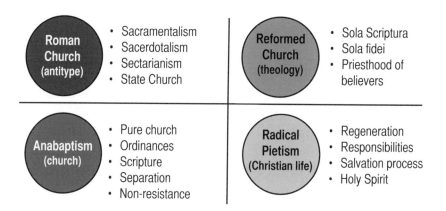

*Figure 17: Specific contributions of the historical
influences to the Brethren*

Roman Church: Antitype. The early Brethren saw in the Roman Catholic system all the seeds that had produced the corruption and deterioration of the church from the primitive model Christ intended. The Roman Church and its practices represented the Babylonian prostitute of Revelation 17, drunk on the blood of the saints. Mack decried the "bestial outcome" of the Catholics that was so loathsome that "the Jews and the Turks are scandalized by the horrible wickedness."[189] The four key doctrines of the Roman system in some ways formed a definition of what the Brethren did not want the church to be, although they would develop their own type of sectarianism in time.

Reformed Church: Theology. The Reformation addressed and corrected the theological errors of the Roman system, but it failed to implement them into the life and structure of the church in the view of the Brethren. Mack saw the outcome of the Reformed Church as a copy of the Roman Church. "What is still more horrible, they go publicly to war," he wrote, "and slaughter one another by the thousands. All this is the fruit of infant baptism."[190] The Brethren would incorporate the three doctrines of the Reformation because they found them to be consistent with the teachings of the New Testament, but they did not accept the state church structure of the Reformed Church.

Anabaptism: Church. It was from Anabaptism that the early Brethren learned a pattern for the nature and organization of the church as the community of faith. Mack knew that the model would be difficult to maintain, and he lamented the "now-deteriorated Baptists" whom he believed had "strayed far from the doctrine and practice of the old Baptists."[191] Mack respected the commitment and the sacrifice of the early Anabaptists and agreed with most of their doctrines, but the later Anabaptists were not so concerned with the forms of primitive church practices, while Mack believed that the church could remain pure only by closely adhering to all the commands of Christ. Still, the Brethren views of the ordinances, the primacy of Scripture, and the relationship between the church and the state were all traits of Anabaptism.

Radical Pietism: Christian Life. Establishing a new church organization was not Mack's objective, but it was necessary to have a setting in which he and his companions could practice the obedience required of the Christian life. Regeneration was the beginning of a life-long process of fulfilling the responsibilities of a disciple of Jesus through the instruction and power of the Holy Spirit. Although Mack had accepted the teaching of the Pietists, he felt their emphasis on a personal faith apart from the discipline of the body of Christ showed a "pernicious hypocritical love."[192] The Brethren would practice discipleship in the context of a community that cared enough to confront sin and displayed a love "which hates sin and punishes wickedness and evil."[193]

New Testament: Foundation and Practice. The early Brethren adopted the contributions of these historical influences because they did not seem to contradict the plain teaching of the New Testament. If any of their ideas or practices fell short of what the Brethren believed to be the commands of Christ, they did not hesitate to criticize them. From the New Testament, the Brethren discovered specific forms they believed were essential to full obedience. The details mattered to Mack. By way of illustration, he depicted a father's expectation of his son's complete obedience.

> If you had been obedient in everything to me for ten or even more years, and I requested you to pick up a piece of straw, and you did not want to do it and did not do it, I would have to consider you a disobedient child. Even if you said a thousand times, "Father, I will do everything; I will work hard; I will go wherever you send me, but it does not seem necessary to me to pick up the piece of straw because it neither helps you nor me," I would say to you, "You are a disobedient wretch."[194]

This insistence on full obedience to the forms and principles of Scripture set the early Brethren apart from their predecessors and their contemporaries.

The Brethren were not innovators, nor did they seek separation out of a spirit of rebellion or jealousy. They did not aim to establish a new organization to rival the state churches in a competition for influence and control. They surveyed what they perceived to be the ruins of the church and picked out a brick here, a frame there, that could help them to restore the original structure according to the blueprint in Scripture. They gratefully acknowledged the insight of a Luther, the courage of a Grebel, the devotion of a Spener, and the passion of a Hochmann, but they would not make any of them the authority for their practice of the faith. They tried to judge the doctrines and patterns of humans by the Word of God, keeping the pieces they deemed true in the comparison and discarding the rest.

When the Brethren organized as a separate sect in 1708, they positioned themselves among four distinct categories of churches. Each of these designations has been used in a variety of ways by church historians, but for our purposes, the names will refer to how the Brethren related to other Christian groups of the time.

1. *Pilgrim Church.* As the name implies, the Brethren could be grouped with other sects that could not find a home within the accepted churches of their day. They were ecclesiastical wanderers, compelled by their beliefs to remain separate from the state churches. In fact, their commitment to always evaluate themselves by the directives of Scripture made it very unlikely they would ever settle on any creed or organizational structure long enough to allow it to become an unchanging tradition. It also meant they would choose to forego the resources of the established churches rather than agree to a system that violated their consciences.

2. *Believers' Church.* The Brethren believed that the true church consisted of only those who had professed faith in Jesus, experienced regeneration, and lived as disciples of the Lord. Others might attach themselves to a religious organization, but they were not members of the body of Christ. For the Brethren, baptism as a believer was an essential public declaration of faith, and communion

was an ongoing sign of continued faithfulness and participation. Since the church was made up of professing believers, obedience to the commands of Jesus was expected and enforced through discipline.

3. *Free Church.* A church of professing believers was not valid if its members professed under compulsion to any human authority. Durnbaugh observed that, for groups like the Brethren, "an uncoerced faith is the mark of true religion."[195] The Brethren would submit themselves, as members of the church, only to the authority of Christ and the Bible. State officials were to be obeyed and respected, but their power did not extend into the beliefs and practices of the church. In the same way, no religious official outside the local congregation had the right to impose a creed or test of orthodoxy against the consciences of the members.

4. *Primitive Church.* Mack was asked by a Pietist, who was critical of the Brethren for wanting to organize into a church, how he could be sure his group had chosen a model that would meet with divine approval. Mack appealed strongly to the initial New Testament church as the true model for a church sanctioned by God.

> We indeed have neither a new church nor any new laws. We only want to remain in simplicity and true faith in the original church which Jesus founded through His blood. We wish to obey the commandment which was in the beginning... If this and its divinity in teaching, words, and commandments were to be acknowledged, then it could be determined whether a church has this divine teaching in it or not. If this is realized, then we think that it would be sufficient to recognize a church before all other churches in the whole world, if she is subject, as a true wife to her husband Christ, to

His commands, yes, if it still strives to be even more submissive.[196]

The early Brethren assumed the church in its primitive stage as first founded by Jesus through the apostles in Jerusalem was the pure church, uncorrupted by the clutter of pride, greed, and error that the intervening centuries would bring. They desired to rediscover and reinstitute the church as it had been at its earliest development before Constantine and the alliance with the state had marred it beyond recognition.

Before we continue the story of the Brethren from the banks of the Eder to the present, we will look more closely, in the next chapters, at five foundational principles the early Brethren deemed essential to the private and corporate lives of those who would follow Christ. In them we will detect again and again the influences outlined in the preceding section of this book. In them, if we are wise, we will also see the contextual rationale for many concepts and practices still valued among the Grace Brethren today.

CHAPTER 8

Believer's Baptism by Trine Immersion

"The fact is incontestable that a congregation or church of Christ could never have existed without the baptism and ordinances as commanded by the true Founder," wrote Alexander Mack.[197] When asked if he meant there was no church if baptism were not observed in the correct manner, Mack replied, "If the early ordinance of baptism had ceased to exist, then, of course, the church of Christ would also have ceased to exist. Even if there had been souls here and there who lamented the great apostasy, they could not have been called a church."[198]

The early Brethren believed the pure church consisted of people who had responded to Christ in faith and demonstrated that fact publicly through baptism. No one could be accepted as part of the community of faith who had not submitted to the rite. Some might profess and proclaim the truth of God, but "we cannot consider them to be the church of Christ just because of their prophesying, if they did not walk in the teaching of Jesus, in baptism and the other ordinances."[199] Mack was careful to say that God alone could judge whether such people were saved, but the fact remained that they could not be positively identified by others as members of the church without baptism.

What was this "early ordinance of baptism" that the Brethren decided was absolutely necessary for individual obedience and corporate existence? In recent years, much has been said about the distinctiveness of the form of baptism practiced by Brethren. The action of trine immersion, involving three separate dips under the water, was the mode intended by Jesus and performed by the apostolic church according to Mack and his companions, but the exact mode was not the point they emphasized most. Although Brumbaugh proclaimed in his history, "From the first trine immersion for adults only was held to be baptism by the Brethren,"[200] the precise form of the ordinance was not addressed in the open letter to the Pietists in 1708 that announced the intentions of the group. Nor was it mentioned in Mack's letter, written to Count Charles August in 1711, protesting the penalty enacted upon a widow and her daughter whom Mack had baptized. Even in his *Basic Questions* (1713) and *Rights and Ordinances* (1715), in which he directly explained the Brethren doctrine of baptism, Mack did not present three immersions as the specific, biblical mode.

That Mack practiced trine immersion could be inferred from his statements that disciples "were to be baptized upon their faith and confession, in the name of the Father, the Son, and the Holy Spirit," and that "the Lord Jesus also commanded that baptism should be performed in these three most exalted names."[201] Mack also quoted Tertullian and a story about Nicodemus that believers in the early church were "immersed three times."[202] His son, writing in 1774, said that Mack "found, in authentic histories, that the primitive Christians, in the first and second centuries, uniformly, according to the command of Christ, were planted into the death of Jesus Christ by a threefold immersion into the water-bath of holy baptism."[203] Among the "trustworthy histories" Mack consulted were almost certainly writings of Gottfried Arnold, Justinian, Bede, Wallfried Strabo, Honorius Augustodunensis, and Tertullian.[204]

Willoughby proposed that Mack "practiced three-fold immersion, but did not consider the actual mode to be a Biblical requirement,"[205] but it seems more reasonable to agree with Stoffer that "the Brethren found the threefold mode of baptism to be of ancient pedigree; then they examined the New Testament and found this mode to be consistent with Scripture."[206] Still, given the religious and cultural climate of the time, the precise form of trine immersion was not the most important of the three priorities Mack emphasized for baptism.

1. *First Priority: Baptism is for believers only.* When Mack wrote a letter to Count Charles August in 1711, he was most concerned to distinguish the "true baptism of repentant sinners after their confession of faith commanded by Jesus" from the "harmful and introduced infant baptism."[207] Both Anabaptists and Pietists were relentless in their opposition to the sacrament which they saw as the chief cause of the immorality of the state churches. If infants were automatically made Christians through a rite practiced upon them, then there was no responsibility for a life of obedience when they became adults.

    Hochmann had stated in his *Confession*, "In regard to baptism, I believe that Christ instituted it alone for the grown up and not for the little children, because one cannot find in the entire holy Scripture one iota of an express command about it."[208] Mack's first two children had been baptized in the Reformed church of Schriesheim in 1701 and 1703,[209] but he later declared, "Children are to be presented to the Lord Jesus in prayer, but baptism should be delayed until they are able to prove and profess their faith."[210] It was natural that the first priority should be believer's baptism since that was the aspect that brought the wrath of the state churches against them. It signaled their departure from the authorized traditions and was taken by the secular officials as an act of rebellion. Mack admitted to Charles August that he was guilty before the state but obedient before God.

Now I will freely and publicly confess that my crime is that Jesus Christ, the King of kings and Lord of lords, desired that we do what we are doing – that the sinner shall repent and believe in the Lord Jesus and should be baptized in water upon his confession of faith.[211]

2. *Second Priority: Baptism must be by immersion in water.* As the news of their action spread, Mack and his companions assumed that Ernst Hochmann and other Pietists would be in full accord with their decision to be baptized, but they were stung by the criticism that followed from those they considered allies. John Gichtel (1638-1710), a prominent Pietist in Amsterdam, wrote,

The natural water is of course not sufficient for the rebirth. It has to be the water of the eternal life, which Christ alone can give. The good souls in Schwarzenau, who have themselves baptized in the natural water, are not deeply enough grounded.[212]

Ernst Hochmann, Mack's mentor in Pietism, who had earlier given approval to the baptism, now expressed more reservations, saying, "I want to advise warmly, however, that they do not begin a sectarian spirit against others who are not inwardly impelled to the outward baptism."[213] The Pietists were concerned with an inward baptism of the spirit and saw little value in the outward form, preferring to avoid it as the beginning of a new sect that would become like all the others. Mack, however, believed that obedience to the command of Christ dictated an outward action that affirmed the inward change of regeneration. He also was convinced that the outward action had an intended form.

The Lord Jesus did indeed not say to baptize the head or some other part of the body of the person, or sprinkle the person a little with water in His name. No, the Lord Jesus did not command this, but rather that the whole person should be immersed in water.[214]

For the early Brethren, baptism must be a physical act performed according to the pattern given in the New Testament to fulfill obedience. If other groups practiced believer's baptism by sprinkling or pouring, it was because "they do not look singly and alone to their Lord and Master."[215] Mack stressed that full immersion was necessary to accurately portray "a water bath or a burial of sins."[216]

3. *Third priority: Baptism should be by trine immersion.* Although Mack said very little about trine immersion specifically, it was certainly not an afterthought. Full obedience meant careful attention to detail in observing the commands of Christ. The real reason that trine immersion received relatively minor treatment in Mack's writings may be that no one was criticizing the Brethren for immersing candidates three times. Mack identified the issues that caused controversy.

> I was criticized because of our baptism, and was called an Anabaptist, for we rebaptize those who were already baptized as infants. I was also severely criticized by those who, although they were baptized as adults but only by aspersion, are despite this baptized by us if they desire to join our church fellowship.[217]

The state churches penalized them for practicing adult baptism, and the Pietists disapproved of their insistence on an outward rite. These were the obvious issues that demanded attention. The tension with other Anabaptist groups over the specific mode only surfaced when one of them wanted to join the Brethren. Within the Brethren sect, trine immersion was the only approved form, but it would be for later generations to refine and articulate a defense of it.

Mack offered no explanation of why Jesus instructed His disciples to baptize by trine immersion. Obedience to the command, not understanding of its reasons, was the essential element to the early Brethren. Later, an argument defending the form would be developed that claimed the Greek construction of Matthew 28:19 demanded a threefold action to picture the trinity. However, even this did little to clarify the rationale behind the command. Mack touched on the real genius of Christ's purposes when he recognized that the baptism Jesus introduced was different from any previous forms.

Mack and the early Brethren did not expand on this observation, but it holds the key to a natural progression in the New Testament from the rite practiced by first century Judaism to the form Jesus gave to His followers as they received His commission to build His church. *Figure 18* below provides a summary of this sequence in which each new development adds a piece to the completed picture presented by trine immersion.

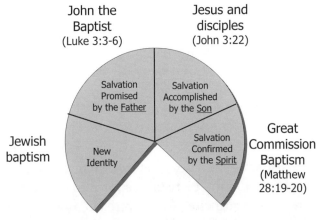

Figure 18: Progression of baptism to trine immersion

1. *Jewish baptism.* Water immersion was already known as an initiatory rite, "a public way of breaking with one's past life and beginning a new one,"[218] before John used it along the Jordan River. It was required of Gentiles who wished to convert to Judaism and of Jews who needed to wash away some ritual impurity before approaching a significant time devoted to God.[219] It was a means of professing a new self-identity with some aspect of religious belief or preparation, and it would have been very familiar to the audiences of John and Jesus. The Brethren recognized this significance of baptism in the burial image of Romans 6 and the cleansing bath of 1 Peter 3:21.[220]

2. *John the Baptist.* John applied the preparatory nature of baptism to his Jewish audience as ones needing to repent and turn from sin to be ready for the coming of God's promised anointed (Luke 3:3-6). John told them that his water baptism was transitory as well as preparatory, for a mightier one was coming who would work a true transformation with the Holy Spirit and with fire. A water baptism of repentance, as presented by John, could demonstrate a willingness to submit to the authority of the Messiah and an eager anticipation of His arrival, but it could only foreshadow the reality of the inward change Jesus would bring.

3. *Jesus and His disciples.* Jesus validated the purpose of John's baptism of preparation by submitting to it Himself, and God used the occasion to powerfully declare that Jesus was the one John had predicted (Matthew 3:13-17). Afterward, Jesus and His disciples conducted baptisms of preparation in a similar manner (John 3:22) but with an added stage of meaning. John had prepared people to follow the coming Messiah, while Jesus, as the Messiah, "perpetuated that baptism during His earthly ministry as a means of bringing repentant ones into

His circle of disciples."[221] Water baptism moved from a sign of anticipation of the salvation promised by God to one of identification with Jesus as the One who would accomplish that salvation.

4. *Great Commission baptism.* After His death and resurrection had fulfilled God' promise of salvation Jesus gathered His disciples to declare that all authority had been given to Him to establish a new order of discipleship (Matthew 28:19-20). Water baptism would continue as a symbol of identification, but it would have new meanings to fit the momentous changes that had been realized through His completed sacrifice. As Tasker observed, this baptism "was not just a revival of John's baptism of repentance, nor even a continuation of the baptism practiced by Himself and His disciples earlier in His ministry. It was essentially a *new* sacrament, by which men and women were to come under the influence of the Triune God."[222] Mack recognized the difference as well, saying, "This was no longer to be a baptism for repentance, but rather a baptism for those who had already repented and who believed in Jesus Christ, the Son of God."[223] The form Jesus gave also added the final piece to the picture of salvation by anticipating the baptism with the Holy Spirit and with fire that would occur shortly at Pentecost to confirm the salvation promised by the Father and accomplished by the Son.

Although Mack did not press the details of trine immersion, he did emphasize a correct form more than either the Anabaptists or the Pietists, and he believed that the Brethren surpassed other groups in their observance of the apostolic mode. Mack concluded that he was correcting "great abuses concerning baptism in these times" that had developed during a period of "great darkness covering the nations."[224] This work was vital, because a willingness to be baptized according to the command of Christ was a necessary fruit of repentance and salvation.

Mack did not equate baptism with salvation, but he said that "the desire for obedience toward water baptism is inseparable from the true rebirth."[225] At the same time, Mack was careful to state that the physical act of obedience without true faith was worthless. More fully, Mack explained the connection between the inward regeneration and the outward ceremony in this way.

> We do indeed believe and profess that eternal life is not promised because of baptism, but only through faith in Christ (John 3:15, 18). Why should a believer not wish to do the will of Him in whom he believes? If it is the will of Christ that a believer should be baptized, then it is also the will of the believer. If he thus wills and believes as Christ wills, he is saved, even if it were impossible for him to receive baptism. . . If, however, a man does not desire to be baptized, he is rightly to be judged as unbelieving and disobedient, not because of baptism, but because of his unbelief and disobedience.[226]

When an opponent insinuated that the Brethren believed that the rite of baptism was the agent of salvation, Mack retorted,

> That would indeed be a good baptism, if all those whom we baptize in water were truly reborn. It cannot be proved that all of those baptized by Christ and the apostles turned out well. If, however, true faith is present, and the Word is grasped or accepted in the water bath by faith, then a considerable rebirth or cleansing occurs in the "washing of water with the word" (Ephesians 5:26).[227]

It seems clear that Mack and the early Brethren did not believe that the physical act of baptism held any efficacious power for salvation, but Willoughby may be right when he says that "in trying to correct the error of infant baptism Mack went to the other extreme."[228] The state churches had made infant baptism the test of orthodoxy and inclusion in their systems. At times, Mack edged towards making believer's baptism by immersion the single requirement for admittance into the circle of the Brethren. He stopped short of condemning all believers who had never practiced the rite as he did, but he could not fully accept them as members of the true church when they had missed such an important command that was necessary to claim the full obedience that he felt should be the hallmark of those who had experienced the rebirth of faith.

CHAPTER 9:

Threefold Communion

By the time the first group of Brethren separated from all the existing churches they knew in order to recapture the primitive church of the New Testament, the prevailing practice of open communion was an enemy nearly as deadly to their concept of the true church as was infant baptism. The one placed people in the church and assured them of God's grace before they could understand their need, while the other extended the promise of salvation to them whether or not they believed or obeyed. Alexander Mack saw a close relationship between the two and insisted that believer's baptism precede and that a life of obedience was required to continue participation in communion.

> The true Householder, Jesus Christ, commanded this only of the members of His household who have entered the Kingdom through true repentance and faith and baptism, and who willingly keep all of the rules of the Householder in obedience of faith.[229]

The image of a household whose master and caretaker is Jesus was central to Mack's understanding of the Lord's Supper. It gave to the Brethren view and practice of communion a distinct emphasis on the human relationships created by membership in the body of Christ. Mack made this clear in his definition of the observance.

> When, however, the believers gathered in united love and fellowship and had a supper, observing thereby the commandments of the Lord Jesus that they wash one another's feet after the example and order of the Master (John 13:14, 15), yes, when they broke the bread of communion, drank the chalice (the cup) of communion, proclaimed the death and suffering of Jesus, praised and glorified His great love for them, and exhorted one another to bear the cross and endure suffering, to follow after their Lord and Master, to remain true to all His commandments, to resist earnestly all sins, to love one another truly, and to live together in peace and unity – that alone could be called the Lord's Supper.[230]

The state churches had removed the "one another" aspects of communion and made it an experience of God's grace through an authorized clerical mediator. The setting had been changed from the table of fellowship to the sanctuary of worship, from the upper room of a home to the lofty spaces of a cathedral. Mack and the Brethren saw a more personal nature to the observance that could be summarized in the following statement: "Invited companions, having been cleansed and prepared by the Master, share a meal of fellowship, in order to identify themselves with His body and His eternal salvation, at His table." *Figure 19* provides a picture of this concept.

1. *Invited companions.* When Jesus gathered with His disciples in the upper room in Jerusalem on the evening before His death, He took the role of host at the event. Mack referred to Jesus as the "Householder,"[231] a term that implied both a familial relationship and a position of authority. He believed that "all who call themselves Christians should

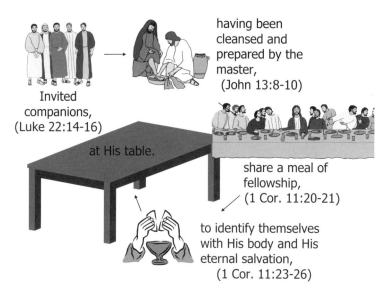

Invited companions, (Luke 22:14-16)

having been cleansed and prepared by the master, (John 13:8-10)

at His table.

share a meal of fellowship, (1 Cor. 11:20-21)

to identify themselves with His body and His eternal salvation, (1 Cor. 11:23-26)

Figure 19: The Brethren picture of the Lord's Supper

live as children of one household. The good Householder has given them rules and laws which they are to keep and respect well and prudently."[232] In the pure church concept of the early Brethren, the Lord's Supper was the place, above all others, reserved only for members of the household. Mack said that Jesus, "the true Householder," permitted only "the members of His household who have entered the Kingdom through true repentance and faith and baptism, and who willingly keep all of the rules of the Householder in obedience of faith."[233] This meant that "even if but one work of the flesh is evident in them,"[234] they should be admonished and called to repentance. If sufficient change did not follow, they should be excluded from the Lord's Supper and from the church.

2. *Having been cleansed and prepared by the Master.* In John 13, Peter objected to having his feet washed by Jesus. When Jesus told him unless He washed him he could have no part with Him, Peter impulsively requested a full bath. Jesus explained that a person who had already bathed was clean but still needed his feet washed. In the immediate

context, the bath may have referred to the ceremonial washing that the disciples would have performed in preparation for the Passover or it may have looked back to the "Levitical ordinance" in which priests were to be bathed at their ordination and were commanded to wash their hands and feet each time they prepared to enter the presence of the Lord.[235] Mack seemed to have a similar view of the relationship between baptism and feetwashing. Baptism showed a participant to be worthy of inclusion in the Lord's Supper while feetwashing demonstrated an awareness and respect for the sacredness of the occasion. By taking the role of the Householder in washing one another's feet the early Brethren recognized their responsibility to serve one another humbly and to maintain the purity of Christ's church.

3. *Share a meal of fellowship.* In the expanded title of *Rights and Ordinances*, Mack referred to himself as "One also called to the Great Supper."[236] The marriage supper of the Lamb (Revelation 19:6-9) was the ultimate event for which Christ was preparing His people, and the Brethren consistently tied that future hope into their observance of the fellowship meal or love feast. In the upper room, Jesus had made this connection by telling His disciples this first practice of the new ordinance would be the last He would share physically with His followers until all it portended would be fulfilled. Thus, the meal provided a transitional symbol "in memory of the last meal eaten with an esteemed friend and in anticipation of another in the future which he has promised."[237] Mack stated the present and future combination in this way.

> By such a supper they portray that they are members and house companions of the Lord Jesus. They will one day observe the Great Supper with the Lord Jesus at the close of the world and enjoy eternal happiness.[238]

Mack insisted this should be an evening meal, and he declared that an observance at any other time of the day was not the Lord's Supper but "a custom which has been introduced by reason and by the worldly spirit through the wrongly praised artfulness of the theologians in their many rational conclusions."[239]

4. *To identify themselves with His body and His eternal salvation.* The apostle Paul marked the bread and the cup as the piece of communion that must be taken in a worthy manner (1 Corinthians 11:27-30). Mack and the early Brethren did not make this distinction. To them, all parts of the communion observance were equally sacred, and only those who had continued in obedience from their repentance and baptism were worthy to participate in any part of the Lord's Supper.

     The state churches had reduced communion to receiving the Eucharist from the hands of an authorized clergyman. Mack and the Brethren placed the bread and the cup back into its New Testament context of a fellowship meal. The elements were not transformed into the body and blood of Christ. They were memorials by which the participants "proclaimed the death and suffering of Jesus, praised and glorified His great love for them."[240] And they were teaching tools by which they "exhorted one another to bear the cross and endure suffering, to follow after their Lord and Master, to remain true to all of His commandments, to resist earnestly all sins, to love one another truly, and to live together in peace and unity."[241] The vertical praise to God and Jesus had to be joined with the horizontal admonition and encouragement to one another. Only then could they say they discerned the body of Christ in a worthy manner.

5. *At His table.* Communion was the gathering of the household at the invitation of the Householder. A family did not share a meal that consisted of nothing more than "a bit of bread and a little wine,"[242] and they did not eat in

isolation from each other. It could be said that the table was the central symbol of Brethren communion because all the other pieces revolved around that setting. The participants did not come to the clergy at an altar to establish a relationship with the Master. They gathered together in fellowship and remembrance because they already had the relationship. The family of God needed to celebrate their birthright and to exhort and remind one another of the privileges and responsibilities that it gave to them.

If baptism was the ordinance through which the Brethren identified themselves with the salvation and people of God, then threefold communion was the continuing observance that renewed their commitment to obey Jesus and to live together as His church. It was a picture of membership in the household of Jesus. It memorialized His suffering that made the family possible, it was a visible expression of the relationships that He had created within the body, and it motivated the participants to a life of obedience and separation from the empty values of the world.

Jesus Himself washed feet and distributed the bread and the cup in the upper room, so it could be argued that the symbols were unnecessary in that setting. However, every future observance of that evening in the history of the church until His return would be celebrated in the material absence of the Host. The symbols of bread and wine were given by Jesus as tools to represent Him and to cause future generations of His followers to remember the life and benefits He purchased for them through His sacrificial death. The meal, the feetwashing, and the bread and cup embodied in experiential form the truth that His disciples would pass on to those who became the new church at Pentecost. And communion would continue, throughout the development of the Brethren movement, to be one of the first things in which every new member was instructed.

CHAPTER 10

The Inward and Outward Witnesses of Truth

Mack readily acknowledged that all the Christian sects of his time appealed to Scripture as an authority for their beliefs and practices, yet he also noted, "To appeal to Scripture and to believe in Scripture are two vastly different things."[243] The Catholic, Lutheran, and Reformed churches all appealed to Scripture as the basis for their creedal statements, but they also depended heavily on the writings of selected church fathers and founders who had worked out the systems and structures that guided the institutions. Some Pietistic groups appealed to Scripture for the foundational principles of their activities, but they believed that the Holy Spirit led them into insights that even Scripture did not address. The Brethren once again took a middle course true to Reformed theology and the Anabaptist application of Scripture with a Pietistic inclusion of the Holy Spirit.

In his letter to Count August, Mack expressed a willingness "to be instructed" if he could "be shown by the learned theologians to be in error."[244] He freely quoted scholars and historians who supported his views along with passages of Scripture to defend his beliefs. At the same time, he warned that appeals by his opponents "to the testimonies of men reveal that they do not possess the divine testimony of Jesus."[245] This divine testimony was the real source of authority and confidence to Mack. He defined it as a "direct calling and impelling by the Spirit of God" which "consists in the fact that the person is made inwardly exceedingly certain of it by the Spirit of God, and is not concerned whether men believe it or not."[246] Such a testimony or calling should certainly agree with careful study of the Bible, but the inward calling confirmed the correct interpretation of Scripture. Thus, while Mack accepted Scripture alone as the authoritative Word of God, he believed that truth from God, consistent with Scripture, could be revealed directly through the Holy Spirit.

Mack explained how these cooperative sources of revelation interacted when he wrote, "That which the Holy Spirit ordained for the faithful was written outwardly. All believers are united in it, for the Holy Spirit teaches them inwardly just as the Scriptures teach them outwardly."[247] This concept included four vital components as pictured below in *Figure 20*.

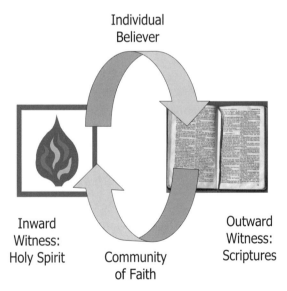

Figure 20: *The Brethren concept of revealed truth*

The inward witness of the Holy Spirit was needed to confirm the words of the outward witness of the Scriptures to the heart and mind of the believer. At the same time, the outward witness of the Scriptures served as a test for the authenticity of the inward witness of the Spirit because the Spirit would not contradict Scripture. In similar fashion, the individual believer and the community of faith provided a safeguard and balance for one another. Individuals could receive truth from God, but the same Spirit who lived in all believers should produce agreement in the body so the subjective interpretation of one person could not stand without confirmation from others. However, the voice of one person could be used by God to cause the whole community to reexamine and reconsider an issue.

If followed consistently, this concept of revealed truth could prevent, or at least slow, the emergence of a closed system of learning. No creed composed by scholars or declaration spoken by a forceful leader could end the ongoing search for God's will in the Bible prompted by the Holy Spirit so long as the Brethren believed God could still speak directly to their hearts. As Mack warned, "How wretched it is to appeal to testimonies of men and to look to men who are considered holy and wise, so that one is led to think or say: 'Truly, if they taught in this way and believed according to the Scriptures, we shall believe it also!'"[248] Mack attributed some of the contentions among the Brethren over issues like marriage and work to "errors which we had absorbed" from "those who were deemed great saints."[249] The fact that they did "continue discussion" on these and other matters showed their aversion to static creeds and confessions. Neither the doctrines of those who influenced them nor even the initial opinions of Alexander Mack would escape the comparative scrutiny of Scripture.

Tom Julien writes, "the most distinctive characteristic of the Brethren movement has been its vigorous opposition to creedalism and its commitment to the Bible as the sole authority,"[250] but Dale Stoffer has shown that "the stance of the earliest Brethren toward creeds may not be so black and white."[251] When six Brethren from Solingen, Germany, were imprisoned in 1717, their Reformed captors questioned them from the *Heidelberg Cathechism* of 1563, a document commissioned by Frederick III, Elector of the Palatinate, to codify Reformed doctrine. One of the Brethren prisoners, William Grahe, later recorded their response, saying, "If the Reformed conducted themselves according to the Heidelberg Catechism, and if only the infant baptism, swearing of oaths, and the sixtieth question were different, we could then soon agree with you."[252] Out of 129 questions in the *Catechism* these early Brethren took exception to only three.[253] Since they had left the Reformed Church to be baptized, the document would have been very familiar to them. They apparently recognized it, with the few exceptions, as an accurate expression of the teaching of Scripture.

The Brethren did not reject the composition or citation of creeds. However, they did oppose the use of a creed or a doctrinal confession as a test of orthodoxy or faith. Their resistance was probably emotional as well as doctrinal since "they had suffered severely from the heavy hand of the authorities who considered the Brethren heretical and who used the creeds to condemn them."[254] The scholasticism of the state churches valued a precise and refined statement of beliefs that could prevent deviations that might fragment the institution. Immorality needed to be limited for the good of society, but heresy must be crushed for the protection of order. Submission to a creed was a sign of loyalty to both the state and the church and a safeguard against the potential dangers of free thinking. Since the early Brethren "felt that they had not yet obtained light on all questions,"[255] a statement written by people could not be accepted as a final word.

To the Brethren, orthopraxy, the living of right actions, was far more important than orthodoxy, the holding of right doctrines. A creed could be useful as a confession or explanation of beliefs, but it could not impose or implant those beliefs into a human heart. A statement of good doctrines required only the ability to read and recite, but a life of good practices required faith. Mack employed the following analogy to illustrate this point.

> This is just as if a king had commands written to his subjects, making great promises along with them if they followed his orders, and great threats if they did not

keep them. Other people who are not subjects of that king are indeed able to read the commands and speak at great length about them. However, if they are not the king's subjects, nor wish to become subjects, they do not respect the threats and do not believe the promises. They do not submit themselves to his commandments, statutes and laws.[256]

Mack assumed the true interpretation of Scripture was given to those who desired to obey, not to those who knew the most. However, the presence of faith would produce a unity of doctrine that would be reflected in a unity of practice. Thus, while a creed could not impart a righteous life, individual obedience would bring the extra benefit of doctrinal unity to the community. The idea is pictured below in *Figure 21*.

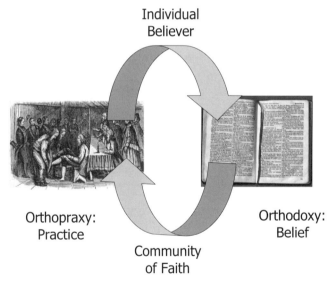

Individual
Believer

Orthopraxy:
Practice

Orthodoxy:
Belief

Community
of Faith

Figure 21: The interplay of orthopraxy and orthodoxy

The realization of such unity was an ongoing process according to Mack. He wrote, "We cannot say that we are completely one in spirit, but we must be one in purpose. That is, we must help one another until we all attain to the same faith and to that unity of fullness in faith of which Ephesians speaks."[257] Mack also said that without "inner ears" opened by faith a person could read but have no inclination or ability to obey.

> Therefore, when a believing person whose inner ears are opened reads the Holy Scriptures outwardly, he will hear as the Lord Jesus intends His teaching to be understood. He hears that which the apostles want to express in their writings. He will also be impelled, through his inner hearing, to true obedience which makes him obey even in outward matters.[258]

Thus, obedience led to a more accurate understanding of the Scriptures which, in turn, led to a more careful attention to obedience, but the cycle had to begin and end with outward evidence. Orthopraxy was a better test of faith than orthodoxy.

It could be said that the ordinances were Mack's creed. The Brethren concluded from their study of the New Testament that, as Brumbaugh observed, "ordinances were vital and creed unnecessary."[259] Holsinger noted that because the Brethren had no written statements or confessions it was "a difficult matter for outside parties to state, even approximately, what they did believe," but "their practice, so far as ceremonials are concerned, could be observed and recorded with some degree of accuracy."[260] The ordinances came to define the Brethren and their beliefs both within their group and in the eyes of outside observers. Baptism, especially, distinguished the Brethren from even their closest spiritual cousins. Perhaps that is the reason that, although he did not press the details of trine immersion, Mack did emphasize a correct form of the ordinances more than either the Anabaptists or the Pietists. Since the form as well as the fact of an ordinance was commanded by Christ, "an unwillingness to submit to the ordinances was taken to represent an *invalid* inner experience."[261]

CHAPTER 11

Separation from Sin and to Obedience

Jesus prayed for His disciples because, although they were not of the world, He was sending them as His witnesses into the world (John 17:16-19). In this way, they were to be sanctified, a word that means set apart or separated. Jesus did not want them to shut out the world or to avoid it. He wanted them to maintain a distinctive identity as His followers within the characteristics and attributes of the world system. Thus, their identity would be defined in part by what they were and in part by what they were not. The church has always had a responsibility to this kind of separation, and it has always stirred turmoil in the religious institutions of the time. The New Testament church was condemned for separating from the legalism of Judaism. The reformers were excommunicated for departing from the abuses of the Roman Church. The Anabaptists and Pietists were persecuted for establishing practices different from those of the national churches. Alexander Mack said he was criticized on all sides for separating from the established churches to observe New Testament practices.[262]

The important factor in each of the above examples is not just that these people separated *from* something, but that they also separated *to* something else. An emphasis on separation *from* alone often results in legalism, conformity to or avoidance of lists of outward forms and prohibitions in order to maintain an accepted definition of righteousness. The separation *from* must be motivated and necessitated by separation *to* something of greater value. For the early Brethren, the goal of separation was the formation of an expression of the church in which there could be greater obedience to the directives of God as revealed in the Bible to their consciences. The goal was not to create an alternative style of worship or a new paradigm for ministry. They were compelled by the call of discipleship and not by the lure of innovation or recognition. Mack said of the early Brethren, "We have left all sects because of the misuses concerning infant baptism, communion, and church system,"[263] but he also insisted, "We indeed have neither a new church nor any new laws. We only want to remain in simplicity and true faith in the original church which Jesus founded through His blood."[264] A clear separation from the other church organizations was being made, but it was being made in order to make an equally clear separation to what they perceived to be the body of Christ as Jesus intended.

Separation focused on three issues, driven by New Testament principles but also by the circumstances and pressures of their setting in the German Palatinate of the early eighteenth century. Their choice of separation *from* involved an evaluation and rejection of existing beliefs and structures so that they stood apart from some of the accepted systems of their time. In this they were seen as rebels or sectarians, unwilling to submit and quick to criticize. Their choice of separation *to* involved a search of the Scriptures and other Christian groups to find the commands of Christ and models for putting them into obedient practice. In this they were sometimes viewed as overly narrow and rigid. The three issues that were prominent themes in their choice are pictured below in *Figure 22*.

1. *Separation from the World System to the Kingdom of God.*
   A basic principle of discipleship among the Brethren was a clear distinction of life between the values and habits of

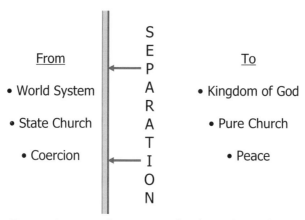

Figure 22: Issues of separation for the early Brethren

unbelievers and the motivations and practices of believers. Mack assumed, "Now then, a true child of God . . . has learned from his heavenly Father at all times a division and separation – namely, that between the pure and the impure, between light and darkness, between His people and the Gentiles."[265] This assumption was in keeping with Mack's view of a pure church as the household of God called to His purposes within the setting of the world. It was not enough that certain individuals lived in this truth, for separation from the world to serve God was the work of the church collectively. To Mack, the separation was already complete inwardly, so that "this body or church is separated from the world, from sin, from all error, yes, from the entire old house of Adam – that is, according to the inner part in faith."[266] Because of regeneration, the desire of every true member of the household was to live a devoted life of obedience to the Master. The outward application of this separation was more problematic.

> However, this body or the church of Christ still walks outwardly in a state of humiliation in this wicked world. It thus happens through divine

permission that Satan is allowed to tempt each member with sins, with various errors, and all kinds of wicked and harmful deeds day and night, in order to test his faith and love. Therefore, the Lord Jesus and the apostles call upon the faithful to watch and pray, struggle and strive.[267]

2. *Separation from the State Churches to the Pure Church.*
    The Anabaptist movement was motivated to separate from the state churches out of a desire to form a pure church, one in which the membership was comprised entirely of people who had made a voluntary, public commitment to be followers of Christ. The practice of infant baptism had all but erased that distinction so that it was necessary to start a new organization. Mack and his companions took the principle a step farther. For the early Brethren, the recovery of a pure church meant a return to the primitive church of the New Testament with its ordinances. Mack stated, "the fact is incontestable that a congregation or church of Christ could never have existed without the baptism and ordinances as commanded by the true Founder."[268] It was not enough to have a church of professing believers. Their profession had to be evidenced by baptism and ongoing obedience to the commands of Jesus. This was seen as a continuation of the pattern of the true church from the time of the apostles. Mack said,

> We believe, and it can also be shown from the ancient histories, that the early form of baptism as ordained by the ordinance of Christ has never ceased to exist. Consequently, the church has likewise never ceased to exist, even if there were but a few members.[269]

> Inclusion in the primitive church necessitated breaking all ties with any religious group that

did not adhere to all the commands of Christ because they were little better, if not worse, than the unbelieving world. The desire to avoid the mistakes of other churches gave the Brethren "a decidedly negative tendency" toward those who disagreed.[270]

3. *Separation from Coercion to Peace.* Both the world system and the state churches were willing to spread and guard their structures and beliefs with violent force. Alexander Mack had personally experienced the threat of both institutions in his lifetime. History shows that the residents in his home village of Schriesheim fled at least three times from advancing armies during his childhood. In 1689, 1693, and 1694, the villagers hid in the surrounding forests and hills until the danger passed and they could return to their plundered homes.[271] Once Mack and his companions broke from the Reformed Church, they were hounded by edicts and soldiers of both political and ecclesiastical officials who wanted to punish or disperse them. William Willoughby is almost certainly correct when he says these experiences "contributed to Mack's unequivocal opposition as an adult to violence and war."[272] Mack himself looked to the Anabaptists for this principle that avoided the use of force for resistance, retaliation, or coercion. He characterized its benefits in describing those who embraced it.

> No Baptist will be found in war, and few in prison or on the gallows because of their crimes. The majority of them are inclined to peacefulness. It is still possible to sleep unconcernedly among them and not need to fear robbery or even murder if one has much money.[273]

This was in sharp contrast to "the seed of Luther, Calvin, and also that of the Catholics."

> Not even with gallows and torture can they keep them, who are of one faith, from murdering one another in their homes, which happens often enough. What is still more horrible, they go publicly to war, and slaughter one another by the thousands.[274]

Avoidance will not produce righteousness, but righteousness will involve some areas of avoidance. This was the balance that the early Brethren struggled to find. Their choice to separate came from a comparison of the existing church systems with the teachings of the New Testament. It was necessary to identify what they were separating *to* before they could evaluate what they needed to separate *from*. Once this had been done, however, the challenge became to keep separation *to* as the focus and measure of the new movement. It is relatively easy to be different and to replace one flawed system with another that is flawed in different ways. It is harder to continue making changes and adjustments to work out the flaws of the new system. The Brethren were clearly different from the state churches, but difference alone only told them what they did not want to be. They were against immoral and selfish patterns of the world system. They were against the infant baptism and open communion of the state churches that did not demand regeneration and obedient discipleship. They were against the coercive use of force by the civil and religious powers to expand influence and maintain conformity. These practices they would separate *from* and reject. The real work would be to define what they would separate *to* and become.

CHAPTER 12:

Freedom of the Local Church

T he structure of the state church system in Germany had come to be defined by the stipulations of the Peace of Augsburg in 1555 and the Treaty of Westphalia in 1648, both of which gave political leaders the right to dictate the religious loyalties of their territories. When the region changed rulers, it could also mean a change in religion. Thus, when Alexander Mack and his companions were baptized in the Eder River in 1708, the official church of the area had changed eight times in the previous century and a half.[275] The baptism by the first eight Brethren marked them outside any of the three competing authorized churches and squarely in the tradition of the Free Church movement.

Three years later, when Mack wrote his letter of defense to Count Charles August, he declared, "We would only appeal to the Supreme Judge, Jesus Christ, who will judge rightly on the day of revelation, and repay everyone according to his works, without regard to persons."[276] He went on boldly to remind the Count that "he, too, has an immortal soul, and will have to give account one day before Jesus, the supreme liege lord, by whom he was placed in authority in this territory, about the way he governed his territory – whether it was according to sacred order or not."[277] For the early eighteenth century in

Germany – or for any time and any place – it was a statement of conviction and courage.

The state church demanded conformity among the local congregations of a geo-political nation or region. A local church either submitted to the creeds and authorities of the approved faith or it had no legal right to exist. Conformity could be enforced through civil agents who might suspend privileges, levy fines, arrest dissenters, banish them from territories, or even impose a penalty of death. Leaders in local congregations were appointed or approved by outside political and religious authorities, and the same could take their positions away. Doctrine was determined through councils of legal experts and church scholars called together by the political ruler to settle disputes and decide questions. Their conclusions were circulated as edicts, confessions, and creeds that established accepted boundaries around the teaching and discussions of the churches. Obedience to the state and church authorities was the assumed duty of every Christian, and those who openly disagreed or associated with those who disagreed could be branded as traitors to the state and heretics to the church. In this environment, there was little tolerance for the view of a personal accountability as expressed by Mack to obey the Scriptures.

The concept of a Free Church that influenced the early Brethren was probably passed on to them through the works of the radical pietist Gottfried Arnold (1666-1714). His *Impartial History of the Church and Heretics*, published in 1699, proposed that "true Christianity had been preserved over the centuries, not by the proud and secure church or prelate, professor, and priest, but by the despised dissenters."[278] He believed the church had fallen into a fatal error when Constantine folded it into the state system of Rome, and this mistake had continued in the state churches that emerged from the Reformation. He concluded there still was a true church that had preserved the original intentions of Christ, untainted by the wealth and power of the world system. The chief characteristics of this church, according to Arnold, were its refusal to bow to man-made pressures and its suffering at the hands of the corrupted church. Edicts, clerical titles, councils, and creeds were tools of the fallen church to exercise control and enforce conformity upon its subjects, but the true church remained free by accepting only the directives and practices of the New Testament.

Arnold's ideas were not new to the radicals of church history. Martin Luther and other reformers had also set out with the goal of correcting abuses and returning the church to its biblical roots. However, they did not envision a suffering remnant. They believed the one true church was destined to spread its influence to all mankind and introduce the kingdom of God in the affairs of the world. To accomplish this, a partnership between the church and the state was advantageous and even essential. The church organization must be protected and nonconformity must be punished to fulfill the mission of the church militant.[279] The Anabaptists and Pietists, in contrast, were unique in their acceptance of the notion that the true church could be called by God to prolonged suffering that would be alleviated only by the return of Christ Himself. For them, conformity to a universal church system amounted to unfaithfulness to the Master who would come someday to vindicate them.

Mack recognized only one Lord and Householder of the church, and His will was expressed through the words of the Scriptures. He and the first Brethren announced that they had separated from all other sects because the others had introduced "man's statutes and commandments."[280] It was necessary to leave behind these corrupted church systems in order to return to what Mack considered pure obedience. Otherwise, Mack said, "We will not be able to meet the test at that time when the Lord will come and require from us the obedience which He has commanded of us."[281] Ernst Hochmann, in his *Confession* of 1702, stated the position adopted by the early Brethren on the relationship between the church and human government.

> Concerning authority I believe that there is in the kingdom of nature a divine order, to which I also gladly

submit in all civil matters according to the teaching of Paul . . . On the other hand, however, to those that strive against God's Word and my conscience, or the freedom of Christ, I grant no power; for it is said: We ought to obey God, etc.[282]

The church had to be free of the intrusive traditions and decrees of political and ecclesiastical authorities who did not observe the primitive forms found in the New Testament. In particular, the church had to be free to enforce discipline among its own members, appoint its own leaders, and establish doctrine from its own study of the Bible. These three areas of governance would be at the core of the Brethren belief in the freedom or autonomy of the local church. Each congregation must be allowed to maintain its own order without interference from an external hierarchy. *Figure 23* illustrates the authority structure in the state churches and in the Free Church system.

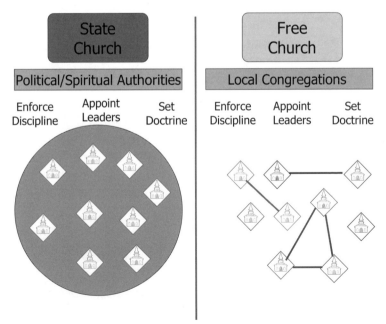

Figure 23: Comparison of the State Church and the Free Church

Since free churches did not recognize the right of political or spiritual authorities to dictate rules for all the congregations in a given region, the associations and affiliations between them were voluntary, based on common origins, similarities of beliefs, or circumstantial necessities. A local church might have obligations to other churches within its own sect, but it was free to cooperate with or separate from other congregations as it chose. While it is true that some harshly criticized other groups and refused to recognize their validity, even so they had no authority to impose their beliefs on others or to deny them their freedom to meet and organize according to their own consciences. Mack's *Basic Questions*, first published in 1713, presented a debate with Eberhard Louis Gruber, a leader of a neighboring sect known as Inspirationists.

The two men disagreed sharply on a number of issues, and it was evident that Gruber considered the Brethren legalistic on baptism while Mack thought the Inspirationists were in danger of apostasy and advised them, "If, then, your salvation and blessedness are dear to you, hasten and bow your necks under the scepter of this great King."[283] Still, in the end, both men could return to their own companions and beliefs without any fear the other would attempt to force a change of conviction through armed agents.

Each individual congregation or sect of congregations was autonomous from the others in their practice of the three areas of governance cited in *Figure 23*.

1. *Accountability and discipline of members.* While the state churches focused their enforcement on doctrinal conformity, the Brethren were more concerned with conformity to obedience in life and practice. This kind of accountability could take place only at the local level, where a person's life and character could be observed in a daily context. The community of faith provided a network of people who could encourage, remind, and admonish one another to remain faithful to their calling. They

could also prevent one who stumbled from continuing a pattern that would be damaging to his or her faith and to the collective obedience of the household. Mack hoped that, in most cases, this accountability would lead to repentance and restoration.

> Even though these faithful members of Jesus may unwittingly also make mistakes and commit sins, they do not do it intentionally, but rather are truly sorry for it in their hearts. They are the kind who suffer because of their weakness. When they are corrected by their fellow members, they listen very willingly, and allow themselves to be told where they have fallen short.[284]

If, however, a member of the body did not respond well to gentle admonitions, the other members were obligated to place that one under the ban, a separation of the person from the life of the church. It was "a firm wall around the church of the Lord"[285] that stopped the spread of the infection. Close friends and family members were expected to observe the ban, knowing that "these believers can then with good conscience also help to exclude and avoid even their beloved fellow members when the latter sin and will not listen to loving admonition."[286] Mack believed that the whole church shared this responsibility because the welfare of the whole church was at stake. A person who would not listen to "loving admonition" was mastered by the "spirit of dissension" which "always works through such a member to bring about the separation of all other members to abolish all order and to be his own master."[287]

2. *Selection of leaders.* Positions of ecclesiastical leadership were often political favors and career stepping-stones

in the state churches. Spiritual qualification and fitness could become little more than secondary considerations. Hochmann spurned this as an artificial system of appointment and declared, "Concerning the office of the Spirit, I believe that Christ, who is the head of the church, alone can appoint teachers and preachers and give them the qualifications therefore."[288] Of course, Hochmann and others may have espoused this view in part because no one in the state churches would confer the office on them. Mack looked for a means in the New Testament and found it in an apostolic succession of the office of elder without the sacerdotal priesthood of the state churches.

> The apostles soon chose others in the service of the household of God to baptize, to administer the ban and the like, so that the divine ordinances might be well maintained. However, at all times they chose only those who were descended from the royal priesthood, that is, those who had the Spirit of Jesus.[289]

Mack made it clear that the choice of leaders was meant to be handled within the local congregation and not by an external power that claimed apostolic privilege.

> On the other hand, after the death of the apostles the faithful church which remained pure and undefiled always chose men from among them who had the Spirit of Jesus and denied themselves. Just as Christ chose His apostles outwardly, so has the church of the Lord (as the body of Christ) in turn chosen those whom they recognized as capable.[290]

Mack discounted the appointment system of the state churches as "characteristic of the false spirits" and said, "When, however, men appointed themselves to the service of the church by their own spirit and their own honor, the great abuse and every evil originated and spread."[291] In contrast, men selected by the local congregation were to shepherd the flock of Christ after the admonition of Paul in Acts 20:18-28.

3. *Belief and obedience by conscience.* Once the state churches issued council decisions and doctrinal statements, they became the measures of orthodoxy for the church. Documents that summarized the teaching of the Bible became replacements for the words of the Bible in determining who was faithful and who was rebellious. Mack and the Brethren wanted to avoid the mistake of establishing yet another creedal sect, and so he made a unique statement when asked if his church would claim to be the sole possessor of truth.

> We indeed have neither a new church nor any new laws. We only want to remain in simplicity and true faith in the original church which Jesus founded through His blood. We wish to obey the commandment which was in the beginning. We do not demand that undoubted divinity be recognized in our church fellowship.[292]

At the same time, Mack did not accept the imposition of a system of laws or beliefs from any human authority outside his local congregation. Mack was not concerned with developing a final statement of doctrine. He was concerned with a continuing process of learning and growing toward complete obedience to the requirements of God. A creed or list of laws ran the risk of omitting some aspect or principle of obedience that might be lost if the church stopped searching the Scriptures. He was determined that "all of the commandments of the great God shall be esteemed great."[293]

It is important to note that Mack applied the principle of freedom or autonomy to the church and not to individual church leaders. There is no evidence that he was ever inclined to become the bishop of a network of congregations that might rival the three authorized churches. A church was not meant to be the business project of a single leader, to satisfy his desire for growth and influence. The leaders were to be the shepherds of the church, making certain that the people were taught and cared for so they could grow in obedience to Christ individually and corporately. Just as Mack did not believe a council should dictate matters of conscience to a local church to maintain conformity, a local church leader should not demand that a congregation unify around his personal beliefs or goals. The safeguard was found in the biblical pattern of multiple elders for each church and in the submission of these elders to the commands of Christ. Mack believed the one Master of the household appointed godly leaders to care for and direct His church together in the patterns and practices He set for them. All members of the congregation, including the leaders, were subject to His authority, for "the faithful dare not be of a different mind in the household of God than God has revealed himself to be in His household."[294]

Brethren Development

CHAPTER 13

European Exodus

Even though the early Brethren held some clear foundational principles, it does not follow that they had a fully developed system of beliefs. In general, their theology, with the clear exceptions of the principles cited in the previous section, was in line with that of the Reformed Church, but the Brethren formed a church of distinctive practices, not one of established doctrines. Both of Alexander Mack's extended writings, *Basic Questions* in 1713 and *Rights and Ordinances* in 1715, were defenses of what the Brethren did more than statements of what they believed. In their quest to recreate the primitive model of the church as found in the New Testament, the Brethren were regularly making adjustments, and they sometimes strayed into questionable trials they later abandoned. They made an attempt at communal living until it nearly bankrupted Mack who, as one of the wealthier members, contributed most of his resources to assist others. They also experimented with a commitment to sexual abstinence, but they eventually decided that marriage was permitted by God, although it was "closer to the image of Christ to remain unmarried."[295] Their beliefs ranged from an adherence to Old Testament food laws to a universal restoration of mankind after the torments of hell.[296]

The Brethren were just one of a number of small separatist groups in the Palatinate who were trying to find security and peace in an unstable environment. The toleration granted in Wittgenstein by Count Henry Albert was challenged by neighboring rulers, especially his brother-in-law, Count Charles Louis, who sustained a campaign of letters to imperial officials in which he referred to the fact that "fanatical and heretical people of low and knavish extraction and unknown vagabonds gathered as a pack from all kinds of places have established their residence in the Schwarzenau area."[297] He dismissed the loophole by which Henry claimed the right to allow toleration to groups outside the three recognized churches by citing article seven of the *Treaty of Westphalia* (called the *Treaty of Osnabruck* by Protestants), which stated that any exceptions must be "examined before competent Judges, who are to determine the same."[298] On this basis, Charles appealed to the Imperial Solicitor to take action against "these sectarian rabble-rousers" who, he had written earlier, "live in such a blasphemous way that they are ruining the territory and its people."[299] Although Henry steadfastly defended his policy of toleration, pressure upon him from higher authorities was mounting.

In the meantime, a second haven of toleration opened in Marienborn, about 75 miles south of Schwarzenau. In 1711, Alexander Mack had been expelled from the region twice for performing baptisms of people who had migrated from Schwarzenau. One of these occasions had prompted his letter to Count Charles August, the local ruler, protesting the expulsion of a widow and her daughter whom he had baptized. The next year, Count Ernest Casimir of Ysenburg-Budingen, which included Marienborn, issued an amazing edict of toleration.

> Some honest people avoid migration to a county because they are not members of the established church of that county, and therefore fear a coercion of conscience. We are convinced from the nature of the religion of the Kingdom of Christ and the spirit of man, as well as from the Holy Scriptures and the example of the great church Reformation and decisions arising therefrom, that the power of the authorities does not

include matters of conscience. We therefore wish to grant everyone complete freedom of conscience. None of our subject or foreigners and settlers in our county, who profess another than the Reformed faith, or even who profess no outward religion at all because of their scruples of conscience, will be caused difficulties or annoyances, if they behave honorably and virtuously and in a Christian manner in their civil conduct toward the authorities and subjects.[300]

The wording was taken as an open invitation by separatists who professed a faith other than Reformed and by Pietists who professed no outward religion. Mack returned to baptize another group of immigrants from Schwarzenau and was again ordered to leave.

Baptisms among the settlers continued until, in May of 1714, Peter Becker and his wife, subjects of Charles, were baptized by the Brethren in Marienborn. This Charles would not tolerate, and the Brethren were given the choice to obey the following order or to leave the territory.

His Grace will respect their full freedom of conscience in the carrying out of their devotions in private meetings in their homes in a quiet way, and will otherwise leave them in peace just as other subjects and those taken under protection. He will, therefore, tolerate their further stay in this county on this condition. However, he positively cannot permit the Baptists to organize a new sect or church congregation and to presume or dare to practice their faith publicly. This is just as little permitted as baptism or rebaptism; it is in fact absolutely forbidden.[301]

Unlike the Pietists, the Brethren model of church required outward forms and practices, and so they refused to submit and chose to leave. A year later, many of the Marienborn Brethren left their homes and migrated to Krefeld, a city in the Lower Rhine region of the Palatinate about 90 miles northwest of Schwarzenau. Under tolerant Prussian rule, Krefeld had become a haven for Mennonite craftsmen and a successful commercial center that gathered religious separatists from throughout continental Europe. Many of them were Pietists who were permitted to hold separate meetings in their homes while they remained part of the Reformed Church.

The arrival of the Brethren and their insistence on rebaptism unsettled the Reformed leaders of the area. John Lobach (1683-1750), a local Pietist, described the new influence of the Brethren in his autobiography.

> It further came to pass that some Anabaptists who had been persecuted and expelled in the South because of their practice of baptism came to this area. They made the acquaintance of the awakened, and also attracted various souls to themselves through their earnestness and zealous love. They taught them that it was absolutely necessary that they be baptized as a symbol of their conversion, and thereby become separated from Babel... Through this means it happened that the hate of the preachers and also other people increased, which God permitted for a holy purpose, and they were considered disloyal heretics.[302]

The Reformed clergy of Krefeld informed the General Synod about the *Dompelaars* (Dutch for "Baptists") and their "innovations which are so damaging to the church of God."[303] Just over six months later, Lobach and six others were imprisoned with a sentence of hard labor for life in nearby Dusseldorf for being baptized by Brethren from Krefeld. One of them, William Grahe, later recorded his memories of the experience as a *Faithful Account*. In early 1719, a group of Brethren, one of whom was Alexander Mack, visited the prisoners.[304] It would be nearly two more years before Grahe could report, "Finally the day of our release came – November 20, 1720, – after we had been in prison for four years less two months and ten days."[305] By that time, most of the Schwarzenau Brethren had fled to Friesland and a group of Krefeld Brethren had sailed for Pennsylvania. The window of toleration for the Brethren in Europe was closing.

John Naas had guided the Brethren in their exodus from Marienborn and their settlement in Krefeld. He was joined in 1716 by Christian Liebe who had only recently been released from punishment as a galley slave for baptisms he performed two years earlier. The two men were both respected leaders among the Brethren. By 1717, the Krefeld congregation had grown to more than one hundred people from the influx of other separatists who were persuaded to join the movement through baptism. Holsinger believed that this mixture led to eventual trouble because "this aggregation of people brought into the Krefeld church almost as many different views on subjects of theology, as most of them belonged to some other denomination before they joined the brethren."[306] In addition, since many of the new members were poor, the Krefeld Brethren "endeavored to practice community of possessions to a fault" until "it became such a burden to support this large mass of immigrants and refugees that several of their most wealthy brethren were impoverished in the attempt to do so."[307]

The resulting tensions needed only a reason to erupt into schism, and a marriage provided the reason in 1717. Peter Becker, whose baptism by Naas in Marienborn had aroused the wrath of the local ruler, had moved with the Brethren to Krefeld. The *Chronicon Ephratense*, published in 1786, reported that the issue arose when a friend of Becker married the daughter of a Brethren member who was also a salaried Mennonite minister. The two key leaders, Naas and Liebe, were divided over a decision to place the groom under the ban, the congregation took sides behind them, and, as a result, "everything was ruined and killed."[308] The turmoil within the church combined with the external pressures of hostile religious and political officials proved too much for the fragile group. Becker chose to leave for America with about twenty families in 1719, while others simply drifted away from the congregation. Naas would follow Becker to Pennsylvania with another contingent in 1733, and Liebe eventually would quit the Brethren altogether. The work in Krefeld never recovered.

Alexander Mack and the Scwarzenau Brethren might have followed Becker's lead in 1719 if they had found the means. Although Count Henry Albert continued his policy of toleration until his death in 1723, there were regular threats that made the residents of the region uneasy. In March of 1719, Christopher Seebach, an outspoken separatist, was expelled from Wittgenstein for publishing criticisms of the local clergy.[309] A court decision later that same year gave Henry's intolerant younger brother, Count August David, a share in the administration of the county.[310] In 1720, imperial officials finally began to address the issues raised by Count Charles Louis ten years earlier.

The Imperial Solicitor instructed a local agent to "investigate carefully the religious enthusiasts residing in the county of Wittgenstein, who do not profess any one of the three tolerated Christian faiths established by the Peace of Westphalia" and to "take action against them according to the imperial statutes."[311] The agent replied that "many pious people resided here for a time, about whom one heard nothing evil, but rather perceived that they conducted themselves quietly and devoutly in all things." He went on to report that these people had since left the area, writing, "That some of the persons mentioned previously as being forbidden in the Roman Empire still reside here, is unknown to me.[312] Mack and about 200 others had indeed left Schwarzenau in May of 1720 for Friesland in the northern region of the Netherlands. They would remain there, in and around the village of Surhuisterveen, for another nine years before making the journey to America.

Increasingly, the Brethren and other separatist groups looked across the ocean for a place of refuge. There, in Pennsylvania, William Penn's "holy experiment" offered hope. In 1682, Penn was granted a charter by King Charles II to found a colony in an undeveloped region of America. Penn had suffered religious persecution himself in England, having been expelled from Oxford and arrested on several occasions for being a member of the Society of Friends or Quakers, and he was determined to make his land a haven for freedom of conscience. In a letter he promised, "I shall not usurp the right of any, or oppress his person. God has furnished me with a better resolution and has given me his grace to keep it."[313] His *Charter of*

Figure 24: William Penn (1644-1718)

Privileges, adopted by the General Assembly in 1701, was an unparalleled statement of Christian religious freedom.

Because no people can be truly happy, though under the greatest enjoyment of Civil Liberties, if abridged of the Freedom of their Consciences, as to their Religious Profession and Worship: And Almighty God being the only Lord of Conscience, Father of Lights and Spirits; and the Author as well as Object of all divine Knowledge, Faith and Worship, who only doth enlighten the minds, and persuade and convince the understandings of people, I do hereby grant and declare, that no person or persons, inhabiting in this Province or Territories, who shall confess and acknowledge One mighty God, the Creator, Upholder and Ruler of the World; and profess him or themselves obliged to live quietly under the Civil Government, shall be in any case molested or prejudiced, in his or their person or estate, because of his or their conscientious Persuasion or Practice, nor be compelled to frequent or maintain any religious Worship, Place or Ministry, contrary to his or their mind, or to do or super any other act or thing, contrary to their religious Persuasion.[314]

The *Charter* guaranteed freedom of conscience and practice according to the religious persuasion of an individual or group, meaning that Anabaptists and Pietists would be accepted as well as people who belonged to branches of European state churches. More astoundingly, perhaps for the first time in church history, practitioners of infant baptism and practitioners of believers' baptism would coexist without either having the upper hand to use violence against the other. The *Charter* guaranteed freedom from governmental coercion in matters of faith as long as the practitioners obeyed the requirements of the civil law. To the Brethren and others who had experienced open persecution from civil and religious authorities, Pennsylvania offered the chance to live and work and worship without being labeled heretics against the faith or traitors against the state. At best, they had enjoyed temporary periods and places of religious toleration in Europe. Now, they saw the possibility of religious liberty, not a concession allowed by the government but a right protected by the government.

CHAPTER 14

The American Transition

A new dynamic in the Brethren commitment to remain true to the primitive church model was introduced when, between 1719 and 1735, nearly the entire movement was transplanted to America, but these people also brought with them an outlook shaped by their experiences in Europe. They found religious liberty in their new home, but their memories of oppression made them very jealous of that liberty and suspicious of anyone who might threaten it. They were members of a German-speaking sect in an English land. For religious reasons, they maintained a distinctive plainness of dress that marked them as outsiders to the prevailing culture. In an atmosphere of freedom and tolerance of faith they struggled to retain a separate identity, and their attempts to do so were often seen as sectarian or backwards. In addition, according to the *Chronicon Ephratense*, the mistrust that had developed among them in Krefeld worsened during their crossing, so much so that they said, "Thus it has happened to us; we have become strangers one to the other, and nearly all love and faithfulness have been lost among us."[315]

Shortly after Peter Becker and his band arrived in 1719, the members scattered to establish individual trades and farms. This may have been more from the necessity of finding land and income than from any real disruption of their relationships. However, it would be three years before they began again to hold meetings together for worship and encouragement. Becker, John Gumre, and George Gantz initiated an effort in 1722 to reconnect the former members of the Krefeld congregation through visits that led to a series of meetings, alternating between Becker's home and Gumre's in Germantown, about six miles from Philadelphia.[316] In 1723, a rumor spread that Christian Liebe, one of the leaders in Krefeld, had come to Philadelphia. Many of the Brethren, along with other German immigrants traveled to Germantown to welcome him. The story turned out to be false, but the gathering of people with a common heritage and language awakened a desire for further fellowship. The Brethren, or Germantown Baptists as they were called in the *Chronicon Ephratense*, lingered for a time of worship and invited others to join them.

> These persons were persuaded by the Baptists to go with them to their meeting, during and after which they heard so much of the Germans' awakening, that they went home very much edified. Soon after, a second visit was made to Germantown, by which both parties were so much edified that the Germantown Baptists promised them a visit in return, which they also made four weeks afterwards with great blessing. These newly awakened ones were thereby stirred up still more in their love, so that at last they threw themselves at the feet of the Germantown Baptists, and begged to be received into their communion by holy baptism.[317]

The application of six people to be baptized forced the American Brethren to consider organizing into a functioning congregation. None of them were authorized to administer the ordinance, so seventeen who had been baptized in Europe formally selected Peter Becker to be their elder. On Christmas day in 1723, Becker baptized the six new members in the Wissahickon Creek, and the group later met at Gumre's home for the first recorded love feast in America. The new church continued to meet until winter set in, then resumed their gatherings in the spring of 1724, at which time "there was given to them such a blessing that the whole region roundabout was moved thereby . . . and as the fame of this awakening spread abroad, there was such an increase of attendance at their meetings that there was no room to contain the majority."[318] As a result of this growth, Becker and others of the Germantown Brethren made visits to clusters of members during the summer of 1724 and organized additional congregations at Coventry in September and at Conestoga in November.[319]

One of the members baptized into the congregation at Conestoga was Conrad Beissel (1691-1768), who had for a time served as an apprentice to Peter Becker in the weaver's trade at Germantown. Beissel believed that God had called him to a great purpose, and, at first, he was reluctant to allow Becker to baptize him until he remembered, "Christ also had permitted himself to be baptized by one who was less than himself."[320] Beissel, apparently a man of considerable charisma, was selected to lead the new congregation, but his spiritual pride soon caused tensions with the Germantown Brethren. He advocated Sabbitarianism or Saturday worship, explaining "that whenever the Sabbath came all his burdens, which rested upon him during the week, were removed, which did not happen to him on Sundays."[321] Beissel promoted celibacy as a more holy way of life and claimed direct insight from God, publishing *Ninety-nine Mystical Sayings* in 1728.[322] Finally, in December of 1728, Beissel and six others from the Conestoga group resolved to "give these people their baptism back again" through rebaptism.[323] The Conestoga congregation split with some following Beissel to form a separate church. Eventually, in 1732, they and others settled and built a compound at Ephrata.

The division at Conestoga presented a new dilemma to the Brethren. In Germany, the various congregations at Schwarzenau, Marienborn, and Krefeld had been formed through forced movements of people away from existing congregations. The groups knew one another and communicated but were largely independent because of distance and limited opportunities for interaction. Even when the controversy erupted at Krefeld, Alexander Mack did not attempt personally to resolve the situation or to call the members to order under his authority. Now, members of a congregation started by leaders from Germantown had withdrawn from fellowship, and, worse, were actively urging others to break away and join them. It is doubtful that the early Brethren had given any thought to the complexity of relationships that could come with multiple congregations. At the beginning, Becker and others had told the new group, "You are in no way to be bound to us, as we are at too great a distance from you."[324] The potential problems of this arrangement apparently were not imagined. It was assumed that both congregations would enjoy continued correspondence and fellowship as occasion permitted.

The uncertainty over the proper accountability between the two congregations can be seen in the response of the Germantown Brethren. Peter Becker stepped in to minister to those who had not followed Beissel until they reformed as a separate congregation and elected their own elder.[325] In the meantime, several attempts were made by the Germantown Brethren to reconcile with Beissel, but he avoided the meetings or refused to listen. When Alexander Mack arrived in 1729, he was immediately apprised of the situation. In 1730, he was able to encounter Beissel conducting a meeting at Falckner's Swamp. Little was exchanged between the two, but the session degenerated into bitter disputes among their respective companions.[326] The Brethren depended upon a mutual commitment to peace and unity to resolve differences between members, and they were prepared to use the ban to discipline an individual who resisted, but they had no mechanism to deal with a recalcitrant group. In theory, a congregation of people could be placed under the ban, but in practice, nobody could inhibit them from continuing to meet. To his credit, Mack resisted any urge to assert superior authority as founder of the church, but that left the field to Beissel, a dictatorial leader who did claim special privilege from God.

Internal division, although troublesome, did not prevent the ongoing growth of the Brethren in America. The arrival of Mack in 1729 and John Naas four years later provided occasions for scattered German settlers to gather, renew acquaintances, and realize the benefits of continued fellowship. Quakers and Mennonites had established Germantown in 1683 as a destination for German immigrants. Most of those who came were, like the Brethren, religious separatists seeking freedom from the oppression of the state churches. They shared a common language and customs as well as similarities in their faith from the influences of Anabaptism and Pietism. It was ripe soil for the Brethren. New congregations were formed, not so much from an intentional campaign of evangelism to those who had no religion, but from a gradual rebuilding of familial and regional connections among the growing German population of religious refugees. Visits were made to settlements to encourage old friends, and, in the process, others seeking spiritual community were attracted. By 1770, Morgan Edwards, a Baptist minister in Philadelphia, could chronicle fourteen congregations of "Tunkers" in Pennsylvania in addition to the compound at Ephrata.[327] Congregations also existed in New Jersey, Maryland, Virginia, North Carolina, South Carolina, and Georgia.

The Brethren were by no means the only sect drawn to the colony of Pennsylvania. They shared the territory with German Quakers, Mennonites, Amish, and Moravians as well as English Baptists, and, later, Methodists, all relatively free to organize and practice according to their beliefs.[328] Eastern Pennsylvania was interspersed with other language groups, but the Germans from the Palatinate were so numerous that the Provincial Council began to fear the possibility of a conspiracy against the English crown. On September 21, 1727, the Council issued a mandate that all Palatine immigrants sign the following *Oath of Allegiance.*

We Subscribers, Natives and late Inhabitants of the Palatinate upon the Rhine & Places adjacent, having transported ourselves and Families into this Province of Pensilvania, a Colony subject to the Crown of Great Britain, in hopes and Expectation of finding a Retreat & peaceable Settlement therein, Do Solemnly promise & Engage, that We will be faithful & bear true Allegiance to his present MAJESTY KING GEORGE THE SECOND, and his Successors Kings of Great Britain, and will be faithfull to the Proprietor of this Province; And that we will demean ourselves peaceably to all His said Majesties Subjects, and strictly observe & conform to the Laws of England and of this Province, to the utmost of our Power and best of our understanding.[329]

Both Alexander Mack and John Naas, along with their respective groups, would have been required to sign the *Oath* before they could enter the colony.

The variety of German separatists also presented a new challenge. In Europe, the Brethren had been distinguished clearly from the Catholic, Lutheran, and Reformed churches by their commitment to a New Testament structure and ordinances. Now, in the melting pot of America, their language would mark them as different from some, but finer definitions were needed when they compared themselves to groups who seemed outwardly to be spiritually kindred peoples. The shared oppression that had made them allies in Germany was replaced by a freedom and a close proximity that gave them opportunity to recognize, highlight, and grow suspicious of their differences. Church nationalism, the concept that the people of a given realm were united by the religion of their ruler, was increasingly replaced in America by denominationalism, the idea that the true church consisted of many denominated groups that could be sectarian without designated territories. In other words, while most of the denominations believed they alone correctly practiced the truth and represented the church God intended for His people, none of them could use the power of the state to force their views on others or to carve a territory that would belong to them exclusively. Without the tool of coercion, each sect had to convince prospective converts through their distinctive character, zeal, beliefs, forms, or personalities.

Into this diversity came Count Nicholas von Zinzendorf (1700-1760) and the *Unitas Fratrum* or United Brethren, known as the Renewed Moravian Church. Zinzendorf had a dream of uniting the German sects of Pennsylvania into a "Congregation of God in the Spirit" based on his belief that "denominations are God's economy, machinery to bring truth and the love of His Son to men according to their capacity, and according to the temperature and atmosphere of the country."[330] His previous attempt to achieve his goal in Germany had met with some initial success before arousing the wrath of the Lutheran authorities. For several years, the count had received reports about the potential for bringing eleven German religious groups into accord.[331] When Zinzendorf arrived in December of 1741, these sects were invited to appoint delegates for a series of synods. At the first meeting, held on January 12, 1742, at Germantown, Zinzendorf proposed that the true church was "a communion of saints who, though outwardly belonging to different denominations, agree in all essential points of doctrine pertaining to salvation."[332] Two weeks later, at the second synod, a question was raised about the real purpose of the meetings. The leaders replied, "The proper object of this assembly of all evangelical denominations is that a poor inquirer for the way of life may no longer be directed in a dozen different ways, but only in one; let him ask whom he will."[333] Then during the third synod, February 21-23, three Indian converts were baptized by sprinkling.

The Brethren, along with three other delegations,[334] withdrew from the meetings. One of the Brethren delegates, George Adam Martin, later recalled, "After my return home I went to my superintendent and said that I looked upon the count's conferences as snares, for the purpose of bringing simple-minded and inexperienced converts back to infant baptism and churchgoing and of erecting the old Babel again."[335] The fear of a new American state church motivated the Brethren to entrench more firmly in their own sectarian system. Their immediate response was to convene a "great meeting" at Coventry, the first of the Annual Meetings that would define the organization of the Brethren church in America. They also began to more vigorously defend and differentiate their beliefs from those of their religious neighbors through publications. Christopher Sauer (1695-1758) had established a printing press in Germantown in 1738. He proved to be very sympathetic to Brethren views, publishing their tracts and pamphlets and supporting many of their positions in his German newspaper. In 1747, the Society of Friends or Quakers produced a German translation of *A Serious Call in Christian Love*, a critique of the practice of "outward baptism."[336] In response, a Brethren author wrote *A Humble Gleam of the Despised Light of the Truth which is in Christ*, arguing for the necessity of both water and Spirit baptism. The beginnings of a new American identity for the Brethren were emerging.

At the same time, an old identity was disappearing. Alexander Mack, the founder of the movement, died in 1735. Of the seven of his original companions from Schwarzenau, six had migrated to Pennsylvania, but only one, Andrew Boni who died in 1741, outlived Mack. John Naas also died in 1741. Peter Becker survived until 1758, but with his passing the leadership of the Brethren was entirely in the hands of people who had little memory of the reasons and challenges that originally had shaped the movement in Germany. While there were capable and dedicated leaders, including Alexander Mack, Jr. (1712-1803) and Christopher Sauer II (1721-1784), their adult experience in the church was limited to the freedoms of the new world. The stories of persecution from civil and religious authorities were revered memories of another time and place. To their fathers, being Brethren was a bold and costly statement of obedience to the instructions of the One Householder. To the sons and daughters, it was becoming a statement of belonging to a particular sect. In Europe, it could mean exile from Germany. In America, it was a mark of being German.

CHAPTER 15:

An Isolated Minority

In 1770, Morgan Edwards offered an apology for the lack of adventure in his survey of the German churches in Pennsylvania.

> I fear this volume will be deemed a heap of dry records without a sufficient number of anecdotes to give them a relish; this is owing to the peace and liberty which the Baptists have ever enjoyed in Pennsylvania. In other provinces they have had their troubles which will make their history interesting to every reader.[337]

That period of relative serenity would be interrupted harshly by the onset of the War for Independence. The adoption of the *Declaration of Independence* by the Second Continental Congress on July 4, 1776, was followed by a new *Constitution of Pennsylvania* which divested the Penn family of governing powers on September 28. The convention, led by its president, Benjamin Franklin, reasoned that "whenever these great ends of government are not obtained, the people have a right, by common consent to change it, and take such measures as to them may appear necessary to promote their safety and happiness."[338] The document gave assurance of continued religious freedom.

And all religious societies or bodies of men heretofore united or incorporated for the advancement of religion or learning, or for other pious and charitable purposes, shall be encouraged and protected in the enjoyment of the privileges, immunities and estates which they were accustomed to enjoy, or could of right have enjoyed, under the laws and former constitution of this state.[339]

Unfortunately, the promises granted to religions were not extended to questions of ethnic background. In 1727, concerns and suspicions that the German population of Pennsylvania might be disloyal to the English crown had prompted the *Oath of Allegiance*. Now, similar fears that the Germans would hold to their oath and fight for the British led to the *Test Act* which demanded that they renounce their allegiance to the king and transfer it by another oath to the state of Pennsylvania. The *Act*, passed on June 13, 1777, stipulated that all white males above the age of 18 were required to subscribe to the following "oath or affirmation."

I, _____, do swear (or affirm) that I renounce and refuse all allegiance to George the Third, King of Great Britain, his heirs and successors, and that I will be faithful and bear true allegiance to the commonwealth of Pennsylvania as a free and independent state, and that I will not at any time do or cause to be done any matter or thing that will be prejudicial or injurious to the freedom and independence thereof, as declared by Congress; and also that I will discover and make known to some one justice of the peace of the said state all treasons or traitorous conspiracies which I know or hereafter shall know to be formed against this or any of the United States of America.[340]

Those "refusing or neglecting to take and subscribe the said oath or affirmation" would be prevented from certain privileges, including "buying, selling or transferring any lands, tenements or hereditaments" and would have their personal weapons confiscated.[341] A certificate was to be issued to those who signed, allowing them to travel freely within the state. Without the certificate, a person venturing outside his or her county or city of residence would be "suspected to be a spy and to hold principles inimical to the United States." Such a person could be arrested and brought before a justice. Any who refused to subscribe to the oath at that time could be jailed.[342]

To the framers of the *Test Act*, it was a simple issue of black and white. Any person who refused to sign the statement must be moved by "sordid and mercenary motives or other causes inconsistent with the happiness of a free and independent people."[343] Furthermore, they reasoned that "whereas allegiance and protection are reciprocal, and those who will not bear the former are not nor ought not to be entitled to the benefits of the latter."[344] To the Brethren, however, the *Test Act* was problematic on multiple levels.

1. *Opposition to war.* The Brethren had no intention of taking up arms against the United States or England or any other nation or people. They could easily agree to the requirement that they would not do anything to undermine the independence of the colonies. However, the *Test Act* also required them to inform on others and turn them in to the authorities, and this was to play the role of a spy and a participant in the conflict.

2. *Opposition to breaking oaths.* Many Brethren apparently had subscribed to the *Oath of Allegiance*, enacted in 1727, in order to enter the colony of Pennsylvania, but now they were told to renounce that promise in favor of a new one. The Brethren were reluctant to bind themselves to a government through a vow or an oath at any time, but once they had made the step, they could not set it aside as if it were of no consequence.

3. *Opposition to the world system.* Christopher Sauer II was
    one of a number arrested for refusal to sign the *Test Act*.
    When he was questioned by an official as to the reasons
    for his stance, he replied, "As you have in your Act that
    they that do not take the Oath shall not have a right
    to buy nor sell, and as I find in the book of Revelation
    that such a time will come when such a Mark would be
    given, so I could not take the Oath while it stood on that
    condition."[345]

Some Brethren, whether through fear or confusion of the
language, did take the "attest" as it was known among them.
The Annual Meeting of 1778, as the first question addressed,
threatened them with the ban if they did not reverse their
choice.

> After much reflection, in the fear of the Lord it has been
> concluded in union, that the brethren who have taken the
> attest should recall it before a justice, and give up their
> certificate, and recall and apologize in their churches,
> and truly repent for the error. If they cannot do this, and
> will justify themselves, the apostle exhorts us we should
> withdraw ourselves from every brother who walketh
> disorderly, and such a brother will be deprived of the
> kiss of fellowship, of the council, and the breaking of
> bread, until he becomes obedient again.[346]

The church showed little sympathy either for the difficulties
the *Test Act* placed on individual members or for the American
rationale of independence. Obedience to the commands of God
should supersede fear or hardship, and the sovereign authority
of God should not be judged by people. The Annual Meeting of
1779 made this clear in its opening statement.

> On account of taking the attest, it has been concluded
> in union as follows: Inasmuch as it is the Lord our God

who establishes kings and removes kings, and ordains rulers according to his own good pleasure, and we cannot know whether God has rejected the king and chosen the state, while the king had the government; therefore we could not, with a good conscience, repudiate the king and give allegiance to the state.[347]

For the Brethren, the experiences of Christopher Sauer II, an elder in the Germantown congregation who had inherited his father's printing business, became both a caution of the peril of the state and a model of an individual willing to suffer for the sake of obedience. Sauer had built the business into a prosperous source of news and materials for the German population in the colonies. He produced a yearly almanac in use from New England to the deep South, a German newspaper, editions of the German Bible, and numerous books and pamphlets, including editions of Mack's "Basic Questions" and "Rights and Ordinances" in 1774. Sauer and fifty-seven others who had refused or neglected the oath were labeled "enemies of the country"[348] and ordered to appear before the officials by June 25, 1778. On May 25, Sauer was arrested from his bed, stripped of his clothes, and forcibly marched to a military camp. His property, both the print shop and his home, were confiscated and sold at auction, leaving him dependent upon contributions from friends for the next two years. Sauer would later write, "And so they have not only broken the Fundamental rule in selling my estate, but have also published me in almost all Newspapers as a Traitor, without any cause and without ever giving me a hearing or a trial."[349]

It was frighteningly reminiscent of stories from Europe where following the dictates of conscience had provoked the power of the state against them. The Brethren wanted to remain separate from any involvement in war, but the state demanded loyalty and service especially in a time of conflict. As the War for Independence lengthened, some states enacted conscription laws to fill the ranks of their militias. Non-resistant people like the Brethren were allowed to excuse themselves from service if they paid money that could be used to hire substitutes. Leaders of such groups were required to be collection agents for the fees. In 1781, the Annual Meeting exhorted the Brethren to "hold themselves guiltless, and take no part in war or blood-shedding, which might take place if we would pay for hiring men voluntarily; or more still, if we would become agents to collect such money."[350] The mistrust of government learned in the harsh persecutions of Europe was awakened more and more in America. Even after the war, when states held annual musters on Independence Day to conduct military drills for all male citizens, Brethren were forbidden to participate or even to watch the parades by decisions of Annual Meetings.[351] The fears spilled into the election process as Brethren were advised that "it would be much better if no votes were given in at elections for such officers (by the Brethren); for so long as there is such division of parties, we make ourselves suspicious and unpropitious on the one side, on whatever side we may vote."[352]

The *First Amendment* of the *Constitution of the United States*, ratified in 1788, promised, "Congress shall make no law respecting an establishment of religion, or prohibiting the free exercise thereof." The Brethren welcomed this guarantee of the continuation of religious liberty, but they also knew how quickly such a decree could be repealed or replaced. It was not a given that the new nation would survive, and a change in government could bring a change in its treatment of various religious groups. No single denomination or faith could impose its beliefs on the others as long as a proper separation between church and state was maintained, but the Brethren had reason to believe that it would not last. Although the Brethren did not have a well defined eschatology, they tended toward a Philadelphian view which assumed that the seven churches of Revelation 2-3 represented seven successive phases of church history. As articulated in a popular tract by Peter Bowman, a Brethren minister, in 1817, the present freedoms were the fulfillment of God's promise of an open door to the faithful church in Philadelphia. Soon after, however, the lukewarm apostasy of Laodicea would prevail, and "thus will Christendom be finally spewn out." Bowman outlined the path from freedom to doom.

> As every sect worships according to its own pleasure, it may be presumed, that the temptation, before spoken of has made its appearance, and that the door is opened to antichrist, that he may go into the temple of God, and seating himself on the throne, exalt himself above all that is called God, or that is worshipped. . . From this it may be inferred, that the door of liberty will be shut again, and the time of the great tribulation will begin.[353]

The agent of these events would be a new alliance between a church and a state on a scale that would far exceed the abuses the Brethren had seen in Europe.

The twin concerns of denominationalism, recounted in the previous chapter, and American nationalism, presented in the current chapter, contributed to an isolationism that plagued the Brethren into the latter half of the nineteenth century. The Brethren viewed the growth of these two trends with grave caution. They were not worried primarily about losing a few members to competition from other churches or losing a few freedoms to intrusion from the government. They feared the rise of a new state church in America that might threaten their very existence. Peter Nead, perhaps the foremost Brethren theologian of the time, wrote in 1850, more than a hundred years after the Pennsylvania synods and nearly three quarters of a century after the birth of the nation, about the danger posed by the proliferation of denominations.

> The sects have long been struggling for the mastery and it is now made manifest, (as respects America) that none can succeed, their jealousy will be subsided, and no doubt a great and mighty struggle will be made to unite them all under one head. And they will no doubt

be successful in bringing about a union, (if not under one creed) of one mind, to persecute unto death the true church of Christ.[354]

The unification efforts of Count Zinzendorf had failed, but they might yet be resurrected. Nead proceeded to describe the role government could play in such a disaster.

And from what source will the false church obtain power to persecute and kill the people of God? We answer from the civil government, the same source from whom the Jews obtained power to crucify Christ. In those times there will be a union of Church and State. At this time we have great, and honest hearted men, at the head of government, who by no means would give their vote to suppress the rights of speech, and of the press, to trample under foot the rights of God and man. But a certain majority of the votes of these United States, can make a change in these matters.[355]

The religious liberty of the United States presented the Brethren with freedoms unparalleled in their history to practice and proclaim their beliefs, but fears of losing those freedoms could lead to a protective stance that focused on shutting out rather than reaching out.

CHAPTER 16

Identity and Mission

In spite of the factors tipping the Brethren toward isolation, the country was ripe for expansion in the final decades of the eighteenth century. The conclusion of the War for Independence left the new United States firmly in control of all land east of the Allegheny Mountains, and within twenty years nearly all territories between the mountains and the Mississippi River had been ceded to the government. The Louisiana Purchase in 1803 extended the country across the Great Plains to the eastern slopes of the Rocky Mountains. Huge sections of land lay open to those looking for new opportunities. Martin Brumbaugh briefly outlined the process of westward expansion.

> At once the long stemmed tide of emigration over the Allegheny Mountains set in. First the hardy pioneer; then the invading army that drove the Indian to the West and North; then the agriculturist, whose coming marked the beginning of permanent occupation. The sturdy Germans were among the first to press to the Ohio and Mississippi Valleys.[356]

Like the earlier spreading of the Brethren to the colonies outside Pennsylvania, this was a geographic and economic migration and not a planned evangelistic strategy. Many Brethren families certainly took their faith with them into new territories, and some settled in close proximity to one another, but their primary focus was on clearing forests, building shelters, and preparing fields. Once established, they began to build connections with other German-speaking settlers in the region. Since a number of Brethren ministers had also migrated westward, they became the catalysts for pioneer congregations to form in the new state of Kentucky (1790), the territories of Ohio (1795), Indiana (1809), Missouri (1810), Tennessee (1811), and Illinois (1812).[357] In 1844, the first congregation west of the Mississippi River since the Missouri venture was organized in Iowa Territory.[358]

However, the geographical expansion was not matched by numerical increases. Pioneering Brethren families moved from established local church networks in the colonies to isolated outposts in the territories. While some formed new congregations and gained new members, others were left with little opportunity for fellowship and never organized. Brumbaugh calculated that "the losses and the gains may be said to balance each other, and there was no numerical gain to the church."[359] In addition, the greater distances placed a growing strain on the ability of the congregations to retain their common identity. Communication between scattered groups was reduced to letters and infrequent visits.

In general, the western congregations continued the practices they had learned before migrating from the East, but as they encountered and assimilated people of different religious backgrounds and as their children grew to take leadership, some alterations and adaptations were inevitable. Just before 1820, when a new wave of Brethren settlers moved westward into Kentucky, they found that the existing congregations had adopted variations in dress and procedures for the feetwashing ordinance as well as views on slavery. These deviations were reported to the Annual Meeting, which sent at least two delegations to investigate.[360] The second committee charged the groups with "non-conformity in dress, and too much excitement in worship." Several councils were convened between 1820 and 1826, resulting in the dismissal of fifteen hundred members.[361]

The Annual Meeting, begun in 1742 as a reaction against Zinzendorf's attempts to gather the denominations of Pennsylvania under one authority, had become just such an authority within the Brethren. Initially, the Meeting may have been rather loosely structured as it searched for a reason to continue. Henry Kurtz, writing in 1867, said that general councils were held in conjunction with regional love feasts and were sufficient for the "first thirty or forty years" in America, but that, sometime in the 1750s or 1760s, "as the churches multiplied, and extended . . . and it thus becoming impracticable for all the churches to be represented at every ordinary love feast, it became a necessity to set apart every year a certain time, and appoint from year to year a place for such a general council."[362] The Annual Meeting provided a forum for the various congregations to present issues or queries for consideration. When the Meeting was still small enough, "all members present had the right to vote on questions," and a unanimous decision was required.[363] Soon, however, delegates were selected from each congregation and a Standing Committee of elders was appointed to preview queries and render answers. Brumbaugh claimed that this system was modeled after the rejected Pennsylvania Synods,[364] but the Brethren officially looked to the Jerusalem Council of Acts 15 for support of the Annual Meeting.[365]

The authority of the Annual Meeting was to be of "a judicial, and not a legislative capacity" with all decisions being based on a direct passage of Scripture or an interpretation "according to the spirit and meaning of the Scriptures."[366] Kurtz said that the decisions of the Meeting as recorded in the minutes of those meetings were "NOT *laws and rules* made and enacted by some legislative authority for the government of others, because we believe Christ to be our only legislator and lawgiver, and *his* laws, contained in the New Testament, are *perfect laws*."[367] At the same time, the minutes were more than "mere traditions of men." He went on to explain his view more fully.

> As in a judicial court there are judges, lawyers, the contending parties, the witnesses, and all the people that choose to attend, yet none of these parties, or all together, can bring in a verdict, but the twelve men specially selected, and called the JURY; so in the church of Christ none but those who are deemed to be impartial (we think,) will be able to give a true "Verdict," and such we deem the conclusions of our Yearly Meetings.[368]

These verdicts soon became binding upon the member congregations of the expanding church. As early as 1805, Annual Meeting declared that any members who "would not heed, nor conduct themselves accordingly" and "cannot convince the Church by evidence from Holy Scripture," should be set back "from the breaking of bread until they learn to do better and become obedient."[369]

In practice, the decisions of the Annual Meeting cumulatively formed the *order of the Brethren*, a catalogue of conclusions intended to guide and hold the membership to the primitive order of the church as determined by the council of elders. In 1848, it was decided that each local church should be provided with two copies of the "Minutes of the Yearly Meetings,"[370] and in 1850, it was "concluded that no district or church has any right to make changes in any thing whatsoever, contrary to the ancient order, without proper investigation before, and the general consent of, the Annual Meeting."[371] The ancient order, as defined by the decisions of the Meeting eventually included a lengthy list of matters.

> The work done by our general Council shows its sphere to be, to determine questions of church polity upon which difference of sentiment may exist; to define the rights and powers of local and district organizations;

order of observing the ordinances of the Gospel; order of worship; of electing church officers; of advancing ministers, ordaining elders, with duties and authority to ministry belonging; hearing appeals from dissastisfied members, and exercising a general supervision over the interests of the Church in the spread of the Gospel, and in the preservation of peace and unity among the churches in all places; appealing to the Scriptures for authority upon which to base its decisions.[372]

The Meeting applied its sphere to issues such as business ventures, style of dress and hair, home decorations, participation in social and civic activities, forms of entertainment, use of new technologies, and interaction with people of other denominations. In all of these areas, Annual Meeting established a uniformity of appearance, behavior, and practice among the Brethren that reflected their plain, agrarian, Germanic culture and lifestyle of the days before expansion.

That identity was challenged with increasing regularity as the broader events of the nineteenth century unfolded. Five interconnected factors pushed the Brethren more and more into the mainstream of American life.

1. *Increasing population and growth of urban centers.* The Brethren had lived for much of their American existence in pockets of semi-isolation from outsiders, but the rapid growth of the former colonies after the War for Independence brought them into more frequent and closer contact with non-Germans. Westward migration extended the opportunity for their separate way of life temporarily, but even those distant settlements attracted more people. As vast as the American continent seemed, there simply was not enough arable land to escape the attention of agents and developers who recruited settlers with promises of plenty and sent them by riverboat and railway to claim their share. At the same time,

the demand for goods and services in the cities drew the Brethren into the new economy as tradesmen and industrial workers. The average Brethren member was having more and more contact with people of different faiths or of no faith, exposed to their beliefs, habits, and innovations.

2. *Education in public common schools.* In the 1830s, the idea of mandatory schooling for children was spreading throughout the States. As Bowman observed, "Thereafter, all religious and ethnic groups were expected to sit down together to learn the basics of arithmetic and the English language, with a generous sprinkling of morality and national loyalty rounding out the daily lesson."[373] As early as 1831, Annual Meeting advised against sending sons to colleges because "experience has taught that such very seldom will come back afterward to the humble ways of the Lord."[374] The educational system intentionally stirred generations of diverse immigrants into the melting pot of an American identity.

3. *Dominance of the English language.* When the parents spoke German at home and taught their children to do the same, a culture of separateness within American society could be maintained. In the colonies, the German language was a mark of cultural and potentially spiritual compatibility in a land of strangers, and these people tended to draw together into small, self-contained societies. However, the birth of the United States supplanted European roots with a call to merge differing backgrounds into a new nation that shared a common language. Refusal to adapt to an English world could mean commercial disadvantage, social ostracism, and national suspicion, but with the adoption of English came a diminishing of distinctiveness. In 1836, the Brethren officially took the name, "Fraternity of German Baptists,"[375] but the ethnic title was already becoming a reference to heritage more than to present identity.

4. *Resurgence of publications.* Holsinger claimed that the appearance of the *Gospel Visitor* in 1851 "ushered in the progressive era in the Tunker Church."[376] The most conservative members of the Brethren would later agree, saying, "Up to the year 1851 peace and union existed in the church. In that year the first paper was permitted to be printed among us."[377] In reality, the movement that would contribute to the division of the Brethren may have been started in 1834 by one who would be seen as a champion of the opposite side. Peter Nead (1796-1877) published *Primitive Christianity, Or a Vindication of the Word of God* in English, presenting a systematic treatment of Brethren beliefs to an audience far beyond the Brethren. Nead composed several additional works and collected them in 1850 as *Theological Writings on Various Subjects.* In addition to the *Gospel Visitor*, a number of other periodicals became available, each presenting a distinct viewpoint on the church and each allowing the members to form opinions and debate issues apart from the Annual Meeting.

5. *Awareness of a mission.* Among the Brethren were some who saw these trends as great opportunities. The increasing contacts with mainstream American society that posed threats to Brethren identity were also constant reminders of the need for a Brethren mission. A query to the Annual Meeting of 1852 asked, "Whether the commission of our Lord and Savior Jesus Christ (Matt. 28:19,20; Mark 16:15) does not require the Church to send brethren to preach the Gospel, where the name of Christ is not known?"[378] For the rest of the decade, various plans were proposed until a committee appointed by Annual Meeting brought a report in 1860 that recommended that the Brethren form District Meetings and take special offerings to defray the expenses of evangelists to be sent out "to have the Gospel preached in every place."[379] While Annual Meeting looked favorably upon

the recommendation, it was decided to "postpone it for the consideration of the next Annual Meeting" because of a low representation of churches.[380]

The postponed decision on the plan for evangelism would itself be postponed by an event that would also interrupt the growing tensions among the Brethren between identity and mission. It would consume their thoughts and energies for the next four years, just as it consumed the resources and unity of the nation. The Civil War would reveal the divisions that had long existed in the United States over the issue of slavery and would unleash a bloody violence between families and friendships. However, largely because the Brethren were united on the issues of slavery and non-resistance, the War would temporarily heal some of their divisions by reminding them of the uniqueness of their identity – not as a plain German sect but as spiritual descendants of the Anabaptists and Pietists who would hold to New Testament principles in the face of severe pressure from the surrounding state. When most American denominations would split with the country along northern and southern loyalties, the Brethren would be one of the few that would remain united in a divided nation.

CHAPTER 17:

Wars and Divisions

John Kline (1797-1864), a prominent elder among the Brethren in Virginia, read the gathering signs on January 1, 1861, and was troubled.

> A move is clearly on hand for holding a convention at Richmond, Virginia; and while its advocates publicly deny the charge, I, for one, feel sure that it signals the separation of our beloved old State from the family in which she has long lived and been happy. The perishable things of earth distress me not, only in so far as they affect the imperishable. Secession means war; and war means tears and ashes and blood. It means bonds and imprisonments, and perhaps even death to many in our beloved Brotherhood, who, I have the confidence to believe, will die, rather than disobey God by taking up arms.[381]

Kline moderated each of the four Annual Meetings during the war years, the first in his southern state of Virginia and the next three in the northern states of Ohio, Pennsylvania, and Indiana.[382] In 1782, Annual Meeting had pronounced that the slave trade "cannot be permitted in any wise by the Church,"[383] and the Brethren never wavered from this resolve. Any slaveholder wishing to be accepted as a member of the church was required to first set them free.[384] As the country was divided into slave states and free states, such a slaveholder was additionally required to provide funds for his slaves to "migrate to a land of liberty."[385] During the War, any Brethren minister who spoke in justification of slavery was to "be dealt with according to Matt. 18."[386]

Both the Federal and the Confederate governments eventually made provisions for non-resistant people to be exempted from military service, but they were required to pay a substantial fine and were sometimes subjected to ridicule, suspicion, and even violence by their more "patriotic" neighbors. Annual Meeting urged faithful endurance.

> We exhort the brethren to steadfastness in the faith, and believe that the times in which our lots are cast strongly demand of us a strict adherence to all our principles, and especially to our non-resistant principle, a principle dear to every subject of the Prince of Peace, and a prominent doctrine of our Fraternity, and to endure whatever sufferings and to make whatever sacrifice the maintaining of the principle may require, and not to encourage in any way the practice of war.[387]

The year before, Annual Meeting had recommended that members contribute to a fund that would help those who could not afford the war fine for not serving.[388] John Kline lived these decisions he helped to enact. The exemptions were in part a result of his letters to government officials. He was imprisoned for nearly two weeks by the Confederate army because of his stance,[389] regularly encouraged groups of Brethren, cared for injured soldiers,[390] led Annual Meetings, and traveled thousands of miles on horse and foot to minister to congregations. On June 15, 1864, Kline was ambushed and shot to death by unknown assailants, although many suspected they were Confederate soldiers.[391] The concerns John Kline had voiced at the onset of the War proved to be sadly true for him.

While the nation turned to the hard work of reconstruction and healing after the Civil War, the Brethren returned to the issues that had filled their attention prior to the conflict. The focus, once again, was on the still unresolved tensions between identity and mission. Three distinct positions and groups were becoming more defined among the membership. They came to be known as the Old Orders, the Progressives, and the Conservatives. These three would eventually separate from one another into three branches of the Brethren movement with common roots but different outlooks on how to express their beliefs in the changing environment of American society. Each sincerely desired to remain true to a New Testament foundation, but each placed a different emphasis on what that meant, and each held a different opinion on the role Annual Meeting should take in guiding the church. These differing viewpoints clashed around the proper balance between identity and mission. The Old Orders were concerned that the distinct identity of the Brethren was being eroded in the pursuit of a larger place in American religious culture. The Progressives thought the strong emphasis on identity was unnecessarily hindering the Brethren from effectively reaching out to people with the core message of the Gospel. The Conservatives could see both sides of the argument but feared a split in the Brethren that would render both points irrelevant. Within the outward struggles of the three factions lay fundamentally different answers to three key questions concerning the church as presented in *Figure 25.*

1. *Old Orders.* Words like plain, simple, apostolic, and ancient were the focus of this group. They viewed the changing trends and influences around them as potential threats to the primitive model of the church. The work of Annual Meeting was to protect the church from infiltration and compromise, and they were increasingly frustrated with its inability or unwillingness to do so with firm decisions of prohibition and denunciation. The Old Orders believed in the authority of Annual Meeting to

	Old Orders	Progressives	Conservatives
What is the church?	Distinct and separate people of God, called out of the corruption of the world.	Distinct and empowered people of God, called into the world as salt and light.	Authorized institution of God, called to shepherd His people and to be a witness.
What is the authority for the church?	Scripture as interpreted and applied by Annual Meeting.	Scripture as interpreted and applied by congregations.	Scripture as interpreted and arbitrated by Annual Meeting.
What is the purpose of Annual Meeting?	To protect the church from infiltration and compromise.	To uphold clear directions and prohibitions of Scripture.	To mediate differences in order to preserve unity.

Figure 25: Key questions in the church (1880)

determine proper practices for the congregations, so they introduced numerous queries about dress, associations, and innovations, hoping that the answers would preserve the order by putting a stop to discussions of change and new methods. Time after time, they were disappointed when Annual Meeting, although supporting some of their positions, worded its replies in terms of advisements and recommendations rather than edicts. An Old Order pamphlet, published in 1883, complained, "Thus, when the order of the church was once broken, one innovation after another crept in among us, to the sorrow of many members."[392] Sunday schools, revival meetings, salaried ministers, and high schools and colleges moved the Brethren closer to the ways of other denominations and away from the simple identity the Old Orders were convinced needed to be defended.

2. *Progressives.* Stoffer said that this group held a "vision for what the church could become if it would loose

itself from the formalism and cultural baggage that were hindering the church's mission."[393] They believed the church had to adapt its methods, without compromising its principles, in order to represent Christ to a changing American culture. To the Progressives, Annual Meeting should not concern itself with innovative strategies unless they were expressly forbidden in the Scriptures. While the Old Orders used queries to push Annual Meeting to support and enforce their views, the Progressives used publications to announce their plans apart from the schedules and procedures of Annual Meeting, and they were frustrated when Annual Meeting required explanations from them. Some of the innovations that were seen as threats to the Brethren identity by the Old Orders were considered opportunities to advance the Brethren mission by the Progressives. They saw the church as an army on the march rather than as an outpost under attack.

3. *Conservatives.* This group was, by far, the largest of the three and included many whose sympathies were strongly with one of the other groups. However, the most important issue for the Conservatives was the preservation of the unity of the church, and Annual Meeting was their chosen means of accomplishing that. Annual Meeting was the place of mediation to calm the fears of the Old Orders and to caution the rhetoric of the Progressives. Both were exhorted to exercise restraint and to demonstrate tolerance toward the other, but this only heightened the sense of frustration as neither left the meetings satisfied and used their respective publications to proclaim their arguments. The Conservatives eventually found themselves in an untenable position. If Annual Meeting made a decision to preserve identity, it angered the Progressives and only encouraged the Old Orders to push for more restrictions. If Annual Meeting favored tolerance on methodological

differences, the Old Orders accused it of compromise and the Progressives accused it of imposing unnecessary cautions and boundaries.

The tension between the three factions opened into division in late 1879 when the elders of the Miami Valley district in Ohio, the central stronghold of the Old Orders, composed a petition that outlined their grievances and voted to send it to the 1880 Annual Meeting. The document reflected the realization that their attempts to stop the innovations of the Progressives were failing. They had concluded that the only way to block the innovations was to conclusively block the people who had introduced them. Once again, they appealed to Annual Meeting to take strong measures.

> Now, as all former efforts have failed – in sending query after query to the annual meeting, the exercising of patience and forbearance from time to time, all of which have accomplished but little, the so-called fast element gaining ground year after year, and one innovation after another being introduced among us, which, if suffered to continue, will lead the church off into pride and the popular customs of the world and the other denominations – we think we feel the propriety of a renewed effort on our part to accomplish the object of this petition.[394]

The Old Orders cited five modernisms that "we do not regard as being in harmony with the spirit of the gospel, neither are they in harmony with the ancient and apostolic order of our church."

> The causes of the trouble must be removed before peace and union can be restored; and among some of these causes are the high schools among us, popular Sunday-schools, with their conventions and celebrations, long,

protracted meetings, and the way they are generally conducted, by singing revival hymns and giving invitations to rise or come forward, a salaried ministry, and the single mode of feet-washing.[395]

The petition chronicled how each of the five had once been prohibited by Annual Meeting with firm admonitions but were now tolerated with warnings and cautions that could be ignored. The Old Orders lamented, "Forbearance, we think, is the door through which these things came into the church, one after another, and now, it seems, there is no door to be found by which to get them out again."[396]

Once again, the response of Annual Meeting fell short of the hopes and expectations of the Old Orders. The Standing Committee introduced a substitute to the petition in an attempt to claim a middle position between the Old Order and Progressive factions.

> *Resolved*, Secondly, that while we declare ourselves conservative in maintaining unchanged what may justly be considered the principles and peculiarities of our fraternity, we also believe in the propriety and necessity of so adapting our labor and our principles to the religious wants of the world as will render our labor and principles most efficient in promoting the reformation of the world, the edification of the church, and the glory of God. Hence, while we are conservative, we are also progressive.[397]

While Annual Meeting expressed significant agreement with the Old Order positions, it would not make them mandatory for all congregations and members, preferring to frame them as issues of conscience and caution. The Old Orders complained, "instead of putting these things *away*, it rather by these would-be restrictions, *recognizes* them as having a legal right in the church."[398] They expressed disbelief that Annual Meeting would bend its authority to the individual thoughts and decisions of members. They exclaimed, "Conscience the guide! One of the most dangerous doctrines ever preached, and it came from the brethren's Annual Conference Meeting."[399]

In December 1880, the Miami Valley Brethren proposed and unanimously passed another petition to be sent to the 1881 Annual Meeting at Ashland, Ohio. It basically repeated opposition to the five innovations listed in the previous petition and requested these be clearly disallowed. Holsinger believed that among the Old Orders "hope had not been entirely abandoned of controlling general conference,"[400] but that hope was crushed when the petition was declared illegal by the Standing Committee and a resolution was passed demanding that "said decision of Annual Meeting of 1880 remain unchanged."[401]

Immediately, the leaders of the Old Orders announced a meeting for August 24, inviting "all the faithful part of the church in the various states and localities, that they may consult with regard to the necessary provisions for the preservation of a unanimity of sentiment in faith and practice, the purity of the church."[402] Resolutions were passed stating that those who agreed would abide by the petition Annual Meeting had rejected. The document explained, "It is manifest that our church is in a confused condition, and that duty requires something to be done for the peace and union of our church."[403] The wording made it clear that the Old Orders felt they were not separating from the Brethren church, but that they were leaving in order to preserve the ancient order of the Brethren. As a result, "it was also intimated... that all those who would vote to stand by these resolutions would absent themselves from the then acknowledged Annual Meeting."[404] The congregations and members that withdrew organized themselves under the name Old German Baptist Brethren.

With the departure of the Old Orders, Annual Meeting turned its attention onto the Progressives, and especially Henry Holsinger (1833-1905) who had long been their chief spokesmen through his publishing work. Holsinger's differences with the leadership of Annual Meeting had begun in 1865 with the *Christian Family Companion*, a publication in which "a free rostrum was announced for the discussion of all subjects pertaining to the welfare of the church."[405] Annual Meeting, however, viewed it differently, saying, "Many Brethren seem to so far disregard the advice of the Annual Council as to send to the *Gospel Visitor* and *Christian Companion* articles opposing, through their editors, the counsel of the old Brethren."[406] As early as 1867, he had been forced to apologize for exclaiming in the midst of a heated exchange, "Thank God, I am not bound to truckle to the prejudice of any man or set of men."[407] Holsinger believed "the church was in great need of reformation,"[408] and that the closed system of reaffirming decisions of Annual Meeting "did not contribute much to the prosperity of the church, either numerically or spiritually."[409] He pointedly advocated many of the innovations the Old Orders mistrusted and criticized the ministers and leader of Annual Meeting for their resistance to change.

These criticisms did not go unanswered. In 1870, Holsinger was summoned by a committee to acknowledge wrong and ask forgiveness for publishing a letter that "was a misrepresentation of the facts" and because "his criticism and language were unbecoming a brother."[410] Again in 1873, he was called before the Standing Committee as a warning for statements he had made in sessions which "grieved a large number of members, as their strong feelings, expressed after the Meeting closed, plainly indicated."[411] As a result, he turned over his publishing enterprise to James Quinter. In 1878, Holsinger partnered with Joseph Beer to publish the *Progressive Christian*, "with the avowed purpose of advocating progressive measures and reforms."[412] At the 1879 Annual Meeting, five districts requested a decision to "prohibit the slanderous and schismatic articles being published in the *Progressive Christian*" and that its editors be required to acknowledge "publishing erroneous statements in regard to church members; charging a part of the Church with idolatry; stigmatizing some of its members with terms of reproach; ridiculing some of the peculiar practices of the Church, and admitting into the paper inflammatory and schismatic articles."[413]

Holsinger saw these actions as attempts by the Old Orders to silence him through the vehicle of Annual Meeting. He said of the Old Orders, "They furnished the ammunition, while the conservatives fired the guns, not intending to injure anybody."[414] Holsinger did not cool the situation when he published an article in the *Progressive Christian* called "Is the Standing Committee a Secret Organization?" In 1881, at the same Annual Meeting that witnessed the withdrawal of the Old Orders, a report was submitted that contained the following paragraph.

> Inasmuch as Bro. H. R. Holsinger has been admonished by the Annual Meeting, again and again, according to the Minutes of Annual Meeting, to cease to publish articles conflicting with the general order of the old Brethren and good feeling of the Church, and still continues to do the same, we now request Annual Meeting to deal with him according to Matt. 18, and the decision of Annual Meeting, either directly or by a committee, and if he does not hear the Church, hold him as a heathen man and a publican.[415]

Annual Meeting decided to "appoint a committee to wait on him in his church and deal with him according to his transgressions."[416] The committee kept its appointment on August 9, 1881, at Berlin, Pennsylvania, Holsinger's home congregation. Holsinger and the church refused to allow the proceedings to go forward, so the committee concluded, "That Bro. H. R. Holsinger cannot be held in fellowship in the Brotherhood, and all who depart with him shall be held responsible to the action of the next Annual Meeting."[417]

After lengthy debate at the 1882 Annual Meeting, Holsinger and those who chose to join him were disfellowshiped from the Fraternity of German Baptists. The Progressives held a meeting at Schoolhouse No. 7, near Milford, Indiana, about a mile west of the Annual Meeting grounds, and sent a memorial to Annual Meeting requesting one final attempt at reconciliation.

> We, your petitioners, would beg leave to say that we feel aggrieved at yesterday's action in the case of Elder H. R. Holsinger and his friends, and feeling that another division in the brotherhood is imminent, and deploring an event fraught with so much evil, we humbly petition for a joint committee, say of twelve brethren, half to be selected by progressive brethren and the other half by your body, and they prepare a plan for a general reconciliation between the annual meeting and all the brethren called progressive, and we hope you will hear us in this our earnest request, so that further division may be prevented.[418]

Standing Committee rejected the memorial on the same grounds by which they had refused the petition of the Old Orders the previous year, saying that "it had not come through the district meeting, thus settling the question of her ruling, therefore the standing committee can not receive anything that does not come in regular order."[419] The reply was not unexpected, and the Progressives proceeded to recommend "a convention of all those favorable to restoring the church to its primitive purity,"[420] and to resolve "that our motto shall be the Bible, the whole Bible, and nothing but the Bible."[421]

CHAPTER 18

Choices and Changes

The 1882 Annual Meeting essentially closed the door on any chance of reconciliation when it passed a petition that a decision of Meeting "shall be *mandatory* to all the churches having such cases as the decision covers." It further stated, "And all who shall not so *heed* and *observe* it, shall be held as not *hearing the Church*, and shall be dealt with accordingly"[422] (italics original). By the end of June, there were three separate branches of the Brethren. The Old Orders had organized themselves as the Old German Baptist Brethren. The Progressives held a convention at Ashland on June 29-30 in which they declared their independence from Annual Meeting, saying, "We therefore reaffirm the primitive doctrines of the church, and disavow allegiance to all such derogatory and subversive ecclesiastical mandates, and declare our intention to administer the government of the church as in the days of the apostles and our faithful brotherhood."[423]

One year later, together with smaller groups known as Congregational Brethren and Leedy Brethren, the Progressives stated that "all sectarian titles that theretofore existed shall be forever dropped, and we will hereafter be known and know each other by the gospel name Brethren."[424] The Conservatives retained the designation Fraternity of German Baptists until 1908 when they adopted the name Church of the Brethren. In numbers, the Old Orders took about 4,500 members, the Progressives took another 5,500 members, and roughly 60,000 stayed with the Conservatives.[425]

Each group claimed to be the true representative of the ancient order of the Brethren, and, indeed, each emphasized a true principle of the Brethren movement. The Old Orders valued the *identity* of the primitive church in purity from the stains of the world. The Progressives were guided by the *mission* of the church to influence the world through the gospel message. The Conservatives prioritized the *unity* of the church as the household of God that should remain undivided. It would be incorrect to assume that each group found it necessary to sacrifice the other two principles in order to maintain its own. It would be more accurate to say that each group affirmed and tried to practice identity, mission, and unity, but that each felt it necessary to sacrifice its association with the other two groups in order to preserve its own focus. To some extent, the chosen principle of each has remained a distinguishing characteristic

	Old Orders	Progressives	Conservatives
Name	Old German Baptist Brethren	Brethren Church	Church of the Brethren
Size	4,500	5,500	60,000
Emphasis	Identity	Mission	Unity

Figure 26: *Three branches of the Brethren after 1883*

to the present day. The features of the three branches of the Brethren are summarized above in *Figure 26*.

In their "Declaration of Principles" at the First General Progressive Convention in June 1882, the newly separated Progressives charged Annual Meeting with a long list of abuses that justified their departure and called themselves "the true conservators of the doctrines of the Brethren Church."[426] In his introductory address for the committee that drafted the "Declaration of Principles, Stephen Bashor said, "Instead of it being a declaration of secession, this document is a reaffirmation of our church doctrine and platform."[427] Despite this claim, as the group organized into the Brethren Church, it faced a series of defining choices that would determine how it would express its beliefs and practices in its cultural and religious setting. These choices focused on the three issues of church government, relation to the culture, and framework of doctrine. Each built upon values that had led the group to separate from the paths of the Old Orders and the Conservatives and each responded to new events and developments in American society. The choices are illustrated in *Figure 27* below.

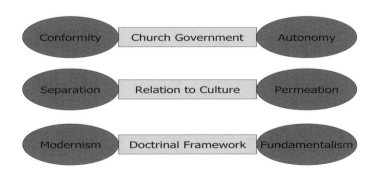

Figure 27: Choices for the Brethren Church after 1883

1. *Church Government: Conformity vs. Autonomy.* In 1881, Holsinger and Bashor published an article in the *Progressive Christian* that attempted to outline the principles of the Progressives. In it, they stated, "Our

doctrine should not come from man but from God, and nothing should be made a test of Christian fellowship or official position but that which can be proven from the gospel."[428] They believed, "if we as a church will be satisfied with the gospel, as our rule of faith and practice, our difficulties will cease."[429] The 1882 "Declaration of Principles proposed how this could be applied in practice to a collection of local churches.

That upon all questions of church government, the doctrines and commandments of men are paralyzing to the life and interests of the church. That in doctrine the church of Christ should universally harmonize, but on questions of government and customs may be congregational.[430]

The Progressives had rejected the centralized authority of Annual Meeting, but they were not clear about what should replace it. At the Dayton Convention of 1883, a committee was assigned to consider church government, but its report was refused as too creedal. A substitute report was offered by P. J. Brown, "I have the honor to report our views in full. They are here set forth – (handed the chairman a copy of the New Testament)."431 It was a symbolic moment, but it did not resolve the issue.

The difficulty lay in balancing the dangers inherent in the extremes of both centralized and autonomous rule. The Progressives knew they did not want a system like the one they had left, but they also recognized that some expectation of conformity among the local congregations was necessary in order to maintain an association of churches at all. A second convention was held in 1887 at Ashland, Ohio, and Bashor introduced a resolution that attempted to clarify the relationship between congregational autonomy and denominational conformity.

It is the sense of this convention that the apostolic idea of congregational church government relates alone to the incidental affairs of the local congregation and not to doctrinal practices and tenets which must be general or universal – the same in all congregations, the doctrinal conditions of membership in one congregation shall be the doctrinal conditions in every other.[432]

The next convention, held near Warsaw, Indiana, in 1892, explained the relationship in more mystical terms.

That the various separate and collective congregations, while absolutely and truly congregational in government, yet each and all have a divine relation to each other, and to the whole church as the body of Christ; and that, therefore, the faith, character, and practice of each and all are under the same divine law of government, under Christ and the Holy Spirit, to each other, as the Word of God teaches.[433]

The concept emerging from these resolutions was of a limited congregational form of church government. Within the Brethren Church were some who wanted absolute congregationalism while others favored a structure that bound individual congregations to common policies and procedures. Both positions were argued in the Brethren publications, but only the collective churches, meeting in General Conference, could speak with authority on the subject.

The 1895 Conference called for a commission "which shall make a study of government and discipline, and report a system of expediency for the Brethren Church which shall be in agreement with, and subordinate to the Word of God."[434] In 1897, the commission returned with "A Manual of Church Expediency for the Brethren Church," a set of policies to standardize observance of the ordinances, establishment of new congregations, credentialing of ministers, and conduct of district and national conferences.[435] Although the document was careful not to depart from what was widely accepted already, the members were not ready to give Conference the authority to dictate such things to the churches, and it was never adopted. Progress on the issue of church government was restricted by older Brethren who feared a return to the mandates of Annual Meeting and by younger Brethren who wanted a structure that could expedite new projects. A middle ground that felt safe and effective to both was hard to find.

2. *Relation to Culture: Separation vs. Permeation.* Although the aggressive plan for evangelism proposed at the 1860 Annual Meeting was interrupted by the Civil War, the zeal for mission did not disappear. However, it was slow to develop because of a related concern. In 1867, a query asked, "Should not our Church adopt some general plan for the spread of the Gospel, as the duty is enjoined upon her by the Savior himself?" The second part of the same query raised the point of contention, "And does not an efficient plan imply some pecuniary provision?"[436] In order to send missionaries to remote locations, it might be necessary to support them financially, and this could open the way for the emergence of a paid ministry. In 1868, Annual Meeting adopted the 1860 report that had allowed that "the funds needed to defray the expenses of said evangelists shall be drawn from the treasuries of the several districts," while advising other ministers "to labor, as they have been accustomed to do, without money and without price."[437] By 1877, missionary work to Denmark was approved,[438] and two years later, every congregation was requested to contribute to its support.[439] A Foreign and Domestic Board was created in 1880, but in 1881, a

query encouraged the work of evangelism but asked that it be done "in a more simple manner" because of the fear that a paid ministry was being encouraged.[440]

The Old Orders had treated the surrounding culture as a threat to the purity of the church. They wanted to be a witness to it, but they approached it with extreme caution lest they be drawn into its habits and patterns. The Progressives agreed that the culture had corrupting influences, but they hoped they could permeate it with the gospel message. The 1882 "Declaration of Principles" announced, "That every possible means for the conversion of souls should be put forth at all times and under every circumstance."[441] At first, the work was mainly focused on gathering and organizing Brethren people who had withdrawn from or been expelled by the Conservatives. However, according to Holsinger, these efforts "opened their eyes more widely to the fact that the Lord had other people to whom the gospel must be preached, and they at once set about to send forth evangelists to the extent of their ability."[442] The "Declaration of Principles," in rather flowery wording, had already affirmed the willingness of the Progressives to use innovative ideas for evangelism.

> That the gospel recognizes the liberty of men and the church to stablish expediences, instruments, and immunities, by which the education and spiritualization of the race may be successfully achieved in different generations and under various circumstances.[443]

Among these devices would be Sunday schools, revival meetings, and salaried ministers.

It was another step in a transformation of the Brethren's relationship to culture. In Germany, the culture was hostile and potentially deadly, and some degree of separation was necessary to protect the very existence of the church. Outreach was primarily proselytizing among other separatist groups with little chance of influencing the state church system. The transition to America placed the Brethren in a new environment of religious freedom, but one that still could be harsh toward a sect whose language and beliefs did not fit the prevailing expectations. After the War for Independence, the Brethren began guardedly to assimilate into American culture, but separation was still required to preserve the order of the Brethren. Growth occurred through an ingathering of scattered German immigrants. In the absence of a persecuting enemy, separation took on a more sectarian aspect with outward distinctions being emphasized as marks of purity. As a generation of Brethren familiar with public education and the English language came of age, however, they more easily moved in the wider circle of American culture and recognized the opportunities for an expanded mission.

City missions and church extension programs were initiated, beginning in the 1890s, in Chicago, Washington, Philadelphia, Dayton, and Montreal with varying degrees of success.[444] At the General Conference of 1900, a proposal for the establishment of a foreign missionary organization was introduced, but the proponents "were informed that there was plenty of room 'out under the trees' where they could go to effect their organization."[445] A group of 52 met under an oak tree on the conference grounds in Winona Lake, Indiana, and formed the Foreign Missionary Society of the Brethren Church with the sole purpose "to carry out the Great Commission of the Lord, Matt. 28:19, 20."[446] By 1909, the Society had tried and abandoned a work in Persia and successfully launched missions in Argentina and French Equatorial Africa. The world outside the Brethren Church was increasingly viewed as an opportunity and not as a threat.

The role of the church was to permeate the culture with the witness of the gospel.

3. *Doctrinal Framework: Modernism vs. Fundamentalism.* Benjamin Franklin once counseled Michael Welfare (Wohlfahrt), a member of the Ephrata Community, that his groups should publish "the articles of their belief, and the rules of their discipline." Wohlfahrt's reply represented well the opinion of the Brethren.

> When we were first drawn together as a society... it had pleased God to enlighten our minds so far as to see that some doctrines, which we once esteemed truths, were errors; and that others, which we had esteemed errors, were real truths. From time to time He has been pleased to afford us farther light, and our principles have been improving, and our errors diminishing. Now we are not sure that we are arrived at the end of this progression, and at the perfection of spiritual or theological knowledge; and we fear that, if we should once print our confession of faith, we should feel ourselves as if bound and confin'd by it, and perhaps be unwilling to receive farther improvement, and our successors still more so, as conceiving what we their elders and founders had done, to be something sacred, never to be departed from.[447]

The Brethren aversion to creeds was born from their commitment to hold the New Testament alone as their standard of faith and practice and from their hard experience of having creeds used and enforced as tests of orthodoxy. Because of this, they published few systematic representations of their beliefs. Peter Nead's *Theological Writings* in 1850 was a clear exception, while R. H. Miller's *Doctrines of the Brethren Defended* in 1876 addressed only the divinity of Jesus and the Holy Spirit, the ordinances, and secret societies, and he carefully said, "We do not put out this work as a document of church authority, binding the church or the brethren by sentiments here expressed."[448] The claim that the New Testament was the creed of the Brethren was good in theory, but in practice it overlooked obvious questions of differing interpretations and applications. In the absence of a clear statement of beliefs, the decisions of Annual Meeting became a creed by default.

The Progressives rejected the authority of Annual Meeting over the congregations, but they offered the New Testament, without interpretation, as their only creed. The 1882 "Declaration of Principles" warned, "he who adds to the gospel, takes from it, or in any way binds upon men anything different from the gospel, is an infidel to the Author of Christianity and a usurper of gospel rights."[449] The document also stated that "in doctrine the church of Christ should universally harmonize,"[450] but it proposed no explanation of what that doctrine might be. The 1892 General Conference "reaffirmed the former position of the church in renouncing all creeds of every description, except the Bible, the whole Bible," but the same Conference offered the ordinances as officially that which "the Brethren Church understands her creed to teach."[451] The Brethren could say with all honesty that the Bible was their creed, but none of them could say with any certainty what they collectively believed the Bible said about specific doctrines. This would leave them vulnerable when doctrinal challenges began to sweep the American religious landscape.

One such challenge came in the form of Dowieism, a phenomenon of divine healing that was a forerunner to the Pentecostal movement. John Alexander Dowie (1847-1907) exploded onto the American religious stage at the Chicago World's Fair of 1893. In 1899, he announced plans to make Zion, Illinois, a city set apart from the evils of the world, and in 1904, he conducted a world tour, gathering converts and money to his project. The Brethren believed in God's power to heal, and Dowie's message was filled with calls for faith, repentance, and baptism. Through the influence of a Brethren elder, he even adopted trine immersion as his only form of baptism.[452] Many members of the Brethren Church were confused or enamored by his wide popularity and apparent success from God. The movement faded when financial discrepancies were revealed, and a stroke in 1906 brought an end to Dowie's career. However, his appeal among the Brethren and the questions he raised demonstrated inadequacies in the Brethren system of doctrinal teaching and in the training of its ministers.

The Progressive Convention of 1887 had passed a resolution to encourage theological education for new ministers.

> *Resolved*, that our ministers of the different states form associations for mutual benefit, and inaugurate a course of study something after the Chautauqua plan so that our ministers have an opportunity to be better acquainted with our doctrine, and that a committee be elected by this convention to carry out the plan; and that the Chairman of this Committee be elected by this body.[453]

In 1888, Ashland College adopted a new charter that cited "the training of Christian ministers" as one of the school's "major functions,"[454] but the Bible department was not designated a seminary until 1906. In the meantime, young ministers flocked to other schools to receive training, and they encountered liberal or modernist systems of theology. One of the most influential was

John Lewis Gillin (1871-1958), who did graduate studies at Columbia University and Union Theological Seminary and eventually became the president of Ashland College in 1907. Gillin began to express modernist views in the classroom and at General Conference. Among these was the idea that "it ought not to be impossible for a man of any theological complexion to find a home in the Brethren Church."[455] At the 1914 Conference, he said that "religious experience" could take the place of an "infallible Bible," and the following year, he claimed that either an Athanasian who believed in the deity of Jesus or an Arian who thought that Jesus was simply a created being could "still be a good member of the Church, these things are of minor importance."[456]

The American church as a whole was experiencing an upheaval caused by debates over two systems of theological thought that came to be known as Fundamentalism and Modernism. Fundamentalism gained its name from the publication of a series of twelve volumes, called *The Fundamentals: A Testimony to the Truth,* that presented and defended what were thought to be the essential doctrines of the Christian faith. Modernism attempted to place Christianity into an interdisciplinary context that drew from the growing fields of the physical and social sciences as necessary tools to properly understand and interpret Scripture in its original historical and social setting. Some main tenets of the two systems are contrasted below in *Figure 28.*

The three defining choices that faced the Brethren Church in the first three decades of its existence exposed weaknesses and strengths in the movement. The Progressives had clearly settled on the side of autonomy over conformity in their church government, but they found that freedom very difficult to apply consistently to the realities of an association of congregations. This tension continues to be a major cause of debate and

Modernism	Fundamentalism
Higher criticism interpreting the Bible as human literature	*Biblical literalism* accepting the Bible as revelation inspired by God
Progressive evolution assuming that society is improving	*Premillenialism* believing that only the return of Christ will redeem fallen society
Social gospel emphasizing the creation of a Christian environment	*Evangelism* emphasizing the need for personal repentance and faith
Life principles as the intended message of the Bible	*Systematic theology* as the essential beliefs from the Bible

Figure 28: Contrasting tenets of Modernism and Fundamentalism

controversy to the present time. On the question of their relation to culture, the Progressives strongly emphasized the mission of permeation with the gospel over the preservation of the ancient order through separation. This choice spurred wonderful advances in domestic and foreign mission efforts and allowed the creative employment of many innovations to reach the culture with the message of salvation. However, at times, the focus on the unbelieving world eroded the identity of the church as the distinct people of God. The balance between the two would also prove to be elusive in the coming years. Finally, although predisposed toward Fundamentalism, the Brethren would especially struggle in the early decades of the twentieth century with the development of a clear and integrated statement of doctrines that would express their beliefs without crystallizing them into an authoritative creed.

CHAPTER 19

A Household Divided

The publication of *The Fundamentals* in 1910-1915 laid down a clear dividing line for the theological debate that swept American Christianity at the turn of the twentieth century. R. A. Torrey, the executive secretary of the project explained its genesis.

> In 1909 God moved two Christian laymen to set aside a large sum of money for issuing twelve volumes that would set forth the fundamentals of the Christian faith, and which were to be sent free to ministers of the gospel, missionaries, Sunday School superintendents, and others engaged in aggressive Christian work throughout the English speaking world... Some of the volumes were sent to 300,000 ministers and missionaries and other workers in different parts of the world.[457]

The project assembled some of the top conservative scholars and leaders from North America and Europe to compose 90 essays that defended what were believed to be essential doctrines of the Bible against modernism in all its perceived forms, including Roman Catholicism, Christian Science, Mormonism, atheism, socialism, and spiritualism.

Because of their wide circulation, *The Fundamentals* became a type of creed that defined who was orthodox and who was a liberal modernist. Some Brethren, who feared that trends of modernism were infiltrating their churches, embraced this systematized theology as a means to return the church to pure, apostolic doctrine. Others saw it as a cause of unnecessary and distracting arguments. J. L. Gillin voiced this concern at the 1915 General Conference.

> Why, then, waste our time and spend our energy in promulgating notions and doctrines which some of us believe and some of us do not believe causing strife and heartburnings where there should be cooperation and common endeavor to promote the ends for which we stand as a denomination.[458]

The Brethren Church was reluctant by principle and unprepared by structure to impose a rigid theological system on its ministers and congregations. Its theology was generally conservative, but its Pietistic heritage wanted to remain open to the possibility of new lessons from the Holy Spirit. This tension was evident in *God's Means of Grace*, a lengthy volume on the distinctive beliefs of the Brethren by Ashland College professor C. F. Yoder (1873-1955), published in 1908. As Yoder discussed the ordinances, his interpretations were often lucid explanations of the original intentions of Jesus. At other times, however, his meanings were drawn from metaphors and connections not based firmly in Scripture. The result was a list of principles and applications that occasionally stretched and confused the central purposes of the observances. Yoder saw trine immersion in the Old Testament requirements for "the cleansing of the clothes, the body, and the heart."[459] The bowing posture of baptism, he wrote, was symbolic of dependence upon God.[460] Feetwashing was a type of "the wedding garment of righteousness," and the bread and the cup represented "the marriage of Christ and the Church."[461] Another writer said that the ordinances illustrated "three great steps in the atonement," with feetwashing corresponding to "Condescension and Humiliation," the bread and the cup representing "Suffering and Death," and baptism picturing "Burial and Resurrection."[462] These images made good illustrations, but they revealed a strongly subjective side to Brethren theology.

The unsettled questions of church government and theological framework threatened the more settled question of the mission of the church. The 1915 General Conference introduced *A Manual of Procedure for Brethren Churches* which stated, "the supreme task of the church" was "the evangelization of the world." It also determined that Conference "shall have no power to interfere with the work of any local church nor with the work of the several District Conferences."[463] The *Manual* did not address doctrinal issues at all and left unanswered the two important questions for the Brethren Church.

1. How can an association of churches pursue a common mission in a unified effort if there is wide diversity of opinion on what the Bible says about key doctrines?
2. How can a unified position on doctrine be reached if no person or organization within the church has the authority to draft or to enforce a statement?

Gillin's hypothetical statement that an Athanasian or an Arian could be a member in good standing in the Brethren Church was essentially correct since there was no official document, other than the New Testament, to decide the issue. In theory, a commitment to the authority of the Bible should have been enough, but in practice, it could become a matter of personal interpretation or application.

That changed at the 1921 General Conference with the introduction and adoption of "The Message of the Brethren Ministry" by the National Ministerial Association of the Brethren Church. (See Appendix A.) A committee of 25 members, which included Gillin, drafted the document, but its content and tone

were largely the work of J. Allen Miller (1866-1935), dean of the
Bible Department or seminary at Ashland College, and Alva J.
McClain (1888-1968), pastor of the First Brethren Church of
Philadelphia. General Conference could not impose a doctrinal
statement on the congregations, but the ministers could adopt
a standard as "the essential and constituent elements of our
message" and "the basic content of our doctrinal preaching."[464]
The Fundamentalist element in the church embraced the *Message*
as the signal of new clarity in the doctrine of the Brethren
Church. Others agreed with its contents, but worried that it was
a radical change from "the traditional Brethren conviction that
fixed statements limit the Holy Spirit's ability to shed new light
on the living Word in response to changing cultural and religious
environments."[465] Ronk summarized its effect on the ministers
when he wrote, "Practically all of the outspoken liberal young
men departed from the fraternity in the next five years; and, the
conservative leaders, with voice and pen, gave unstinted energy
in elucidating the doctrines of the Message."[466]

"The Message of the Brethren Ministry" seemingly settled the
doctrinal debate between Modernism and Fundamentalism in
the Brethren Church at the time. McClain, from his perspective
thirty years later, cited four important results that came from
the adoption of the document:

> First, it provided a rallying point for the evangelical
> ministers of the church, and was widely endorsed
> and used by congregations, district conferences, and
> ministerial examining committees. Second, a number
> of liberally inclined ministers left the Brethren Church
> and entered other denominations. Third, Dr. Gillin
> stopped attending the General Conference, and the few
> remaining ministers who had supported the "liberals"
> suffered a marked decline in influence. Fourth, the
> churches temporarily at least gained a larger voice in the
> affairs of Ashland College, and began a definite agitation

to place on its faculty more men of unquestioned loyalty to the great truths of the Christian faith.[467]

There were unintentional results, however, that profoundly changed the nature of future debates within the Brethren Church. For the first time in the history of the movement, a formal statement of doctrines was the standard of orthodoxy. Although General Conference could not impose the document upon the congregations, the National Ministerial Association had bound its members to a list of interpretive assertions. The 1921 General Conference recognized the potential of such a step and amended the original motion to adopt with the caution "that this declaration of faith shall be used only as the message of the Brethren Ministry, and not as a creed for the denomination."[468] Yet, as Ronk observed, "The Message of the Brethren Ministry was accepted as the Brethren norm in theology. No one cared to disturb it."[469]

A statement of *faith* will almost always become a statement of *fellowship*. The question it asks changes subtly from "What do you believe?" to "Over what are you willing to disfellowship?" The measure of "a good Brethren" began to shift from obedience to the commands of Jesus to adherence to a system of theology. The four results that McClain observed were not signs of a clear victory in the controversy between Fundamentalists and Modernists in the church. They were signs that the debate had been driven underground temporarily. The supporters of fundamentalism had made it uncomfortable or unsafe for the supporters of modernism to voice their beliefs and had banished their opponents' most vocal representative from positions of influence, but the ideas of liberal theology could not be so easily eliminated. In the meantime, the fundamentalists assumed a mandate to move ahead with other advances of their views into the system of the Brethren Church. McClain joined the faculty of the seminary division of Ashland College in 1925 and skillfully articulated the tenets of fundamentalism in his teaching and writing. Some of the points of doctrine were new to the previously undefined theological grid of the Brethren. Ronk identified dispensational Calvinism, and especially the doctrine of unconditional security,[470] as concepts introduced primarily through McClain. Stoffer added a "view of salvation as punctiliar rather than as a process" and "the conception of baptism as a sign and seal of an inward grace rather than as a condition of salvation"[471] to the list. To some it was a "narrow theological system" which "allowed for no deviation from even its more minute details."[472]

McClain hoped to see the seminary become a graduate level program instead of a department in the college, but he resigned in 1927 because of ill health and disappointment that the administration had "no apparent serious interest in placing it on a graduate basis."[473] In addition, he felt "it had become clear that 'liberal' tendencies in life and faith still existed on the campus."[474] McClain moved to California to teach in the Bible Institute of Los Angeles, but he continued to work out the details of a graduate seminary program.

In 1929, Louis S. Bauman (1875-1950), pastor of the influential First Brethren Church of Long Beach, offered to house the endeavor. News of the proposal aroused the attention of the Ashland administration members who worried that a separate campus could split the donor base. McClain and Bauman accepted an invitation to meet with the Ashland College Board of Trustees on April 24, 1930. In that gathering, McClain outlined his terms for a seminary program at Ashland, making it clear that the rival location in Southern California would go forward unless the administration adopted his plan.[475] In essence, the plan required the college to fund a graduate seminary program until it could become financially autonomous through tuition and shared or independent endowments. Given the realities of the Depression and the possibility of divided donations, the trustees approved unanimously, "although there was some apparent hostility on the part of the college administration and its sympathizers on the board."[476] Ashland Theological Seminary opened in September 1930 with a fourfold emphasis on "orthodox belief, spiritual living, thorough scholarship, and practical application."[477]

The seminary was born in tension with much of the administration and faculty of the college. McClain instituted "The Message of the Brethren Ministry" as "a statement of Christian faith" in the initial seminary catalog.[478] The college had no such requirement, and some of the college teachers, in McClain's opinion, "were expressing critical attitudes toward some areas of Christian truth."[479] In 1933, after several attempts to persuade the administration to address this friction, McClain appealed to the board "recommending the adoption of an official statement of faith as a standard by which the fitness of teachers could be determined."[480]

Against the wishes of the administration a committee was appointed to draft the document. The committee returned with a statement, "prepared in its original form by Professor McClain, covering the fundamental Christian doctrines held in common by most evangelical believers, but omitting the distinctive doctrines of the Brethren denomination."[481] The statement was passed with the provision that "the board would not require each teacher to sign it."[482] In retrospect, McClain saw this as a "compromise,"[483] Homer Kent, Sr. (1898-1981), a past student and future colleague, called it "an empty victory,"[484] and Albert Ronk (1886-1972), Brethren Church historian, marveled that McClain "insisted on certain policies for the college administration, even going over its head to the trustees."[485]

In 1934, as Moderator of the General Conference, McClain declared to the delegates that the college was faced with a choice among three roads.

> First, there is the road of *Modern Liberalism*, a complete break with Biblical and historical Christianity, and a policy of unhindered "academic freedom" for all teachers to express their opinions in matters of faith and morals. Second, there is the road of *Christian Faith*, an educational policy which puts spiritual things

first, which carries the Christian view positively into every class room, and which tolerates no teacher or teaching either indifferent or antagonistic to the Word of God. Third, there is the road of *Compromise*, a kind of "no man's land" exposed to fire from both sides, an unhappy attempt to cater to two parties engaged in irreconcilable conflict.

McClain concluded, "To take either the way of compromise or the way of undisguised infidelity will mean the doom of the institution."[486] McClain believed "The Message of the Brethren Ministry" represented the road of Christian faith, but the board of the college had taken the road of compromise in not demanding that all teachers sign it. McClain and Bauman hailed the change in administration in 1935 as a sign of progress. From conversations with the incoming president Charles Anspach (1895-1977), they believed he was in agreement with their theological position and vision for the school. McClain told the board, "His program for the institution, as outlined by him upon several occasions, is the program we have believed in and prayed for through the years."[487] Anspach presented his policy, saying, "It is our duty to assist young people to develop high ideals, clean and wholesome forms of recreation, and Christian standards of living."[488] He later recalled that among the priorities given to him when he accepted the position were "readmission to the North Central Association, stabilizing of the finances, and the improvement of public relations."[489] Reconciling an existing internal dispute was not on his new job description.

However, when Anspach included several local ministers whom McClain considered "religious modernists" in his inaugural program, the seminary faculty protested.[490] A rift opened between the two men that would quickly widen. McClain later wrote his perspective.

Yet within a few months the new president's almost cynical violation of his solemn promises had precipitated a conflict which virtually wrecked the seminary at Ashland, lost to the college at least half its church constituency, and led to a division of Brethren churches into two national conferences. To be sure, one man by himself could not have done all this. There had been existing differences, some trivial, and others more serious, but none that could not have been handled without such far-reaching results if the actions of Dr. Anspach had been tempered with more wisdom and good will.[491]

In another article, McClain called Anspach's conduct "superficial and childishly stubborn."[492] Anspach sought a constitutional change that would add six positions to the board of the college, but McClain saw it as an attempt to "permit a substantial increase of non-Brethren membership on the board, and depriving the church districts of their former elective powers, thus making the board self-perpetuating."[493] Kent cited Anspach's proposal at the April 1936 board meeting to "establish a double standard of conduct for college students upon the campus – a stricter standard for the pre-seminary college students and a more lenient standard for the regular college students" as "the thing that stirred up the most resentment from the seminary and its supporters."[494] Anspach defended the intent of the policy in an article.

The college shall encourage the type of behavior which shall be in conformity with Christian standards. It does not permit on campus, dancing, card playing, smoking, etc., and discourages such practices off campus. It does not, however, pledge all students to refrain from such practices off campus, as a condition of entrance. Sixty-five percent of our students live within twenty-five miles of the college and approximately fifty percent live in their own homes. Under such circumstances we cannot require that all students live the completely separated life.[495]

The seminary faction was not disposed to accept such explanations, and two board members, Bauman and Charles Ashman, Sr. (1886-1967), resigned.

A cycle had formed in which every action of the administration was scrutinized critically for flaws and departures from the position represented by McClain's application of the "Message of the Brethren Ministry" to the seminary and by his desire to apply it equally to the college. He and his supporters seemed to hold the administration to that position even though the "Message" had not been made an official standard for the college. The administration, on its part, increasingly looked for ways to appease and later silence the constant challenges to its authority to set policy for the school. Behind the question of which theological or moral position was right was the question of how a faction that disagreed with the decisions of the administration should present its case when it had no institutional authority to impose changes.

The two board members chose resignation when they felt their voices were not being heard, but they did not let the matter rest. Both were members of the Southern California District, and its leaders sent an open letter to Anspach on June 16, 1936, in which they accused the administration of working in harmony with "an organized effort on the part of a small group connected with the college to wrest the college from the control of the church and deliver it over, body and soul, to a group of Ashland people."[496] In particular, the letter protested the expansion of the board, the "policy of a double standard of conduct on the college campus," and a reduction of the seminary faculty from four to three members. Anspach replied on June 26 and proposed a meeting between representatives of the Southern California District and representatives of the board and faculty of the school.[497] Instead, the District made their open letter public on July 31, less than a month before the 1936 General Conference.

The General Conference appointed a committee of seven to "thoroughly investigate the condition which is causing the disturbance at this conference."[498] Anspach informed the committee members that they could not begin without an invitation from the Board of Trustees. When the invitation finally came in 1937, only one member of the committee attended the meetings in June and wrote the subsequent report. Earlier in the year, at a faculty meeting, a set of Rules and Regulations was introduced which stated that a teacher could be dismissed "for inefficiency or neglect of academic duty, immorality, or conduct unbecoming to a gentleman."

McClain moved that "for teaching anything contrary to the college Statement of Faith" be added to the list of causes, but his motion was soundly defeated with only the three seminary teachers and two college teachers voting in favor.[499] Bauman and Ashman, who had resigned in 1936, came to the June board meetings as the elected representatives of the Southern California District although the new constitution required two candidates for each position. The existing board elected two alternate members and refused to seat Bauman and Ashman.[500] The board also requested the resignations of McClain and Herman Hoyt (1909-2000) from the seminary faculty because of "incompatibility," a charge not included in the "Rules and Regulations." The board later explained its action.

> It is true that no charge was made against the life and teaching of these men. They were given a lengthy examination, as were the rest of the faculty, as to the causes of the ill-will and dis-affection on campus . . . Since these two men were also in the spirit of rebellion against the administration and the great majority of the Board, there was no other course except to demand their resignation... Knowing the impasse which had been reached, and freely confessing it, these men refused to resign for reasons best known to themselves, thus forcing

the hand of the Board. They were dismissed on the definite charge of incompatibility by vote of 19 to 3.[501]

That evening, at a prayer meeting of those sympathetic to the two teachers, "The Brethren Biblical Seminary Association" was formed. Later that summer, a group of officers met in Philadelphia and decided "that the name of the school would be 'Grace Theological Seminary,' and that its temporary location would be in the Ellet Brethren Church, Akron, Ohio."[502]

The Grace Brethren

CHAPTER 20

New Beginnings

The General Conference of 1937 was faced with the reality of two competing schools within the Brethren Church. McClain would later point out that other denominations "had more than one school, often differing widely in their theological viewpoints,"[503] but the antagonism between the factions made any cooperation untenable, and it was reflective of growing division in other areas of the church. Ronk observed that the "Message of the Brethren Ministry" had "produced a status quo with smoldering embers. But little fuel was required to kindle anew the spirit of controversy."[504] This time, however, the fundamentalist definition of orthodoxy was based on the interpretation of a written statement of faith that McClain and others hoped to make the standard for all aspects of the Brethren Church. The problem was not in the content of the document that, although it went well beyond the traditional tenets of the Brethren movement, was carefully and precisely worded. Tension was created when some applied it to organizations within the church to halt a perceived slide into modernism. Positions on organizational boards became a means of securing a majority that would ensure that the *correct* side of the debate would be emphasized.

Thus, in 1935-1936, changes had been made in the Publishing Company of the church that had replaced the business manager and editor with men of fundamentalist leanings.[505] At the 1937 General Conference, R. Paul Miller (1891-1964), field secretary for the Home Mission Board, was dismissed by the board then reinstated in response to a majority vote from the Conference.[506] As the 1938 Conference approached, Miller himself identified the issue when he stated that fundamentalists were watching the growing polarization of the Brethren Church and they were "very anxious that one certain faction shall gain control."[507] Both Miller and Bauman, who served as secretary-treasurer of the Foreign Missionary Society, refuted accusations that they used their organizations to further the cause of fundamentalism and the new seminary.[508] At the 1938 Conference, Miller was again relieved of his duties for having an "inharmonious spirit."[509] Another attempt to reinstate him was defeated, and the Conference was adjourned. However, a request was made for the delegates to remain seated, Bauman was named chairman, and a motion was passed to "resolve the gathering into a Committee of the Whole." From this meeting, held after the official adjournment of Conference and with a partial representation of delegates, a National Home Mission Council was formed with Miller as its field secretary.[510] Bauman hinted that the action might have been planned beforehand when he later wrote, "The members of the Home Mission Board were duly warned that their opposition which resulted in the defeat of that resolution would mean the creation of a new home mission board."[511]

The congregations of the Brethren Church increasingly took sides in the conflict, aligning themselves with the organizations controlled by one faction and withdrawing support from those on the other side. By the time of the 1939 General Conference, the lines were drawn with theological titles being assigned to each group. Hoyt stated the indictment that at Ashland College, "Legalism, the teaching that men may save themselves by their own works, was a prevailing spiritual atmosphere of the institution."[512] Meanwhile, George Ronk (1881-1964) published a series of articles in which he charged that members of the "Grace" group were Antinomians who believed in eternal security and discounted the necessity of living in obedience to the principles of the Sermon on the Mount and other moral teachings of the New Testament.[513] The names stuck, and real discussion was lost in accusations and defenses. At the Conference, the Credential Committee refused to seat 81 delegates because their churches were "out of fellowship in their District" or had taken action "that did not abide by the Committees of Conference."[514] Since all of the rejected delegates were from churches that supported the Grace faction, the Ashland group controlled the Conference. McClain recalled, "the supporters of Grace Seminary (now held to a fixed minority) refused to vote upon any motion throughout the Conference. Other delegates, noting the situation, did not even bother to present their credentials."[515] Both sides later looked back with shame on the animosity that was displayed in the sessions. Charles Mayes, editor of *The Brethren Evangelist*, observed, "If the Lord tarries our grandchildren will read the report and be shocked."[516]

The expelled delegates and their supporters held separate meetings after the evening sessions of the General Conference, and it was there the National Brethren Bible Conference was organized, later to be named the National Fellowship of Brethren Churches. The Grace group did not form a new denomination in 1939. In part, this was because of concerns raised by a series of lawsuits over church property in which the Ashland group claimed the Grace group had given up all rights by refusing to support General Conference and Ashland College. In the case of the First Brethren Church of Dayton, Ohio, the court ruled, in 1941, "a local Brethren Church may withdraw its support from any conference or board and still continue to be a Brethren Church."[517] The result was, as Kent explains, "Both groups claim to be The Brethren Church. Both groups have claimed that the other has departed from true Brethrenism."[518] They held separate annual conferences; the Grace group in Winona Lake, Indiana, and the Ashland group in Ashland, Ohio. Each developed its own foreign and domestic mission agencies, publications, women's organizations, and ministerial associations, and each supported its own school. Official division, however, was not finalized until 1986 when the Grace group incorporated as the Fellowship of Grace Brethren Churches.

The structural results of the division in 1939 became fairly easy to measure. More congregations remained with the Ashland group, but the overall membership was split nearly evenly. Perhaps more importantly, "those elements that added vitality and zeal to the church – an aggressive home mission program, a successful foreign mission program, nearly all the young ministerial recruits – were inherited by the Grace group."[519] It is harder to assess the perspectives and patterns developed and lost during the struggle. In the bitterness of the disputes, the Grace Brethren had strongly staked out positions that would continue to mark their new fellowship. By doing so, they had also cast aside certain traits that would be slow to recover. Both the gains and the losses would shape the course of the decades to come and would raise a new set of choices. The issues were the same ones the Progressives had faced in the years after 1883: church government, relation to culture, and doctrinal framework. The options, however, were different since they were outgrowths of the choices that had been made by the Progressives. These are illustrated below in *Figure 29*.

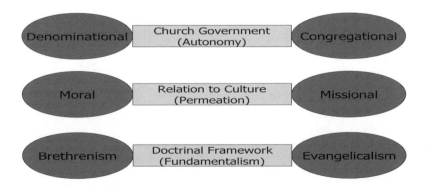

Figure 29: Choices for the Grace Brethren after 1939

1. *Church Government: Denominational vs. Congregational.*
   Kent strongly affirmed that the Grace group was
   committed to maintaining the autonomy of the local
   congregation.

   > In all of their conferences, both national and
   > district, the Grace group of churches has been
   > most careful to maintain the congregational
   > principle of church government. It recognizes
   > the sovereignty of the local church. Conference
   > actions, therefore, are not mandatory; they are
   > advisory . . . Though there is the recognition of
   > the independence of the local church, yet there
   > is also a recognition of the need of the individual
   > churches to work and council together as they
   > did in New Testament times.[520]

   In this, the Grace Brethren held to the long-
   standing belief that a regular meeting of the scattered
   congregations was in keeping with the New Testament
   pattern seen in Acts 15, but the purpose centered
   on cooperative efforts rather than binding decisions.
   McClain, in an address to General Conference several
   years before the separation, had stated, "it would be a
   major disaster, in my judgment, for the Brethren Church
   to shift to any other system."[521] Yet he also saw a potential
   danger in congregational government which he likened
   to the gathering specter of fascism.

   > But here again, as in other matters, the easiest
   > way to lose our position is not by repudiation,
   > but by wrong definition and perversion of a
   > Congregational Principle... We have only to drive
   > the Congregational Principle to an unscriptural,
   > non-cooperative extreme and men will begin
   > to say (as they have said), "Let us abandon this

system. It has made us nothing but trouble. We cannot accomplish anything permanently worth while as long as some churches ignore the rights of others, declining to recognize any authority but their own." Just as in civil government we have seen anarchistic individualism lead directly to ironclad dictatorship of a central government, so in the church the surest road to centralization of ecclesiastical authority is an extreme non-cooperative congregationalism.[522]

Congregationalism, then, was the balance between anarchy and dictatorship; between a disintegration of all associations and a burdensome fellowship through coerced conformity. The Brethren consistently had tried to practice this balance throughout their history, and consistently they had struggled to define the principle in a way that would avoid the drift toward one extreme or the other.

McClain believed the way to achieve the balance was through the application of an agreed upon statement of faith like the "Message of the Brethren Ministry." Its application to the ministers of the church had seemingly solved the modernist crisis, but its application to the Ashland campus had been frustrated. McClain thought that he had learned a valuable lesson from his experiences at the college, however. He said, "It is not enough to *have* a statement of faith. It is also necessary to bind the statement legally into the institution, and then have men who have the will to support it."[523] He cared for the first condition of attaching the document to the institution by drafting a "Covenant of Faith of Grace Seminary" in 1938.

With the new board of the seminary, he "took the original Ashland Statement of Faith, enlarged its content, added a very complete biblical documentation, and then included it as one of the purpose clauses in the Ohio Charter, to which each trustee and teacher is required 'to subscribe annually in writing.'"[524] In addition, the preamble of the "Covenant" declared that it "cannot be changed or diminished."[525] Although it was intended primarily for the seminary board and faculty, Hoyt said ten years later that it was "held by the members of the Brethren Church."[526] The second condition of McClain's solution to the risks of congregationalism was found in a greater emphasis on trained ministers as the overseers of the congregations, and specifically ministers trained through Grace Seminary.

In 1850, Peter Nead issued a warning about turning the autonomy of the local congregation into an autonomy of the ministers.

> Though preachers have a right to preach the Gospel, and to administer the institutions, yet they must bear in mind, that they are amenable to the church for their conduct, and in no case proceed contrary to the counsel of the church. It is their duty, in transacting the affairs of the kingdom of grace, to always take counsel of the church, when it can be done. He must not think, because he is a preacher of the word, that he is above every member, and can pursue any course he may see proper. It is certain that every member has an equal voice – that is, as much authority in managing the business of the church as the preachers have. Whenever preachers are entrusted with all the power (which is quite contrary to the Gospel,) in managing church business, the church is sure to become corrupted: therefore, let the church keep an eye upon their preachers, and see that they always proceed according to the Gospel of Jesus Christ; and it is

the duty of the preachers not "to shun to declare the whole counsel of God."[527]

Those words expressed the principle of congregationalism not just *between* local churches but *within* local churches. They were written at a time when a professional ministry did not yet exist in the Brethren movement and when higher education was frowned upon by Annual Meeting. While Nead and McClain would have agreed on the right of the church to operate free of outside interference, they would have differed on who was to lead the local congregation and on what basis the leadership was given. Nead would have assumed that the minister was responsive in all his functions to both the directives of Annual Meeting and accountability to the local congregation. McClain would have made the minister accountable to a statement of faith for his doctrine and to the local congregation for his character, but the minister, by virtue of his advanced education and training, should be the clear leader of the operations of the church. This definition of "the Congregational Principle" would result in a growing organizational distinction between the salaried pastors and the membership of the local church.

2. *Relation to Culture: Moral vs. Missional.* The Progressives had decided they were called by God to influence the surrounding culture with the Gospel of Jesus. They would be in the world without conforming to it. The Grace Brethren inherited most of the domestic and foreign work that had been established prior to 1939. The National Home Missions Council, formed in September 1938 under the leadership of R. Paul Miller, continued and expanded the existing works in Kentucky and among Spanish-Americans in New Mexico.[528] By 1949, new fields had been opened among the Navajos in New Mexico and Jewish populations in Los Angeles.[529]

Since Grace Seminary began with almost all of the students who had previously attended the school at Ashland,[530] the fellowship had a rich pool of young ministers to start new congregations. From the 74 congregations that aligned with the Grace group in 1939, the number rose to 137 by 1953[531] and to 284 by 1980.[532] Likewise, "practically all of the foreign missionaries and members of the board of trustees accepted the Grace viewpoint in the controversy."[533] The Foreign Missionary Society inherited ministries in Africa and Argentina, and, by 1953, it had added works in Brazil, Mexico, France, and the territory of Hawaii.[534] Grace Seminary provided most of the new personnel for the mission agencies from its stream of graduates.

The one obstacle that could slow the mission of the Grace Brethren was the temptation to settle for behavioral morality. For most of their history, the Brethren had assumed and even promoted their distinction from other denominations. Separation from the world included separation from the mistakes and inconsistencies of those who called themselves Christian. One writer said the Brethren had "a decidedly negative tendency" toward people who disagreed with them.[535] The Grace Brethren, however, began early in their existence to show a desire to be accepted into mainstream evangelicalism. To accomplish this, they would have to highlight areas of common agreement while downplaying areas of distinction with other evangelical groups. The focus of nonconformity became separation *from* the immoral behaviors of the culture, but the corresponding issue of what they should separate *to* was unclear. Clouse characterized the separated life of evangelicalism as "restrictions that forbid smoking (tobacco), drinking alcoholic beverages, dancing, attending theaters, and similar amusements."[536] Following such regulations could give the appearance of deep spirituality and the hope of cultural influence, but it overlooked the real need of people and the culture for a transforming encounter with the message of salvation through faith.

3. *Doctrinal Framework: Brethrenism vs. Evangelicalism.* The historic commitment of the Brethren to the forms of the New Testament did not fit easily into the evangelical mainstream with its emphasis on fundamentalist statements of doctrine and personal experiences of conversion. The Grace Brethren wanted to blend a clear connection to their Brethren heritage with a close adherence to the doctrinal precepts of fundamentalism. Hoyt attempted to merge the two by showing that the distinctive practice of the ordinances was an integral part of a correct doctrinal position and was a model for other evangelical groups.

> Among Brethren Churches forming the National Fellowship of Brethren Churches there is a decidedly Biblical and praiseworthy fundamentalism, and many associated with other denominations recognize this fact and marvel. Such orthodoxy, however, is no mere accident. It must be traced to a basic and a proper view in true fundamentalism, namely, that the Scriptures include several well defined and providentially ordered rites intended to set forth and conserve Biblical truth in concrete form.[537]

Thus, the emphasis on the Brethren form of the ordinances shifted away from a *commitment to recovering the primitive church.* Instead, correct form demonstrated a *commitment to the systematized theology of fundamentalism.* The Brethren practice of the ordinances was seen as a measure of true orthodoxy, and it was argued that they should be accepted and adopted by the broader evangelical church community.

Bauman said the Brethren practiced "golden baptism" since "there is no denomination of evangelical Christians that does not give assent to the validity of trine immersion, by receiving into its fellowship, without rebaptism, those baptized by trine immersion."[538] Likewise, he stated, "practically all authorities of every creed in the matter of church history are agreed that in the primitive church the Love Feast was first celebrated, and was followed by the bread and wine of the Eucharist."[539] Whereas the Brethren had long conducted their beliefs regardless of the opinions of surrounding religious sects, the Grace Brethren were inclined to try to convince fellow evangelicals they needed to adopt those beliefs. The ordinances illustrated how carefully the Grace Brethren studied and applied even the details of the Bible, but they were pieces of a larger theology that now included elements foreign to the historic Brethren movement. Among these, according to one writer, were unconditional election, eternal security, dispensationalism, and a greater emphasis on grace over obedience.[540]

Perhaps the most profound change that the Grace Brethren adopted from fundamentalism was a willingness to encapsulate their beliefs in a document. A revision and update of "The Message of the Brethren Ministry" was begun in 1953 and resumed by an appointed committee in 1967.[541] The resulting "Statement of Faith of the National Fellowship of Brethren Churches" was approved by the 1969 National Conference. It should be noted that "The Message of the Brethren Ministry" was adopted in 1921 by The National Ministerial Association of the Brethren Church and was applied to ministers as a statement of "the basic content of our doctrinal preaching and teaching." "The Covenant of Faith of Grace Seminary," adopted in 1938, required an annual subscription in writing from "each member of the faculty and Board of Trustees." The "Statement of Faith" was adopted by National Conference as "a statement of those basic truths taught in the Bible which are common to our Christian faith and practice" among the congregations of the Fellowship. (See Appendix B.) In this way, the audience shifted from those holding designated positions of oversight within the church to all those associating themselves with local Grace Brethren congregations. Faith in Jesus Christ was still the one condition for membership in the body of Christ, but membership in the local church now involved some level of agreement with the listed doctrines of the *Statement of Faith*.

Since the Brethren saw baptism historically as "the material symbol by which believers are formally initiated into the local church,"[542] there was a general practice, of requiring a baptismal confession for local church membership. Baptism, among the Grace Brethren, had become detached from any essential role in entering the universal church, but it continued to be used as the "public ceremony of the believer's entrance into the local congregation,"[543] signifying by its distinctive form an acceptance of the beliefs of the Fellowship. It was the one article of the "Statement of Faith" that required a visible response in a physical action. Thus, the form of the ordinances took on a denominational importance. The Grace Brethren believed the Bible specified the forms of trine immersion baptism and threefold communion. Therefore, it was important that people who joined Grace Brethren churches should practice the ordinances in the correct forms. Alexander Mack and the first Brethren had separated from the state churches and formed a new congregation around obedience to the primitive forms of the ordinances. The principle was upheld by decisions of Annual Meeting for nearly 150 years, and it was one clear constant throughout the two major divisions in the Brethren movement. Now, it would become the focus of three periods of contention within the Fellowship that would force the Grace Brethren to deal more specifically with the three questions of church government, mission, and doctrine in an association of autonomous congregations.

CHAPTER 21:

Testing
Autonomy

J ohn Lewis Gillin, who would later play a leading role in the fundamentalist-modernist controversy at Ashland College, wrote a dissertation in 1906 for his Ph.D. at Union Theological Seminary in which he attempted to trace the sociological factors that shaped the development of the Brethren movement. He encapsulated his theory of the "consciousness of kind" in the following statement.

> Whenever a number of persons have deliberately come to the same conclusion on a doctrine or an ideal, and on the basis of that similarity have united in association for a common purpose, their zeal for the accomplishment of that purpose varies directly with the development of the consciousness of kind. That is to say, their zeal will be great or small, on the one hand, according as they are conscious of their likeness to each other, and, on the other, according as they recognize their unlikeness to their opponents.[544]

Simply put, when a stimulus or significant change is introduced into a society, groups of people naturally look for others who respond in a similar manner. They associate with one another and begin to share and shape common beliefs and behaviors to deal with the change. This association blossoms into a consciousness of kind or recognition that they are indeed a group in contrast to the beliefs and behaviors of others around them. Finally, the group establishes goals that preserve their points of identity while moving them forward in a path beneficial to the group.

In Gillin's theory, however, "an organization never develops very far before its leaders formulate and seek to enforce a policy of uniformity."[545] Gillin believed that such efforts were futile and that the Brethren would continue to discover differences within their ranks as new changes were introduced into their environment, so that tensions and even divisions were inevitable. It was hardly an encouraging theory, but the path that produced the Fellowship of Grace Brethren Churches seemed to fit the pattern. The eight dissidents in Schwarzenau, the immigrants from Germany to Pennsylvania, the Progressives, and the Grace group all broke from settings where they felt centralized religious control prevented them from practicing their faith according to conscience. In each case, they reformed in a way they hoped would restore the New Testament intentions of the church. The one constant in each of the transitions was a group of Brethren gathering with others of like mind to turn away from one form of church government they found oppressive to set up another. In each case, the new system attempted to address key issues about the balance between association and autonomy, but the answers proved elusive. In each case, differences within the ranks of the new group led some to seek a policy of uniformity and others to resist and eventually to leave.

For the Grace Brethren, the issue first erupted in 1959, "when two churches in Southern California permitted the reception of members without baptism by trine immersion," causing "widespread apprehension and dismay."[546] The following year, an appointed Committee on Denominational Interests publicly raised the concern that the action of the two churches, if "condoned by the National Fellowship, in the seating of their delegates" could place in legal jeopardy "the property of all the congregations participating in the National Fellowship."[547] The concern came from a legal case between the Ashland and Grace groups, finally settled in 1957, over the rights to the church property in Leon, Iowa. It was the last of four such challenges brought by the Ashland group which claimed, among other charges, that the Grace group had "departed in certain particulars from the fundamental faith of the Brethren,"[548] and so had begun a new denomination with no rights to Brethren property. The dismissal of one charge was based in part on the testimony of the Grace defendants that "they have never accepted, and upon their affirmation stated they would never accept anyone into the Brethren Church without triune immersion."[549]

Just before the 1959 National Conference, Alva McClain had sent an open letter to pastors in the Fellowship in which he warned that "no better basis for a successful law suit could possibly be found than an official departure from the Brethren practice of trine immersion as a requisite for church membership."[550] Understandably, the Grace Brethren were sensitive to opening a way to new legal charges. Therefore, the Committee recommended that Conference once again reaffirm its position that trine immersion "is a requirement for entrance into the membership of The Brethren Church," but that "no final disposition be taken by this conference before 1962."[551] The two churches in California were admonished to refrain from accepting any new members without trine immersion until a final decision could be reached. The recommendation for delay revealed an important dilemma among the Grace Brethren. While Conference, along with the national organizations and district conferences of the Fellowship, supported the position that required trine immersion for local church membership and desired to avoid any legal risks, it was reluctant to disenfranchise any local congregations by action of Conference.

Some saw more ominous consequences than even legal penalties. In his 1959 letter, McClain said, "Once we abandon the Brethren doctrine of baptism, as set forth in our statement of faith and confirmed by unbroken usage, we shall not ultimately be able to save the great truths for which it stands."[552] In 1961, James Sweeton warned the National Fellowship of Brethren Ministers, "Let us keep one important point clear: to change any ordinance is to concede to all persons the right to change any other ordinance."[553] Still, a Committee on Findings in the Baptismal Problem proposed a solution in 1963 that would disqualify any pastor and congregation which "shall practice or advocate the practice of any other form of baptism" while allowing "churches which receive members without trine immersion" to remain in the Fellowship and to "have their delegates seated in National Conference with voting privileges on all matters except those involving the subject of water baptism in relation to church membership."[554] Plaster recognized the significance of this decision adopted at the 1964 National Conference.

> What was it that turned Conference back from its original stance that member churches could receive only trine immersed individuals as members? While many factors and personalities certainly contributed to the change, the fundamental value that launched the Progressive movement had won out. The Conference had determined that it would not impose membership standards upon local churches which the Fellowship saw as autonomous. There were some checks and balances built into the decision, but the result was a victory for the principle of congregational autonomy.[555]

For at least 160 years the Brethren had affirmed the need for trine immersion baptism for local church membership in the case of a person who had been baptized previously in a different form. A decision of Annual Meeting in 1804 stated, "they ought to be baptized in the proper order."[556] The requirement was suspended temporarily in 1821,[557] but by 1834, Annual Meeting reinstated it with the declaration that "hereafter it should not be done otherwise."[558] So it remained until the 1964 Conference. All Grace Brethren churches were obligated to teach and practice only trine immersion baptism, but they were permitted to enact a policy in the local church to accept into membership people who had received another form of baptism or no baptism at all. The *National Fellowship of Brethren Churches Manual of Procedure* was revised to reflect that membership in the Fellowship consisted of "churches which subscribe doctrinally to the Message of the Brethren Ministry as an outline of faith and practice, and which in the performance of the ordinances practice baptism by trine immersion only and the threefold communion service only."[559]

The next fifteen years were relatively peaceful and constructive for the Grace Brethren, but a second conflict was developing. The word "only" in the *Manual of Procedure* led some to fears of restrictive denominationalism. In addition, the 1969 *Statement of Faith* presented the ordinances in a manner that was different from previous documents. In every official list since 1883, the three parts of the communion observance had been treated as separate commands, but the "Statement of Faith" clearly reduced the number of ordinances to two: "baptism of believers by trine immersion" and "the threefold communion service, consisting of the washing of the saints' feet, the Lord's Supper, the communion of the bread and the cup."[560] These two documents raised the issue of whether any of the three parts of communion could ever be practiced separately from one another. In 1979, David Hocking, pastor of the Long Beach Grace Brethren Church, wrote an article for the *Brethren Missionary Herald* in which he stated, "While we maintain our 'distinctives' we also need to be careful that we do not alienate people by our exclusiveness or our 'Brethrenness.'"[561]

One month after the 1980 National Conference, Hocking began a series of sermons that outlined his views on denominationalism and the ordinances, including his belief that feetwashing and the love feast were not obligatory for the church. At the conclusion of the series, he led the congregation in an observance of the bread and the cup alone. By the next National Conference, some were calling for Hocking and the

Long Beach church to be removed from the Fellowship for violating the *Manual of Procedure* and the "Statement of Faith."

Conference moderator Knute Larson requested that the Long Beach church provide a position statement concerning its subscription to the "Statement of Faith" or face dismissal from the Fellowship, and he proposed a two-year study committee to address the primary question: "How does a fellowship of churches maintain Biblical direction and unity in light of its concern for local church autonomy and disciplines?"[562] It was the same question of church government that had plagued the Brethren throughout their history, and it was related once again to the questions of relation to culture and doctrinal framework.

The ordinances, sometimes referred to as the "distinctives" of the Grace Brethren, were the focus because they were the only matters of *practice* in the Fellowship's doctrinal statement. If trine immersion and threefold communion were only Brethren traditions, they should not be included in the "Statement of Faith" and they could be unnecessary impediments to the mission of making disciples. However, if they were specific commands of Christ to define and teach discipleship, then they were essential to the mission of the church and mandatory to those who claimed to be His followers. As James Custer had urged in his 1978 Moderator's Address to National Conference, "While our distinctives *do* give us an identity, and declare our determination to obey all that God has commanded us, may they be more than relics and totem poles of distinction."[563]

The two-year study committee held open forums with Grace Brethren ministers, and "it soon became evident that the essential question, which overshadowed all others, was the role of the ordinances."[564] The issue centered on two questions: "Does our constitution line up as well as possible with Biblical principles?" and "Does the limitation 'threefold only' about communion represent clear Biblical teaching?"[565] A survey of 466 responding ministers, conducted in 1982, showed that 77.4 percent agreed without reservations with the article on ordinances in the "Statement of Faith,"[566] but the controversy was far from settled. A flurry of correspondence ensued, with some calling the "only" clause in the *Manual of Procedure* an offensive sign of creedalism and others believing the whole doctrine of the ordinances was at stake in any agreement to alter a strict requirement of their form. The opinions reflected appeals for calm and bursts of anger, desires for discussion and cries for swift action. One pastor cited a heritage that "not only tolerates a great deal of diverse opinion about church practices and ordinances but also protects with vigor the autonomy of local congregations and the freedom of these churches from direction by any central authority."[567] Another charged that those who wanted to remove the clause "categorically rejected the truth of Communion as set forth in our Statement of Faith!"[568]

The study committed was extended until 1984 and presented its *Unanimous Report of the FGBC Study Committee* to that year's National Conference with the following proposal.

> Therefore we advise that in FGBC churches the word "communion" be reserved exclusively for the threefold service, since it is our understanding that when "the communion of the bread and cup" is separated from the meal, it does not carry the same spiritual and symbolic impact as when it is joined together with the meal, and therefore, is not that which fulfills what Christ commanded to be perpetuated. If a church practices the Eucharist (the Bread and Cup) separately from the threefold communion service, it must clearly teach that this does not fulfill the obligation of the believer to do what Jesus instituted and what the New Testament church practiced as "communion."[569]

The conclusion of the committee followed the opinion expressed by David Plaster, one of its members, two years earlier that "I must honestly state that while the Biblical data clearly indicates to me three parts of the communion service, it does not clearly direct us relative to the absolute necessity of practicing them always together."[570] It was another departure from an historic Brethren position, motivated in large part, by a desire to protect the autonomy of the local congregation from the imposition of any Conference decision or creedal statement. The ordinances would be preserved and practiced, but they would remain subject to a careful study of the New Testament and not be allowed to become creeds in themselves. The identifying principle of the Grace Brethren would be, as one correspondent had insisted, "the absolute authority and finality of the Word of God."[571]

The principle would be tested yet again in a third period of contention which surfaced at the 1989 National Conference when a motion was made "to rescind the membership resolution of 1964 and to modify the Bylaws to require that all members of local churches, other than for a medical exception, had to be trine immersed in order for a church to hold membership in the FGBC."[572] James Boyer summarized the rationale for the motion.

> During the years that the policy has been in effect the situation has gradually but drastically changed. The number of churches using this provision has increased in number and in geographical distribution, until now that which started as a *tolerated exception* has come to be considered as an *acceptable option*[573] (emphasis original).

The motion was tabled, but because it had stirred significant confusion and animosity, the matter was referred to the Fellowship Council for a three-year period of study and discussion.[574] The issue combined certain elements of the previous two controversies in that it centered on the necessity of trine immersion baptism for membership in a local Brethren church according to the *Manual of Procedure* and the "Statement of Faith," but it touched the deeper question of whether this was a New Testament mandate or a Brethren policy. The presenters of the tabled motion, who called themselves Conservatives, argued that "anything other than trine immersion is not valid

Christian baptism."[575] Therefore, people who had been baptized as believers by a form other than trine immersion needed to be instructed about the correct form. If they accepted the Brethren position but stood by their former baptism, they became "guilty of a disobedience of the worst kind, willful rebellion."[576]

Once again, lines were drawn and labels were employed as "the terms 'open' churches (churches that allowed non-trine immersed members) and 'closed' churches (those who required all members to be trine immersed) became buzzwords."[577] The terms only further confused the situation, since some "open" and "closed" congregations held their respective positions as a matter of individual church policy and not as a doctrinal mandate that ought to be binding on every congregation. Plaster witnessed how widespread and angry the contention became.

> Representatives of a group now calling themselves "conservatives" addressed the international missions board, calling for them to repent and deal with churches abroad that had non-trine immersed members. Home missions was charged with hypocrisy for allowing two different church constitutions for home missions churches; one with a "closed" membership policy and one with an "open" membership policy. Grace College and Seminary was accused of promoting a "new hermeneutic" that denied the direct statements of scripture and its own Covenant of Faith.[578]

A series of regional forums were organized for ministers to ask questions and discuss the challenges facing the Fellowship. Members of the Conservative Grace Brethren Association largely ignored or refused invitations to participate. Jim Custer, who moderated the forums, summarized the core issues that surfaced in the meetings.

> The focused issue is a two-pronged question. First, is triune immersion the biblical mode of baptism that

Christ commanded, and is it universally required of every New Testament disciple? Second, what are the requirements mandated in the New Testament for membership in the local congregation, and is baptism one of those requirements? ...The vast majority of debate grows out of the second question, not the first.[579]

At the 1992 National Conference, Moderator Plaster attempted to refocus the issue on the central questions that he believed needed to be discussed and resolved.

Does the New Testament make any specific requirements for membership in the local church? What is the relationship of church membership as defined by our culture and laws compared to the relationship sustained by first-century believers to the local church? What should a fellowship of churches, a para-local church group that had no direct biblical warrant, require of its member churches and why?[580]

Plaster and others recognized as a key issue the relationship of the New Testament command for baptism to the modern practice of local church membership. Underneath this was a foundational issue of church government: Would the Fellowship assume the mantle of a denomination and demand conformity to a practice that was not clearly commanded in Scripture?

If it was a New Testament mandate that all members must be baptized, then the baptism-membership issue really was a Statement of Faith issue. If, on the other hand, it was preference, no matter how good the reasons, it was a matter that had to be left to the decision of local churches.[581]

The Conference decided it was an issue of preference or church policy and voted to add a new paragraph to the Bylaws that read, "Requirements and responsibilities for membership by the several local churches shall be established by each church and shall not determine the church's membership in the Fellowship."[582] A small number could not accept the decision and chose to leave the Fellowship. Their statement to the Conference reflected the importance of the baptism-membership issue to them, but it also referenced what they believed to be two other notable differences between the groups.

> We also take exception to the tendencies toward denominationalism inculcated by the Fellowship Council which takes to itself more and more power and control each year. We cannot continue under such a system… There is a new way of interpreting Scripture at work in our Fellowship. It looks at truth with a subjective eye and seeks to divide God's Word into levels of certainty or clarity.[583]

The rest remained united in that they were willing to allow different policies around a shared belief as expressed in the report of the Fellowship Council.

> The Scriptures reveal that while baptism does teach and illustrate doctrinal truth, obedience in it functions as an evidence of discipleship. We believe that triune immersion is an essential part of the discipleship process. However, the relationship of baptism to membership in the local congregation is to be determined by the policy of each local church as are all the other privileges and responsibilities of membership.[584]

The agreement that was concluded among the remaining churches of the Fellowship was not one of uniformity about the relationship between baptism and local church membership. It was an agreement that local church autonomy would take precedence over the attraction and convenience of an enforced uniformity from a centralized authority structure.

Unfortunately, "the energy, the momentum, the vitality, and the steady growth experienced in the earlier years after the founding of the Grace Brethren movement in 1939 evaporated in the face of conflict that sometimes became malicious and hurtful."[585] From 1965 to 1992, the number of congregations in the United States increased from 204 to 308, then the count fell back to 273 after the division.[586] Despite increased energies in starting new churches, the number has remained fairly static since that time. The three disputes changed the Grace Brethren in relation to their Brethren heritage and to their evangelical surroundings. Robert Clouse described the Grace Brethren as "an old coin which has passed from hand to hand so often that the inscription on it is almost undecipherable unless it is held to the light at just the proper angle."[587] The great question for the Fellowship as it emerged from the series of disputes was whether it would remain Brethren in the sense of continuing the work of making the church what Christ intended for it to be or it would settle into an evangelical model that adequately relieved the tensions of its unique heritage. Clouse believed it was essential for the Grace Brethren to know their historical and theological roots because "rediscovery of past attitudes and behaviors may lead to an understanding of the dangers involved in an uncritical acceptance of the state, modern capitalism, and the excesses of evangelical Christianity."[588]

CHAPTER 22:

Testing Fellowship

The Grace Brethren had affirmed their commitment to the sovereign autonomy of each local congregation in an association of churches, but conflicts leave scars. The mood following the departure of the Conservative Grace Brethren in 1992 was a mixture of sadness and optimism with a lingering atmosphere of caution and weariness. Plaster observed, "Discussion that might lead to any disagreement has been suppressed."[589] However, it might be more accurate to say that such discussion could find little reason or motivation to take place. The Fellowship was left with a coalition of ministers and churches that had agreed that the requirements and responsibilities of membership should be determined by local congregations and not by a mandate of Conference, but within that coalition there were diverse positions on practice. Some required trine immersion baptism of all applicants for membership, while others accepted a previous baptism by single immersion as sufficient. Both were allowed and so there was no need to discuss or debate the merits of either. Since National Conference had removed itself as the body of arbitration in the matter, there was "no real forum within the Fellowship for the discussion of new ideas, theological questions and issues, and consideration of changes."[590]

The weakening of communication and the loss of trust may have been the most profound effects of the series of conflicts within the Fellowship. Changes to several organizations within the Fellowship illustrated the problem. One was a definite shift in the position and perception of Grace Theological Seminary. Previously, the seminary had provided doctrinal stability in the debates, its faculty serving as voices of caution or affirmation. It also had been a source of relational commonality as most of the ministers in the Fellowship had received graduate training through that institution. However, the baptism and church membership controversy of 1989-1992 opened a rift in the seminary faculty that produced confusion and disenchantment among the students. Instead of moderating the conflict, some faculty members were seen by others in the Fellowship as inciting it. The seminary enrollment, because of this and other factors, plunged from more than 400 in 1982 to less than 200 in 1992 and threw the institution into a financial crisis. When several faculty positions were eliminated, rumors concerning the reasons further damaged the seminary's reputation for stability.

At the same time, the National Fellowship of Grace Brethren Ministers had been at the center of many of the debates, and its membership was plagued by mistrust over accusations and statements made in the emotion of the time that could not be recalled or easily forgotten. One observer wrote, "What has happened to us is comparable to biological warfare. The minds of dear brethren have been infected with the virus of mistrust. Words have been used in violation of their meaning. Rumors have abounded. Motives have been judged."[591] Friendships were strained or severed and new alliances formed while some chose to become more independent of the Fellowship and focus their energies on their own local congregations. The people in the churches received most of their information about the Fellowship from their pastors, so the congregations largely followed their lead. McClain's vision of ministers trained at Grace Seminary serving as the guardians of the doctrinal and organizational integrity of the Fellowship appeared to be evaporating.

With the May/June 1996 issue, the Brethren Missionary Herald Company ceased publication of the *Brethren Missionary Herald* magazine. The first issue had appeared in January 1940 with McClain commenting, "Thus the entire name contains three important words, each one indicating a specific task, and which taken together suggest the threefold policy and program of the magazine."[592] It was distinctly *Brethren* in its reporting of selection and viewpoint of stories, it connected its primarily American audience to the progress and needs of *missionary* work among the Grace Brethren in the United States and throughout the world, and it served as a *herald* to the Fellowship of vision and initiatives from the leaders of the various national organizations. Although subscriptions to the publication had declined for a number of years, its demise, after more than fifty years as the major source of news and information for the Fellowship, left a vacuum of accessible stories about people and events among the Grace Brethren. Several national organizations, including Grace Brethren International Missions, Grace Brethren North American Missions, and CE National, had begun their own newsletters to bring their work to the attention of the people and churches of the Fellowship, but now there was no unifying publication to tie their messages into a common vision.

The need for renewed venues of connection was recognized, and a number of significant steps were taken to address the fragmentation that was revealed by the 1992 division. The leaders of several of the national organizations, seeing the need to begin restoring communication and healing relationships, initiated regional Focus Retreats of ministers in 1993. National Conference, "in an effort to attract younger men and women and their families,"[593] began to emphasize locations conducive to vacations and a Bible conference format. A Fellowship Coordinator was hired in 1998 and tasked with promoting communication and cooperation between the churches and organizations. The Brethren Missionary Herald Company made a commitment in 2002 to "nurture Great Commission teamwork between the people and churches of the FGBC by building bridges of communication."[594] BMH launched a new publication called *FGBC World* to bring stories of the Fellowship to the churches.

In 2005, the first Equip Conference was held to provide continuing education for ministers and church leaders. Moderators of the Fellowship annually stressed the need for a common vision among the congregations. Increasingly, the planting of new congregations in the United States and around the world emerged as a common priority although a common strategy and model proved to be more elusive.

Each of these efforts, along with others on regional, district, and local levels, has helped to renew hope and energy in the Fellowship. However, as was the case in 1883 and 1939, the refocusing that came after conflict and division left the Grace Brethren with questions about the same three issues of church government, relation to culture, and doctrinal framework. The answers their predecessors had given shaped the new choices that faced them now. The progression of these choices is seen below in *Figures 30-32.*

1. *Church Government: Independent vs. Fellowship.* What began in 1708 as the concept of autonomy of the local church from the intrusive control of the state church became a choice of autonomy from the centralized authority of Annual Meeting in the 1880s. The Brethren Church then made the decision to remain congregational in its government rather than replacing Annual Meeting with a denominational structure. The Grace Brethren firmly upheld the sovereignty of the local church through three conflicts over the application of doctrinal statements and bylaws to congregations in the Fellowship. One of the most significant benefits of this choice has been the freedom of local congregations to assess and respond to the opportunities, needs, and challenges of their contexts without the burden of denominational mandates and procedures that might hinder them. They can form associations that allow

Figure 30: Choices for the Brethren Church after 1883

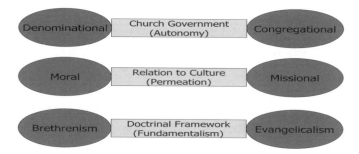

Figure 31: Choices for the Grace Brethren after 1939

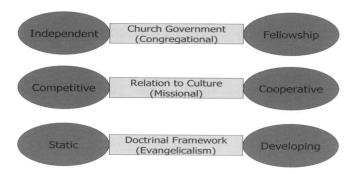

Figure 32: Choices for the Grace Brethren after 1992

them to address the goals and objectives they have set for their ministries more directly. This means, however, that associations within the Fellowship have been made completely voluntary among its members. The national organizations cannot assume a certain amount of support from Grace Brethren churches because none are mandated. Likewise, participation in district functions and projects can be solicited but not required.

Much has been written about the health and structure of an autonomous local church, but relatively little has been said about how a number of such churches maintain cohesion in association with one another. Member churches in the Fellowship of Grace Brethren Churches are still obligated to subscribe to the *Statement of Faith* and to pay annual membership fees to the Fellowship. These payments are used to support the office of the Fellowship Coordinator and the preparations and operations of National Conference, but they do not contribute to the budgets of any of the national organizations. Otherwise, the congregations can operate in apparent independence from each other, but the result can be a breakdown of any real ties of fellowship. Only the churches can place mutual obligations on themselves through a vote at National Conference, but then some group or person must be empowered with the authority to enforce the decisions, and autonomy is seemingly threatened. Having rejected the mandates of an Annual Meeting and the dictates of a denominational statement, the Grace Brethren look to find a unifying vision or purpose that will draw the congregations together in a cooperative effort.

2. *Relation to Culture: Competitive vs. Cooperative.* The Progressives wanted to pursue innovations such as Sunday School and financial support for missionaries because they believed God had called them to permeate the culture with the message of salvation. Later, while some groups settled for a moral influence on society, the new Fellowship emphasized the mission of the church to make disciples who have committed their lives to

following Jesus. More recently, the Grace Brethren have focused that mission on planting new congregations and training new leaders to shepherd them. However, differing models of a church and a wide variety of methods for accomplishing the mission have consistently weakened attempts at close cooperation between existing congregations. Autonomy gives each church the freedom to develop its own strategies, models, and methods, but an insistence on this aspect of autonomy can create an environment of good initiatives stubbornly competing for attention and influence. In a Fellowship of churches with no officially recognized center of authority, influence can be gained, at least temporarily, by gathering and managing resources or by building partnerships with key individuals and organizations to achieve an authority by consensus. Competition of this sort does not seek to destroy or discredit other viewpoints for the most part, but behind its outward civility, it still falls short of true cooperation.

Cooperation in the Fellowship can take place only when autonomous churches and ministers willingly suspend or limit their autonomy for the sake of accomplishing a mutual goal. Leadership in such ventures is not a position of authority but a permission from peers to influence based on a trust that grows from relationships. Initially, people may be drawn to a leader's competency or ability to get things done, but in the long term they will feel safe following only if the leader's motives and values have been proven publicly and personally through experience and over time. A compelling vision alone does not produce sustained cooperation without the relational trust necessary to allow participants to give control of some of their resources and ideas to others. Competition jealously guards autonomy but hinders regional, national, and international efforts that are beyond the scope of any single congregation. Meanwhile, cooperation demands a limitation of autonomy to capture the principle that the collective resources of the churches and skills of the people are essential to fulfilling Christ's mandate for His church.

3. *Doctrinal Framework: Static vs. Developing.* Tom Julien, writing soon after the 1992 division, characterized a tension that has plagued the Brethren from the beginning.

> Like Rebekah, the Brethren movement has always had two sons within it, each striving to be born. One is the tendency toward protectionism, often expressed in traditionalism or legalism. The other is the desire for proclamation, expressed in what one historian called 'a willingness to be contemporary, to change,' as long as this change does not affect foundational doctrines and practices.[595]

Protectionism seeks to produce a system that will eliminate questions and debates by establishing a final authority, whether a Standing Committee or a creedal statement, that will bring conformity. The desire for proclamation, on the other hand, agrees that an unchanging foundation is necessary, but it requires freedom to adapt and to try different methods and strategies. The *Covenant* of the Fellowship states, "The sovereign congregations which are members of this corporation are united in accepting the Holy Scriptures as the sole guide and authority in all matters of faith, doctrine and practice."[596] The *Statement of Faith* serves as "the current expression of a never ending effort to clarify an understanding of the primary doctrines we accept,"[597] and it can be amended through a lengthy but attainable procedure.[598] The Bible alone remains an unchangeable standard for the Fellowship.

This principle has been true throughout the history of the Brethren, yet it has been accompanied continuously by the reality that people of good intentions may interpret the unchangeable standard differently. The *Constitution* of the Fellowship states the ideal that "doctrinal practices or tenets . . . must be general or universal," but it follows with the practical application that "the basic doctrines of one congregation shall be the same as the basic doctrines of every other."[599] In any association of churches, interpretive differences will at times bring tensions between member congregations or ministers, but in a movement that values an ongoing quest to understand and obey the commands of Scripture for the church, the tensions must be accepted. Denominational structures address them by appealing to a group, individual, or document that has been authorized to mandate orthodoxy and discipline those who will not submit, so that the doctrinal framework is made static through enforcement. The Grace Brethren chose not to use their documents in this way, leaving questions of specific interpretation open within the boundaries of a changeable *Statement of Faith*. The danger to the Fellowship is not that its members *cannot* discuss doctrinal differences. The danger is that either, because of a lack of trust, they *will not*, or, because of a lack of opportunity or concern, they *do not* enter into such discussions.

The Fellowship of Grace Brethren Churches is dependent on its members for its existence, but they are not dependent on the Fellowship for theirs. If the Fellowship disbanded and the individual local congregations all became independent, most of them would continue to function as churches, seeking ways to fulfill the commission to make disciples and establishing new associations as needed or desired. The name "Grace Brethren Church" would disappear from their signs, but the doctrinal beliefs and practices could be unchanged. The national organizations would broaden their constituencies through offering their services and expertise to new alliances in order to continue operations. Church planting and mission initiatives that currently look to agencies and resources of the Fellowship would find other means of support to keep their work alive. To some extent, all of these changes already are taking place while a claim to the Fellowship and its values is maintained. This may not be a betrayal of the Fellowship or of the Brethren movement, but it involves a redefinition of what it means to belong to an association of local congregations when there are few organizational or legal obligations to bind the members to one another.

CHAPTER 23

Being Brethren

When Alexander Mack and his seven companions began the Brethren movement in Germany, they believed they were recovering the original intentions of Jesus for His church. Every branch that has sprung from that first group has claimed to be the guardian of the pure essence of Brethrenism. Conrad Beissel gave back his baptism and founded the Ephrata compound, saying that the Germantown Brethren had corrupted its origins. The Old Orders, Conservatives, and Progressives all said they were preserving the order of the Brethren when they divided from one another in 1881-1883. The modernists and fundamentalists in the Brethren Church both felt they were the keepers of the real Brethren heritage. When the Ashland and Grace groups separated in 1939, each believed they held the doctrinal and legal right to be called Brethren. The Conservative Grace Brethren walked out of the 1992 National Conference convinced they were honoring their Brethren roots while those who stayed in the Fellowship stood firm in their belief that they had done the same. There are other branches, not involved in the history of the Grace Brethren, who would also claim to be true descendants of Mack. A chart of the major branches with the dates of division appears below in *Figure 33*.

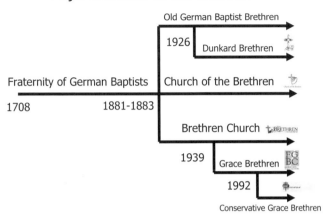

Figure 33: Major branches of the Brethren

Most likely, none of the six major branches would be immediately recognizable to Alexander Mack. Each, from the Old German Baptist Brethren who may have changed the least to the Grace Brethren who perhaps have changed the most, have adopted doctrinal tendencies, church structures, and practices that were not part of Mack's original model. Of course, it must be remembered that Mack and his friends separated from the state church systems so hat they could practice full obedience to what they found in the New Testament. They were not intending to start a new church, much less an association of churches with the complications that distance and numbers bring. At the same time, each of the six branches rightly can claim to be a true descendant of the original Brethren in the sense that each bears distinctive marks of that heritage. Each would say it is an expression of the primitive New Testament church model in its present context. The differences between them stem from divergent interpretations of what the Bible teaches and from variations in the choices each group made in response to the three issues of church government, relation to culture, and doctrinal framework.

Being Brethren cannot be measured by how closely a group adheres to the outward appearances and structures of the early examples. By its very nature, Brethrenism does not easily settle into a crystallized system because it is always seeking to better understand and follow the mandates of Scripture for the church. The first Brethren borrowed and adapted their theology from the Reformers, their model of the church from the Anabaptists, and their view of the Christian life from the Pietists. Why should that process of evaluation, keeping what fit with the Bible and discarding what did not, have ceased after 1708?

The concepts of salvation by faith alone and the priesthood of every believer did not originate on October 31, 1517, when Luther nailed his ninety-five theses to the Castle Church doors in Wittenberg. The idea of believers' baptism as an expression of a personal decision of faith and communion as a memorial in the hands of common believers were not new when Blaurock and Grebel renounced their association with the Reformed Church on January 21, 1525, in Zurich. Spener and Hochmann were not the first to return to the New Testament to discover a model for the Christian life, and Mack did not break new ground when he led his seven companions into the waters of the Eder outside Schwarzenau. Similarly, progress did not begin with the Progressives in 1883, nor did the 1921 *Message of the Brethren Ministry* capture previously unknown doctrines. Local church autonomy was not created through the three controversies in the FGBC, and the correct forms of the ordinances were not discovered by the Brethren.

None of these changes to the existing models and practices of the church were innovations. They were corrections, adjustments, and recalibrations based on study and interpretation of the principles and directives of Scripture. They did not settle questions about church government, relation to culture, and doctrinal framework once for all, but the best of them advanced the refining process within the church, so, as Michael Wohlfahrt told Benjamin Franklin, "Our principles have been improving, and our errors diminishing." At the core of being Brethren lies this restless desire to study, apply, and improve that should prevent the establishment of a static model for the church. At the same time, the quest for the true biblical intent for the church also should curb the tendency toward change simply for the sake of innovation or growth. The primary goal of any local church should not be size or excitement. It should be to honor the Householder and to serve His purposes according to His values. It is certainly not wrong to have both inward obedience and outward success, but the first should never be sacrificed to attain the second.

Earlier in this book, I examined five foundational principles of Alexander Mack and the early Brethren. They were believer's baptism by trine immersion (Chapter 8), threefold communion (Chapter 9), the inward and outward witnesses of truth (Chapter 10), separation from sin and to obedience (Chapter 11), and freedom of the local church (Chapter 12). The Brethren were not the only group to believe and practice these principles, but collectively they were the real "distinctives" of the movement at its beginning. Times and settings change over the years, and the way each principle is applied may shift in its emphasis to meet the demands of the surrounding issues and challenges. Mack spent a great deal of energy arguing for believer's baptism and threefold communion because they were the cornerstones that would mark his break from the state churches and his establishment of a primitive church model. Separation for the Brethren in colonial Pennsylvania focused on their stance against participation in war because that was the point that was directly challenged through the *Test Act*. The Progressives championed freedom of the local congregation from the edicts of Annual Meeting differently than Mack in his detachment from the state churches or the Grace Brethren during the conflicts of the later twentieth century. It was not that the biblical principles changed or became less important with time, but the circumstances that brought them into the center of attention came and went, peaked, and subsided.

For this reason, it would be unfair to compare directly the present treatment of the five foundational principles to the emphasis they received in 1708. However, it may be helpful to reframe the five principles into four statements that capture their application to the context of the Grace Brethren three centuries later. In doing so, I will make a definite change in the style of this book. When relating history and development I have tried to gather, sift, and report what the documents of the time say about the people, events, and influences that shaped the Brethren. Now, I will attempt to paint a picture of what the distinctive beliefs and characteristics we hold can make us at our best. These statements are not unique to the Grace Brethren movement. Since the principles are indeed biblical, many individual congregations and groups of churches have and will reach very similar conclusions about what Jesus, the Householder, intends them to be. Each of the four statements will be followed by a series of sub-points that describe how I believe it should be applied in Grace Brethren churches today. Each statement will also be followed by an explanation of how the ordinances of baptism and communion in the forms that Jesus gave to His church can refocus our attention on the truths of our real "distinctives."

We hold the Bible as our authority.

- Our hermeneutic or method of interpreting the Bible is based on a strong belief in the inspiration of Scripture and a diligent attention to grammar, context, and history.
- We remain non-creedal, consistently resisting a man-made document as a measure of orthodoxy while using such documents to communicate our current understanding and to encourage continued study.
- We repeatedly return to a set of biblical expectations of discipleship as opposed to a growing list of traditions and behavioral rules.
- The Bible forms the basis for any authority vested in organizational structures or offices, and any person holding a position of influence is held to the principles and instructions of Scripture.

- The teachings of the Bible remain our model for structure and practice within our local churches.
- We expect the Holy Spirit to provide personal insight and direction without imposing those convictions on others in the body.

The path that led Mack and his group to the banks of the Eder River involved a clear disavowal of any human leader, state government, or organized church structure or statement as the arbiter of what constitutes truth and obedience. The Brethren were certainly willing to learn from and agree with people like Hochmann or documents like the *Heidelberg Confession*, but these were regarded as confirmations and not sources of the truth. Only the Bible, as the inspired communication of God, could provide the determinative basis for the formation of a local church or the conduct of the Christian life. The ordinances and principles we observe were not imposed on the church by a decision of Annual Meeting or the declaration of a doctrinal statement. They are practices drawn from the study of the New Testament, and if, like Mack's early views on marriage and work,[600] they are found to lack support in Scripture, they should be dismissed. The idea of conforming to a practice such as trine immersion baptism simply because it is part of our Brethren heritage is decidedly un-Brethren as is the idea of setting aside a New Testament ordinance because it has become inconvenient or unpopular.

Because we hold the Bible as our authority, we should not allow our natural desires for cultural relevance or evangelical acceptance to take precedence over our commitment to Scriptural integrity. Every method, program, vision, or initiative should be measured by the stated goals and guidelines in the Bible before they are evaluated for feasibility and effectiveness. Since the New Testament gives relatively few specifics about schedules, structures, and events, there is wide freedom for creativity, ingenuity, and diversity within the list of symbols and principles Jesus said He wants His people to observe. However, we should not neglect these clear commands while giving more time, energy, and attention to gatherings and events that are worthy but biblically optional. The physical practice of these commands may not require a great amount of time, but the proper explanation and instruction of them will require a significant effort among our leaders to understand them personally and to communicate them adequately. Such effort is necessary if the ordinances and principles are to be considered expectations of discipleship to Jesus and not just traditions or events unique to a local church or an association of churches.

No Grace Brethren leader should treat the practices of trine immersion baptism and threefold communion as if they were matters of preference or tradition or denominational policy. It is important to the identity and mission of the Fellowship that its leaders base their understanding and convictions on careful study of the forms and functions presented in the Bible. Then they can observe them and teach them to their people from that foundation, modeling the truth that the Bible is our authority. At the same time, the ordinances should not be used as measures of doctrinal orthodoxy or of loyalty to the Fellowship of Grace Brethren Churches. No minister should practice trine immersion baptism or threefold communion simply to conform to the expectations of the Fellowship or the constitution of a local church. No participant in a Grace Brethren church should engage in the ordinances simply to meet an institutional membership requirement. The Brethren left behind the national churches to avoid those compromises of conscience. The sole authority of the Bible in faith and practice means that there should be no coercion on obedience other than the stated truth of God's Word.

We live as the body of Christ.

- We recognize the equality of all members within the body, most notably in our practice of communion around a table of fellowship and baptism as a voluntary declaration of faith.

- We welcome the diversity of gifts, experiences, and perspectives among the members submitted to the will and directives of God.
- We value the privileges and the responsibilities of the relationships created by our spiritual induction into the body.
- Our definition of church as an organic union rather than as an organizational affiliation stems from the biblical picture of the body composed of individual members.
- We emphasize the shepherding role of elders as leaders chosen by character, motivated by service, and empowered by trust.
- We guard the autonomy of each local congregation as a self-governing expression of the body, cooperating voluntarily with other local churches to accomplish common purposes or benefits given by God.

From its inception at Pentecost the church was designed to be a diverse community united by a common faith through the baptism of the Holy Spirit into a new organism which superseded all racial, gender, social, and economic distinctions between its members (1 Corinthians 12:12-13; Galatians 3:26-29; Colossians 3:11). The people who entered it were to see themselves as being connected like the stones of a building, the members of a household, or the parts of a body. The act that first outwardly identified them as a group of Christ's followers at Pentecost, just as it later identified the Brethren as a group committed to obeying Jesus in Germany and in America, was water baptism. That public self-identification with the salvation promised by the Father, accomplished by the Son, and sealed by the Holy Spirit and with the people who had also received it marks us as the members of the body in our intention to live as disciples of Jesus. Likewise, our periodic observance of communion renews our commitment to the responsibility and accountability of fellowship, to the need for maintaining a pure relationship with Jesus, to the obligation to remember the life and benefits purchased by His sacrifice, and to the mission of proclaiming His death until He comes. These are the benefits and the works of Christ's household.

Threefold communion, as presented by Jesus to His disciples in the upper room, is without a doubt the central piece of worship and devotion in the household of Christ. It is the symbol Jesus has given to define our relationships with Him and with one another. It is also the one specific gathering that is commanded for the members of the body, and it is the one event that is designated as a coming together of the church (1 Corinthians 11:18). There is no better way to demonstrate our unity with Christ and with one another. The symbol does not give us unity, but it provides a vivid reminder and expression of the unity that Christ has given and prepares the way for the lessons, conversations, and actions that are essential for unity to grow. Threefold communion takes more time than a simple observance of the bread and the cup, but it restores the intended relational aspects of the ordinance. It combines a remembrance of the source of new life with an immediate application of how that new life expresses itself in the fellowship of the body. There is no priest but Jesus, and we His followers share and handle the symbolic food and drink, towel and basin, and bread and cup equally at His table as members of His household. We are invited into a special setting and temporarily immersed in symbols of the life of our body, so that we are reminded and taught to live as the body in everyday settings.

We practice a proper separation *from* sin and *to* obedience.

- We continue our heritage as a product of the pilgrim church that has constantly sought to improve on existing models with the goal of ever-greater obedience to the directives of God as revealed in the Bible to our consciences.

- We are committed to the principle of non-coercion in matters of faith and conscience as opposed to the enforcement of a determined human model.
- We hold our citizenship in heaven above our rights and obligations to any political, social, or religious entity.
- We affirm our identity as followers of Christ and intentionally invite those outside the body to become followers as well.
- We center on the principles of discipleship in the Great Commission as guides to our use of innovations and as guards against legalism.
- We encourage obedience among the people of God by example, instruction, training, and discipline.

Separation can define the identity of a group by clarifying its values and priorities. At times in their history, the Brethren used an imposed separation from the world or from other Christian groups improperly to build a behavioral conformity that only weakened any real unity of identity. However, a voluntary separation to the revealed will of God distinguishes us as true disciples who listen to the voice of our Master. The baptisms at Pentecost marked the participants as members of a separated community that placed its faith in the salvation that God had provided through Jesus and had communicated and sealed by the Holy Spirit. Similarly, the Anabaptists and early Brethren, through adult baptism and closed communion, separated themselves to a church composed only of those who had received salvation by faith. Jesus Himself excluded Judas from the bread and the cup, and Paul later warned that believers should examine themselves before sharing the symbols. Each time the church is invited to the Lord's Supper, we renew our pledge to be the distinct, separated household of Christ.

It is from our identity that we launch into our mission to live as disciples in this world and to urge others to join us in knowing and following Jesus. By reaffirming who we are we clarify the invitation that we declare to a lost world. We offer them the

Good News that they can be separated *from* the kingdom of darkness and separated *to* the kingdom of God's Son. We call them to leave behind bondage to sin and death and to enter into the yoke of righteousness and life. The ordinances properly exclude all who have no relationship with Jesus, but they gladly include all who receive salvation by faith, distinguishing them as members of the body of Christ, separated to His fellowship and service forever. We must never refuse the water to receive new declarations of identity with the salvation and people of God or fail to offer an empty seat at the table of the Lord to welcome those who accept His invitation into the benefits of the New Covenant.

We seek to fulfill the entire Great Commission.

- We view evangelism as one necessary piece of the command to make disciples, seeking opportunities to proclaim the Good News through word and action.
- We recognize that the development of Christ-followers is the central objective of the Great Commission.
- We understand conversion to be a work of God in the human heart, accomplished and sealed by His power and not by our skill or technique.
- Our understanding of salvation looks for a continuing process of growth rather than a single event, action, or experience.
- We are convinced that disciples should gather in local churches for mutual encouragement and edification, and we endeavor to spread these local expressions of the body of Christ.
- We believe that, until the rapture of the church, the work of the Great Commission is not accomplished until the gospel is proclaimed to all people and those who respond in faith are taught to obey all that He commanded.

The state churches used the ordinances as an easy means to incorporate every possible person into the church. Baptism was administered to infants, so they were made part of the national religious community before they could possibly be aware that such a thing existed. Communion was given with the blessing of the clergy in order to offset anything otherwise lacking in a person's spiritual life. In this way, the national churches could claim many members even if there were far fewer actual disciples. However, the commission given by Jesus to His followers did not settle for expanding numbers or recording decisions. In Matthew 28:19-20, the command to make disciples is followed by two clauses that name two essential elements in the process. The first is baptism, the public, voluntary self-identification of the individual with the triune God and the salvation He provided. No one who willfully refuses to submit to that requirement should be considered an obedient follower of Jesus. The second element in the process of making disciples is teaching them to obey all that Christ commanded. The initial identification involves an obligation to follow through with growth in understanding and service. Discipleship is measured by current obedience and not by a past experience.

After the division of 1939, the Grace Brethren tended toward a view of salvation as a point in time with a strong emphasis on faith alone rather than as a process with an expectation of obedience after conversion. As McClain asserted, "Either Christ will save you by grace through faith plus nothing, or He will not save you at all!"[601] This position distanced the Fellowship from any hint of baptismal regeneration and fit well with the sharp delineations of fundamentalism and the fervor of evangelicalism to reach the lost, but it diminished the urgency of a life of obedient discipleship. The ordinances provide valuable lessons that bridge the gap that is opened between salvation by faith alone and the obligation to take up the cross daily and follow Jesus, the reality of being saved *from* sin and punishment and the reality of being saved *to* a life of devotion and fellowship. Baptism reminds us of the change that God has accomplished for us through Christ while also positioning us for the responsibilities of a new life as Christ's followers. Communion celebrates the life and benefits of the new covenant that Jesus instituted through His sacrificial death while also illustrating our need to receive continual renewal and cleansing and to recognize, care for, and participate in the household of Jesus.

Since discipleship involves learning to obey the commands of our Master, the ordinances should be taught as essentials in the process. Baptism is the means by which we identify ourselves as disciples of Jesus, and communion is the means by which we demonstrate our continuing commitment to live as His disciples. They do not accomplish salvation, nor are they the only measures of faithfulness, but, as outward practices given to and expected of the church, they are more than suggestions or options. We need to approach this matter carefully because it has been a stumbling block in the Brethren movement before now. Exhortation should not become coercion, but we should encourage a sense of voluntary obligation to express our involvement in the identity and mission of the church through the practices Jesus gave. They are the personal reaffirmations and public testimonies that we are actively engaged in the process of following our Lord in fellowship with the disciples of His household.

CHAPTER 24

Continuing
the Quest

History is a tool that can be used to understand how we reached the present and to inform our choices as we try to realize a desired future. It gives us the advantage of seeing the outcomes of words, actions, and strategies that have been applied to circumstances and events that may be similar to our own. History is not an infallible guide—sometimes mistakes appear to work and decisions of integrity seem to fail—but it allows us to evaluate somewhat dispassionately from a distance of time.

The Brethren have specialized in comparing the beliefs and practices of others with the expectations and commands of Scripture, and we certainly should do the same with our own history. The words and plans of Mack, Holsinger, and McClain are not the pattern we must follow. These men would be among the first of our spiritual ancestors to remind us to look to the New Testament for our directions. They attempted imperfectly to apply the intentions of Jesus to their time and place, just as we try imperfectly to apply them to ours. The ideal of the primitive church is not an outward form frozen in the time of a mythical golden age. It is the careful implementation and consistent utilization of Christ's timeless principles and purposes for His church in the setting of the present time.

By far, the most damaging events in the history and development of the Brethren movement have been internal struggles. Wars, persecutions, and hardships have usually drawn the membership together against a common threat. Disagreements, misunderstandings, and suspicions among the membership have brought division. One proposed solution is to find and promote a compelling vision that will unite the ministers, churches, and members in a cooperative effort of shared resources. It is an attractive dream, but it contains an inherent weakness in the context of the Fellowship. A few eloquent and forceful speakers could accomplish the communication of such a vision. A model and strategy could be designed by a group of talented innovators and organizers. The shared resources and energy necessary to implement and sustain the vision, however, would demand negotiation on issues of funding, authority, and control. That kind of communication requires time and patience. It also requires solid relationships of trust that can work through honest differences and inevitable misunderstandings, and that means even more time and patience are needed. Divisions have occurred in Brethren history when individuals or groups of people have grown frustrated with the slow process of negotiation and either have tried to impose their wishes on others or have decided that separation was the only way to maintain freedom.

The autonomy of each congregation is an important principle that safeguards us against coercion of conscience as we seek to obey Jesus. Autonomy should not be interpreted as a freedom from any spiritual authority or accountability, however. The church is both an organism and an organization. New Testament imagery focuses primarily on the organic nature of the church as the body of Christ, composed of individual disciples who have responded in faith to the message of salvation. These people are sheep who need shepherds, living stones being fit together into the temple of God, diverse members who together form a functioning body. The church has also become an organization with physical resources that need to be maintained, employees who need to be supervised, and legal responsibilities that need to be met. Both the organic and the organizational aspects of the church require leaders who are entrusted with the authority to give direction to others. The first is the shepherding role of leadership outlined in the New Testament and entrusted to a group called elders or overseers. The second is the administrative role that cares for the realities of church operations in the context of modern society.

Both types of leaders are needed in the Fellowship of Grace Brethren Churches, but a key question must be answered clearly: Does the organization serve the organism or does the organism serve the organization? A corporate model of leadership may be helpful for the organizational aspects of the church, but it is not the model presented in the New Testament for the organic leadership of the household. Organizational leadership focuses on accomplishing necessary tasks through people who have the appropriate skills, experience, and techniques. Organic leadership focuses on shepherding God's flock through people who have the required character and faithfulness to model a consistent and growing life of obedience to Jesus and the credibility and spiritual gifts to equip others to grow in obedience. The development of teams of elders who understand and practice the biblical role of shepherds in local churches may be the greatest need of the Fellowship. They are in the only leadership position expressly authorized by God in the New Testament for the care and oversight of the church.

The Fellowship of Grace Brethren Churches is an entity far more complex than Alexander Mack could have imagined when he and his companions began their meetings. Mack wanted freedom from the errors and control of the state churches to organize and worship according to his beliefs, but it is doubtful that he ever envisioned the dynamics of an association of autonomous congregations. Over the years, the introduction of properties, facilities, salaried ministers, mission agencies, and the like have brought tremendous advantages to the local church and to the Fellowship, but they have also created organizational and administrative issues that have greatly complicated and, in some cases, blurred the two roles of leadership. The national organizations of the Fellowship have administrative leaders, including boards of directors or trustees, to manage and maintain their operations, but the national organizations are best suited to be responders, supplying tools and services in their respective areas of expertise, to the needs and vision of the churches. No person or group has been entrusted with the shepherding role to monitor and direct the spiritual health of the collective member churches.

Again, some would see the need to appoint a visionary leader who could articulate a strategy and guide the churches of the Fellowship into a grand future. However, by what process can such a leader be selected, and, if one were agreed upon, would the autonomous churches really follow? In the end, would we find ourselves, having elected a leader like the other denominations have, wishing for deliverance from mandated programs and expenses that we do not believe in or understand fully? Perhaps the solution lies in the shepherds God has already

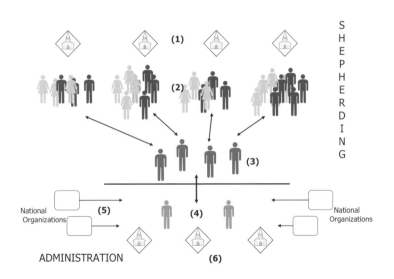

Figure 34: Model for leadership and cooperation in the Fellowship of Grace Brethren Churches

provided within the individual congregations. Since we are a fellowship of churches, and since a team of elders is the New Testament model for church leadership, it would follow that a representative collection of elders are in the best position to give direction to cooperative efforts among the association of congregations. Some of the pieces for the general model shown above in *Figure 34* are already in place.

(1) The individual congregations are grouped into geographical districts or regions of churches. It is not necessary for the regions to be equal in size, although some restructuring might be beneficial to ensure that each region has enough members to remain viable. Each church is autonomous under the oversight of elders selected by the congregation on the basis of faithfulness to the church and godly character that is recognized both inside and outside the congregation.

(2) The elders of each congregation select one or two of their members to represent them in a district pool of elders. Churches should be encouraged to make their choices from their complete list of elders and not just paid ministers. These representatives serve as liaisons between the district and its member congregations in discussing and communicating cooperative efforts between the churches.

(3) Each district pool then chooses one or two representatives to serve on a board of elders for the Fellowship. This board is responsible for crafting a vision for the Fellowship by gathering input from and reporting progress to the district pools who, in turn, inform the elder teams of the local churches. The goal of the board is not to dictate policies or programs to the districts. It is to explore and discover possibilities for cooperative opportunities among the regions of the Fellowship.

(4) At this point, the focus of leadership moves from shepherding to administration as the board provides direction for a staff of people who possess the skills to develop tools and materials that will help churches to implement the vision. The staff creates an annual budget to fund their work, the

monies being collected through annual fees from the member churches.

(5) The staff uses the funds to contract with the national organizations for services needed in the communication and promotion of the vision. This does not preclude the organizations from working with individual districts or congregations, but they contribute their expertise to the vision of the Fellowship as one means of serving the churches.

(6) Since the individual congregations are still self-governing, they choose their own level of involvement in the vision, forming partnerships with other churches and obtaining specific services and resources from the national organizations.

Obviously, this model is very sketchy in details, and it must be left to others more skilled in designing strategies to debate its merits, reveal its flaws, and provide improvements or alternatives. It is presented here as a starting point, because I believe that without continued cooperation on projects that further Christ's purposes for His church in a way that preserves the freedom of the local congregations, the Fellowship will find no real reason to exist. In choosing a Fellowship model of church government, a cooperative approach to reaching our culture, and a view of doctrine as a developing process of study and refinement, I believe we have chosen well. Furthermore, I believe these are choices that fit the intentions of Christ for His church in the pages of Scripture. Putting those choices into consistent practice, however, will require more than new phrases and tools. It will require the application of God's commands to all aspects of His household by all members of His household.

The Message of the Brethren Ministry

The Message which Brethren Ministers accept as a divine entrustment to be heralded to a lost world, finds its sole source and authority in the Bible. This message is one of hope for a lost world and speaks with finality and authority. Fidelity to the apostolic injunction to preach the Word demands our utmost endeavor of mind and heart. We, the members of the National Ministerial Association of The Brethren Church, hold that the essential and constituent elements of our message shall continue to be the following declarations:

1. Our motto:

    The Bible, the whole Bible and nothing but the Bible.

2. The authority and integrity of the Holy Scriptures.

    The ministry of The Brethren Church desires to bear testimony to the belief that God's supreme revelation has been made through Jesus Christ, a complete and authentic record of which revelation is the New Testament; and, to the belief that the Holy Scriptures of the Old and New Testaments, as originally given, are the infallible record of the perfect, final and authoritative revelation of God's will, altogether sufficient in themselves as a rule of faith and practice.

3. We understand the basic content of our doctrinal preaching to be:

    (1) The Pre-Existence, Deity and Incarnation by Virgin Birth of Jesus Christ, the Son of God;

    (2) The Fall of Man, his consequent spiritual death and utter sinfulness, and the necessity of his New Birth;

    (3) The Vicarious Atonement of the Lord Jesus Christ through the shedding of His own blood;

    (4) The Resurrection of the Lord Jesus Christ in the body in which He suffered and died, and His subsequent glorification at the right hand of God;

    (5) Justification by personal faith in the Lord Jesus Christ, of which obedience to the will of God, and works of righteousness, are the evidence and result; the resurrection of the dead, the judgment of the world, and the life everlasting of the just;

    (6) The Personality and Deity of the Holy Spirit, Who indwells the Christian and is his Comforter and Guide;

    (7) The personal and visible return of our Lord Jesus Christ from heaven as King of kings and Lord of lords, the glorious goal for which we are taught to watch, wait and pray;

    (8) The Christian should "be not conformed to this world, but be transformed by the renewing of

the mind"; should not engage in carnal strife, and should "swear not at all";

(9) The Christian should observe, as his duty and privilege, the ordinances of our Lord Jesus Christ, among which are: (a) Baptism of Believers by Trine Immersion; (b) Confirmation; (c) the Lord's Supper; (d) the Communion of the Bread and Wine; (e) the Washing of the Saints' Feet; and (f) the Anointing of the Sick with Oil.

Covenant and Statement of Faith

FELLOWSHIP OF GRACE BRETHREN CHURCHES

Section One. *Covenant.* The sovereign congregations which are members of this corporation are united in accepting the Holy Scriptures as the sole guide and authority in all matters of faith, doctrine and practice.

Section Two. *Statement of Faith.* The Fellowship of Grace Brethren Churches has a corporate commitment to a basic body of beliefs founded on God's revealed truth. The Statement of Faith is the current expression of a never ending effort to clarify an understanding of the primary doctrines we accept.

It is the understanding of this Fellowship that, although individual Grace Brethren Churches remain distinct, autonomous legal entities, congregational church government relates alone to the incidental affairs of the local congregation and not to doctrinal practices or tenets which must be general or universal the same in all congregations. The basic doctrines of one congregation shall be the same as the basic doctrines in every other.

Accordingly, the Fellowship of Grace Brethren Churches, Inc., believing the Bible, the whole Bible, and nothing but the Bible to be the infallible rule of faith and of practice and feeling the responsibility to make known the divine message of the Bible, presents the following articles as a statement of those basic truths taught in the Bible which are common to our Christian faith and practice.

1. THE BIBLE. The Word of God, the sixtysix Books of the Old and New Testaments, verbally inspired in all parts, and therefore wholly without error as originally given of God (2 Tim. 3:16; 2 Peter 1:21).

2. THE ONE TRUE GOD. Existing eternally as three persons the Father, the Son, and the Holy Spirit (Luke 3:22; Matthew 28:19; 2 Cor. 13:14).

3. THE LORD JESUS CHRIST. His preexistence and deity (John 1:13), incarnation by virgin birth (John 1:14; Matthew 1:18-23), sinless life (Heb. 4:15), substitutionary death (2 Cor. 5:21), bodily resurrection (Luke 24:36-43), ascension into heaven and present ministry (Heb. 4:14-16), and coming again (Acts 1:11).

4. THE HOLY SPIRIT. His personality (John 16:7-15), and deity (Acts 5:3-4), and His work in each believer: baptism and indwelling at the moment of regeneration (1 Cor. 12:13; Rom. 8:9), and filling (Eph. 5:18) to empower for Christian life and service (Eph. 3:16; Acts 1:8; Gal. 5:22-23).

5. MAN. His direct creation in the image of God (Gen. 1:26-28), his subsequent fall into sin resulting in spiritual death (Gen. 3:1-24; Rom. 5:12), and the necessity of the new birth for his salvation (John 3:35).

6. SALVATION. A complete and eternal salvation by God's grace alone received as the gift of God through personal

faith in the Lord Jesus Christ and His finished work (Eph. 2:8-9; Titus 3:5-7; 1 Peter 1:18-19).

7. THE CHURCH. One true church, the body and the bride of Christ (Eph. 1:22-23; 5:25-32), composed of all true believers of the present age (1 Cor. 12:12-13); and the organization of its members in local churches for worship, for edification of believers, and for worldwide gospel witness, each local church being autonomous but cooperating in fellowship and work (Eph. 4:11-16).

8. CHRISTIAN LIFE. A life of righteousness, good works and separation unto God from the evil ways of the world (Rom. 12:12), manifested by speaking the truth (James 5:12), maintaining the sanctity of the home (Eph. 5:22-6:4), settling differences between Christians in accordance with the Word of God (1 Cor. 6:1-8), not engaging in carnal strife but showing a Christlike attitude toward all men (Rom. 12:17-21), exhibiting the fruit of the Spirit (Gal. 5:22-23), and maintaining a life of prayer (Eph. 6:18; Phil. 4:6), including the privilege, when sick, of calling for the elders of the church to pray and to anoint with oil in the name of the Lord (James 5:13-18).

9. ORDINANCES. The Christians should observe the ordinances of our Lord Jesus Christ which are (1)baptism of believers by triune immersion (Matt. 28:19) and (2)the threefold communion service, consisting of the washing of the saints' feet (John 13:1-17), the Lord's Supper (1 Cor. 11:20-22, 33-34; Jude 12), and the communion of the bread and the cup (1 Cor. 11:23-26).

10. SATAN. His existence and personality as the great adversary of God and His people (Rev. 12:1-10), his judgment (John 12:31), and final doom (Rev. 20:10).

11. SECOND COMING. The personal, visible, and imminent return of Christ to remove His church from the earth (1 Thess. 4:16-17) before the tribulation (1 Thess. 1:10; Rev. 3:10), and afterward to descend with the Church to establish His millennial kingdom upon the earth (Rev. 19:11-20:6).

12. FUTURE LIFE. The conscious existence of the dead (Phil. 1:21-23; Luke 16:19-31), the resurrection of the body (John 5:28-29), the judgment and reward of believers (Rom. 14:10-12; 2 Cor. 5:10), the judgment and condemnation of unbelievers (Rev. 20:11-15), the eternal life of the saved (John 3:16), and the eternal punishment of the lost (Matt. 25:46; Rev. 20:15).

Endnotes

Notes for Introduction

1. John Lewis Gillin, *The Dunkers: A Sociological Interpretation* (New York: AMS Press, 1906), 60.
2. Donald F. Durnbaugh, ed., *European Origins of the Brethren* (Elgin, Ill.: The Brethren Press, 1958), 122.
3. Ibid., 160.
4. James Quinter, *A Vindication of Trine Immersion as the Apostolic Form of Christian Baptism* (Huntingdon, Pa.: The Brethren's Publishing Co., 1886), 232.
5. Alexander Mack, *The First Brethren Tract* in William R. Eberly, ed., *The Complete Writings of Alexander Mack* (Winona Lake, Ind.: BMH Books, 1991), 10-11.
6. Henry R. Holsinger, *History of the Tunkers and the Brethren Church* (Oakland: Pacific Press Publishing Co., 1901), 35.
7. Mack, *First Brethren Tract*, 13.
8. Merle D. Strege, *Baptism & Church: A Believers' Church Vision* (Grand Rapids: Sagamore Books, 1986), 29. *Gemeinschaft* and *Gemeinde* are German words used by the early Brethren to indicate a community bound together by a common center of belief. They preferred these words to the designation *Kirche* or church.
9. Carl F. Bowman, *Brethren Society: The Cultural Transformation of a "Peculiar People"* (Baltimore: The Johns Hopkins University Press, 1995), 76.
10. Dale R. Stoffer, *Background and Development of Brethren Doctrines 1650-1987* (Philadelphia: The Brethren Encyclopedia,, 1989), 71.
11. Alexander Mack, *Basic Questions* in William R. Eberly, ed., *The Complete Writings of Alexander Mack* (Winona Lake, Ind., BMH Books, 1991), 23.
12. E. H. Broadbent, *The Pilgrim Church* (Grand Rapids: Gospel Folio Press, 1999), 404.
13. Ibid., 17.
14. Stoffer, *Background and Development*, 84.
15. Broadbent, *The Pilgrim Church*, 181.
16. *The Brethren Encyclopedia* (Philadelphia and Oak Brook, Ill.: The Brethren Encyclopedia, 1983), 1100.
17. Holsinger, *History of the Tunkers*, 26.
18. Mack, *Basic Questions*, in Eberly, ed., *The Complete Writings of Alexander Mack*, 25-26.
19. Durnbaugh, *European Origins of the Brethren*, 11.

Notes for Chapter 1

20. Richard E. Averbeck, "The Focus of Baptism in the New Testament," *Grace Theological Journal* 2 (Issue 2: 1981), 288.

21. F. F. Bruce, *The Book of Acts* (Grand Rapids: William B. Eerdmans Publishing Co., 1988), 70.

22. Craig S. Keener, *The IVP Bible Background Commentary: New Testament* (Downers Grove, Ill.: InterVarsity Press, 1993), 329.

23. I. Howard Marshall, *The Acts of the Apostles* (Grand Rapids: William B. Eerdmans Publishing Co., 1982), 82.

24. Keener, *The IVP Bible Background Commentary*, 330.

25. Homer A. Kent, Jr., *Studies in the Gospel of Mark* (Winona Lake, Ind.: BMH Books, 1981), 149.

26. Everett F. Harrison, *Acts: The Expanding Church* (Chicago: Moody Press, 1975), 66.

27. Kent, *Jerusalem to Rome: Studies in Acts* (Winona Lake, Ind.: BMH Books, 1972), 156.

28. Marshall, *The Acts of the Apostles*, 83.

29. Gillin, *The Dunkers*, 51.

30. Broadbent, *The Pilgrim Church*, 181.

31. Martin G. Brumbaugh, *A History of the German Baptist Brethren in Europe and America* (Mount Morris, Ill.: Brethren Publishing House), 1899, 25.

Notes for Chapter 2

32. Bruce L. Shelley, *Church History in Plain Language* (Dallas: Word Publishing, 1995), 50-51.

33. Acts 14:23 indicates that elders (plural) were appointed in each local church (singular). Acts 20:28-31 and 1 Peter 5:1-4 provide two examples of apostles entrusting the care of the flock to these elders. The qualifications for the role listed by Paul in 1 Timothy 3:1-7 and Titus 1:5-9 reflect the pattern for selecting candidates who are known for their character and faithfulness.

34. Justo Gonzalez, *The Story of Christianity: Volume 1, the Early Church to the Dawn of the Reformation* (San Francisco: Harper & Row, 1984), 63.

35. Broadbent, *The Pilgrim Church*, 30.

36. Gonzalez, *Vol. 1*, 106.

37. Broadbent, *The Pilgrim Church*, 41.

38. Philip Schaff, *History of the Christian Church: Volume III, Nicene and Post-Nicene Christianity* (Grand Rapids: William B. Eerdmans Publishing Co., 1979), 11.

39. Gonzalez *Vol. 1*, 106.

40. *Edict of Toleration*, from the Latin text of Lactantius. A.D. 311.

41. Shelley, *Church History*, 94.

42. "Edict of Milan," A.D. 313.

43. Broadbent, *The Pilgrim Church*, 41.

44. Gonzalez, *Vol. 1*, 107.

45. Schaff, *Vol. III*, 13.

46. Shelley, *Church History*, 94.

47. *Proclamation of Theodosius*, A.D. 380.
48. Augustine of Hippo, *The Advantage of Believing*. A.D. 391.
49. Shelley, *Church History*, 128.
50. Augustine of Hippo, *Epistulum quam vocant fundamenti*. A.D. 396.
51. Shelley, *Church History*, 96.
52. J. H. Moore, *The New Testament Doctrines* (Elgin, Ill.: Brethren Publishing House, 1915), 123.
53. Shelley, *Church History*, 125.
54. Joseph R. Shultz, *The Soul of the Symbols: A Theological Study of Holy Communion* (Grand Rapids: William B. Eerdmans Publishing Co., 1966), 99.
55. Marlin Jeschke, "Making the Lord's Supper Meaningful," in Dale R. Stoffer, ed., *The Lord's Supper: Believers Church Perspectives* (Scottdale, Pa.: Herald Press, 1997), 141.
56. "Sermon of Leo I," delivered on the anniversary of his papacy. A.D. 441.
57. Ibid.
58. Shelley, *Church History*, 146.
59. *Codex Justinian, Book 1, Title 1: De summa trinitate*. A.D. 529.
60. Shelley, *Church History*, 96.
61. Broadbent, *The Pilgrim Church*, 165.
62. Strege, "Ecclesiology and the Lord's Supper: The Memorial Meal of a Peaceable Community," in Stoffer, ed., *The Lord's Supper*, 120-121.
63. Gonzalez, *Vol. 1*, 124.
64. Broadbent, *The Pilgrim Church*, 44.

Notes for Chapter 3

65. Martin Luther, *Disputation of Doctor Martin Luther on the Power and Efficacy of Indulgences*, 1517.
66. Shelley, *Church History*, 238.
67. Gonzalez, *The Story of Christianity: Volume 2, the Reformation to the Present Day*, 10.
68. Adapted from Shelley, *Church History*, 246.
69. Gonzalez, *Vol. 2*, 53.
70. Schaff, *History of the Christian Church: Volume VII, Modern Christianity: The German Reformation*, 177.
71. *Exsurge Domine*, 1520.
72. Luther, *The Freedom of a Christian Man*, 1520.
73. Luther, *Address to the German Nobility*, 1520.
74. Luther, *Against the Murderous, Thieving Hordes of Peasants*, 1525.
75. Gonzalez, *Vol. 2*, 34.
76. Luther, *On Secular Authority*, 1523.
77. Broadbent, *The Pilgrim Church*, 163.
78. Gonzalez, *Vol. 2*, 37.
79. Schaff, *Vol. VII*, 51.
80. Broadbent, *The Pilgrim Church*, 167.
81. Luther, *Debate at Leipzig*, 1519.
82. Luther, *The Freedom of a Christian Man*, 1520.

83. John Calvin, *Defense of Orthodox Faith of the Sacred Trinity against the Prodigious Errors of the Spaniard Michael Servetus,* 1554.
84. Albert T. Ronk, *History of the Brethren Church: Its Life, Thought, Mission* (Ashland, Ohio: Brethren Publishing Co., 1968), 13.
85. Gillin, *The Dunkers* 47.

Notes for Chapter 4

86. Shelley, *Church History*, 247.
87. William R. Estep, *The Anabaptist Story: An Introduction to Sixteenth Century Anabaptism* (Grand Rapids: William B. Eerdmans Publishing Co., 1996), 14.
88. Schaff, *History of the Christian Church: Volume VIII, Modern Christianity: The Swiss Reformation*, 77.
89. David R. Plaster, *Finding Our Focus: A History of the Grace Brethren Church* (Winona Lake, Ind.: BMH Books, 2003), 5.
90. Gonzalez, *Vol. 2*, 55.
91. Schaff, *Vol. VIII*, 77.
92. Estep, *The Anabaptist Story*, 14.
93. Schaff, *Vol. VIII*, 75.
94. John D. Rempel, *The Lord's Supper in Anabaptism* (Scottdale, Pa.: Herald Press, 1993), 36.
95. Gonzalez, *Volume 2*, 53-54.
96. Thielman J. van Braght, *Martyrs Mirror*, Joseph F. Sohm, trans. (Scottdale, Pa.: Herald Press, 2004 [1660]), 396.
97. Durnbaugh, "Believers Church Perspectives on the Lord's Supper," in Stoffer, ed., *The Lord's Supper*, 70.
98. Estep, *The Anabaptist Story*, 20.
99. Ibid., 29.
100. Broadbent, *The Pilgrim Church*, 165.
101. Shelley, *Church History*, 254.
102. Durnbaugh, "Believers Church Perspectives on the Lord's Supper," in Stoffer, ed., *The Lord's Supper*, 70.
103. Jeff Bach, "The Agape in Brethren Tradition," in Stoffer, ed., *The Lord's Supper*, 163.
104. Broadbent, *The Pilgrim Church*, 165.
105. Estep, *The Anabaptist Story*, 29.
106. Shelley, *Church History*, 251.
107. Gonzalez, *Volume 2*, 56.
108. Van Braght, *Martyrs Mirror*, 741-742.
109. *The Schleitheim Confession of Faith*, Article I. 1527.
110. Ibid., Article III.
111. Ibid., Article IV.
112. Ibid.
113. *"The Dordrecht Confession of Faith*, Article XIV. April 21, 1632.
114. George Hunston Williams, *The Radical Reformation* (Philadelphia: The Westminster Press, 1962) in Stoffer, *Background and Development*, 45.
115. *Second Diet of Speiers*, April 1529.

. 116. "The Augsburg Confession" was later endorsed by John Calvin and remains today the recognized creed of the Lutheran faith. Its charges against the Anabaptists include some real differences of doctrine and some misunderstandings or misrepresentations of Anabaptist views. Each charge begins with the declaration, "They condemn the Anabaptists" followed by an offensive doctrine attributed to the Anabaptists. These include the giving of the Holy Spirit apart from the sacraments (Article V), salvation apart from infant baptism (Article IX), eternal security of the believer (Article XII), refusal to hold civil office (Article XVI), and the annihilation of condemned souls (Article XVII).

117. Van Braght, *Martyrs Mirror*, 442-443.

118. Ibid., 392, 397.

119. *The Dordrecht Confession of Faith*, Article XIII.

120. *The Schleitheim Confession of Faith*, Article V.

121. Ibid.

122. Shelley, *Church History*, 252.

123. Menno Simons (1496-1561) became an Anabaptist in 1536 and traveled among Anabaptist groups in northern Europe. His teaching placed a strong emphasis on the repudiation of violence. His followers were called Mennonites.

124. Shelley, *Church History*, 252.

125. Pieter Jansz Twisck, *Confession of Faith, According to the Holy Word of God*, Article XXI. 1600.

126. Ibid.

127. Ibid., Articles XXII and XXIII; Emmert F. Bittinger, *Heritage and Promise: Perspectives on the Church of the Brethren* (Elgin, Ill.: Brethren Press, 1983), 79.

128. *The Bern Disputation*, 1538. Quoted in Estep, *The Anabaptist Story*, 191-192.

129. Twisck, *Confession of Faith, According to the Holy Word of God*, Article XI.

130. *The Schleitheim Confession of Faith*, Article VI.

131. Ibid.

132. *The Dordrecht Confession of Faith*, Article XIV.

133. Shelley, *Church History*, 248-249.

134. Ibid., 254.

Notes for Chapter 5

135. Broadbent, *The Pilgrim Church*, 281.

136. Gonzalez, *Volume 2*, 207.

137. Johann Arndt, *True Christianity*, Peter C. Erb, trans. (New York: Paulist Press, 1979 [1606]), xiii.

138. Ibid., 23.

139. Shelley, *Church History*, 329.

140. Herman A. Hoyt, *All Things Whatsoever I have Commanded You* (Winona Lake, Ind.: Grace Theological Seminary, 1948), 55.

141. Stoffer, *Background and Development*, 19.

142. Broadbent, *The Pilgrim Church*, 282.

143. Philip Jacob Spener, *Pia Desideria*, Theodore G. Tappert, trans. (Eugene, Ore.: Wipf and Stock Publishers, 2002 [1675]), 88.

144. Ibid., 93.
145. Ibid., 96.
146. Ibid., 99.
147. Ibid., 103.
148. Ibid., 104.
149. Ibid., 115.
150. *Letter from One Friend to Another on the Question: What is Pietism?* William Willoughby, trans., in Floyd E. Mallott, *Studies in Brethren History* (Elgin, Ill.: Brethren Publishing House, 1954), 302.
151. Ibid., 319.
152. Bach, "The Agape in Brethren Tradition," in Stoffer, ed., *The Lord's Supper,* 162.
153. Stoffer, *Background and Development*, 253.
154. *The Brethren Encyclopedia*, 57.
155. *The Brethren Encyclopedia*, 614.
156. Durnbaugh, *European Origins*, 37.
157. Stoffer, *Background and Development*, 36-37.
158. Ernst Hochmann, *Confession of Faith*, in Martin G. Brumbaugh, *A History of the German Baptist Brethren in Europe and America* (Mount Morris, Ill.: Brethren Publishing House, 1899), 84.
159. Dale R. Stoffer, *Anabaptized Pietism: The Schwarzenau Brethren,* in Stephen L. Longenecker, ed., *The Dilemma of Anabaptist Piety* (Bridgewater, Va.: Penobscot Press, 1997), 41.
160. Task Force on Brethren History and Doctrine, *The Brethren: Growth in Life and Thought* (Ashland, Ohio: Board of Christian Education, 1975), 166.
161. Dale W. Brown, *Understanding Pietism* (Grantham, Pa.: Evangel House Publishing, 1996), 67.
162. Spener, *Pia Desideria*, 63.
163. Stoffer, *Anabaptized Pietism*, 39.
164. Hochmann, *Confession of Faith*, in Brumbaugh, *A History of the German Baptist Brethren*, 84.
165. Brown, *Understanding Pietism*, 48.
166. Ibid., 49.
167. August Francke, *A Guide to the Reading and Study of the Holy Scriptures* (Philadelphia: Hogan, 1823), 116.
168. Stoffer, *Background and Development*, 5.
169. Donald F. Durnbaugh, *Brethren Beginnings: The Origin of the Church of the Brethren in Early Eighteenth-Century Europe* (Philadelphia: The Brethren Encyclopedia, 1992), 64.

Notes for Chapter 6

170. *Peace of Augsburg,* Article 16. 1555.
171. Ibid., Article 17.
172. *Treaty of Westphalia*, Article XXVIII. 1648.
173. Ibid., Article XLIX.
174. Task Force on Brethren History and Doctrine, 6.
175. *Edict of the Elector Palatine* in Durnbaugh, ed., *European Origins*, 48-49.

176. Gillin, *The Dunkers*, 47.
177. Shelley, *Church History*, 304.
178. *Treaty of Westphalia*, Article LXIV.
179. Eberly, *The Complete Writings of Alexander Mack*, 1-2.
180. Stoffer, *Background and Development*, 66.
181. William G. Willoughby, *The Beliefs of the Early Brethren 1706-1735* (Philadelphia: The Brethren Encyclopedia,, 1999), 16.
182. Mack, *First Brethren Tract*, 10.
183. "*Hochmann von Hochenau to Grebe and Mack*, July 24, 1708. In Durnbaugh, *European Origins*, 113.
184. Ibid., 9.
185. Ibid., 13.
186. Lawrence W. Shultz, *Schwarzenau Yesterday and Today: Where the Brethren Church Began in Europe* (Milford, Ind.: Lawrence W. Shultz, 1977), 35.

Notes for Chapter 7

187. Holsinger, *History of the Tunkers*, 26.
188. Ibid., 27.
189. Mack, *Basic Questions*, 40.
190. Ibid.
191. Ibid., 37.
192. Ibid., 38.
193. Ibid.
194. Mack, *Rights and Ordinances*, in Eberly, ed., *The Complete Writings of Alexander Mack*, 52.
195. Donald F. Durnbaugh, *The Believers' Church: The History and Character of Radical Protestantism* (New York: The Macmillan Co., 1968), 32.
196. Mack, *Basic Questions*, 39.

Notes for Chapter 8

197. Mack, *Basic Questions*, 23.
198. Ibid.
199. Ibid., 24.
200. Brumbaugh, *A History of the German Baptist Brethren*, 549.
201. Mack, *Rights and Ordinances*, 48.
202. Ibid., 58.
203. Alexander Mack, Jr., introduction to the first American edition of his father's writings. In Alexander Mack, *A Plain View of the Rites and Ordinances of the House of God* (Mount Morris, Ill.: The Brethren's Publishing Co., 1888), ix.
204. Mack, *Rights and Ordinances*, 50, 57-58.
205. Willoughby, *Beliefs of the Early Brethren*, 66.
206. Stoffer, *Background and Development*, 74.
207. Mack, *Letter to Count Charles August*, in Eberly, ed., *The Complete Writings of Alexander Mack*, 19.
208. Hochmann, *Confession of Faith*, in John S. Flory, *Literary Activity of the German Baptist Brethren in the Eighteenth Century* (Elgin, Ill.: Brethren Publishing House, 1908), 6.

209. William G. Willoughby, *Counting the Cost: The Life of Alexander Mack* (Elgin, Ill.: The Brethren Press, 1979), 28-29.

210. Mack, *Basic Questions*, 31.

211. Mack, *Letter to Count Charles August,* 18.

212. John George Gichtel, *December 10, 1708,* in Durnbaugh, *European Origins,* 129.

213. Hochmann, *Hochmann von Hochenau to Count von Solms,* November 2, 1708. In Durnbaugh, *European Origins,* 126.

214. Mack, *Rights and Ordinances,* 59.

215. Ibid., 60.

216. Ibid.

217. Ibid., 45.

218. Leland Ryken, James C. Wilhoit, and Tremper Longman III, eds., *Dictionary of Biblical Imagery* (Downers Grove, Ill.: InterVarsity Press, 1998), 73.

219. Averbeck, "The Focus of Baptism in the New Testament," 290.

220. Mack, *The First Brethren Tract,* 12.

221. Averbeck, "The Focus of Baptism in the New Testament," 288.

222. R. V. G. Tasker, *The Gospel According to Matthew* (Grand Rapids: William B. Eerdmans Publishing Co., 1981), 275-276.

223. Mack, *Rights and Ordinances,* 48.

224. Ibid., 60.

225. Mack, *Basic Questions,* 35.

226. Ibid., 28.

227. Ibid., 35.

228. Willoughby, *Counting the Cost,* 96.

Notes for Chapter 9

229. Mack, *Rights and Ordinances,* 61.

230. Ibid., 62.

231. The German word used by Mack is *Haus-Vater* which literally means "father of the house."

232. Mack, *Rights and Ordinances,* 44.

233. Ibid., 61.

234. Ibid., 63.

235. L. S. Bauman, *The Faith Once for All Delivered unto the Saints* (Winona Lake, Ind.: BMH Books, 1977), 65. See also Exodus 40:12-15; 31.

236. Ibid., 43.

237. Joseph W. Beer, *The Jewish Passover and the Lord's Supper* (Lancaster, Pa.: Inquirer Printing and Publishing Co., 1874), 230.

238. Mack, *Rights and Ordinances,* 62.

239. Ibid., 63.

240. Ibid., 62.

241. Ibid.

242. Ibid., 61.

Notes for Chapter 10

243. Mack, *Rights and Ordinances*, 81.
244. Mack, *Letter to Count Charles August*, 19.
245. Mack, *Rights and Ordinances*, 94.
246. Mack, *Basic Questions*, 25-26.
247. Mack, *Rights and Ordinances*, 83.
248. Ibid., 95.
249. Mack, *Basic Questions*, 39.
250. Thomas Julien, "Brethrenism and Creeds," *Grace Theological Journal* 6 (Issue 2: 1985), 373.
251. Dale R. Stoffer, "The Brethren, Creeds, and the Heidelberg Catechism," *Old Order Notes* 22 (Fall-Winter: 2000), 7.
252. William Grahe, *Faithful Account*, in Durnbaugh, *European Origins*, 249-250.
253. The three questions Grahe cited are numbers 60, 74, and 101 in the *Heidelberg Cathechism*. Question 60 asks, "How are you righteous before God?" The Brethren would have objected to the section of its answer that stated that a believer is "still inclined to all evil," since they believed that full obedience was not only possible but expected. Question 74 reads, "Are infants also to be baptized?" and question 101 asks, "May we then swear religiously by the name of God?" The *Cathechism* answered both in the affirmative, but the Brethren would have disagreed strongly.
254. Willoughby, *Beliefs of the Early Brethren*, 77.
255. Stoffer, *Background and Development*, 68.
256. Mack, *Rights and Ordinances*, 83.
257. Mack, *Basic Questions*, 37.
258. Mack, *Rights and Ordinances*, 84.
259. Brumbaugh, *A History of the German Baptist Brethren*, 33.
260. Holsinger, *History of the Tunkers*, 207.
261. Emmert F. Bittinger, *Heritage and Promise: Perspectives on the Church of the Brethren* (Elgin, Ill.: Brethren Press, 1970), 87.

Notes for Chapter 11

262. Mack, *Rights and Ordinances*, 45.
263. Mack, *First Brethren Tract*, 10.
264. Mack, *Basic Questions*, 39.
265. Mack, *Rights and Ordinances*, 64.
266. Ibid., 66.
267. Ibid.
268. Mack, *Basic Questions*, 23.
269. Ibid.
270. Gillin, *The Dunkers*, 51.
271. Willoughby, *Counting the Cost*, 23-24.
272. Ibid., 25.
273. Mack, *Basic Questions*, 40.
274. Ibid.

Notes for Chapter 12

275. Donald F. Durnbaugh, *The Believers' Church*, 121.
276. Mack, *Letter to Count Charles August*, 18.
277. Ibid.
278. Durnbaugh, *The Believers' Church*, 11.
279. In Roman Catholic theology, the church was divided into three categories: The *church militant* was comprised of all believers on the earth still fighting for righteousness. The *church triumphant* was made up of those in heaven, having overcome sin. The *church suffering* or *expectant* was comprised of those who had not completely triumphed in earthly life and so were in Purgatory for a time before joining the church triumphant. Reformed theology substituted the *church latent*, the elect on earth who had not yet come to repentance and faith, for the church suffering.
280. Mack, *First Brethren Tract*, 10-11.
281. Ibid., 11.
282. Hochmann, *Confession of Faith*, in Flory, *Literary Activity*, 7-8.
283. Mack, *Basic Questions*, 41.
284. Mack, *Rights and Ordinances*, 71.
285. Mack, *Basic Questions*, 33.
286. Mack, *Rights and Ordinances*, 71.
287. Ibid., 69.
288. Hochmann, *Confession of Faith*, 7.
289. Mack, *Rights and Ordinances*, 54.
290. Ibid., 55.
291. Ibid.
292. Mack, *Basic Questions*, 39.
293. Mack, *Rights and Ordinances*, 53.
294. Ibid., 75.

Notes for Chapter 13

295. Mack, *Rights and Ordinances*, 89.
296. Mack included a discussion "on blood and strangled animals" in *Rights and Ordinances* (pp. 87-88). He also expressed his belief that there would be a real punishment of unbelievers, but that it would eventually end. However, they would never "attain that which the believers have achieved in the time of grace through Jesus Christ if they obey Him (*Rights and Ordinances*, 98).
297. *Count Charles Louis to Count Henry Albert, August 29, 1709*, in Durnbaugh, *European Origins*, 133.
298. *Treaty of Westphalia*, Article VII. 1648.
299. *Count Charles Louis to Imperial Solicitor, November 14, 1709*, in Durnbaugh, *European Origins*, 138.
300. *Edict of Count Ernest Casimir, March 22, 1712*, Article I, in Durnbaugh, *European Origins*, 152.
301. *Ysenburg Councilors to Deputy Administrator Wiszkemann, May 24, 1714*, in Durnbaugh, *European Origins*, 185.
302. John Lobach, *Autobiography*, in Durnbaugh, *European Origins*, 203.

303. *Minutes of the General Synod of the Reformed Church, July 9-16, 1716*, in Durnbaugh, *European Origins*, 204.

304. Grahe, *Faithful Account*, in Durnbaugh, *European Origins*, 257.

305. Ibid., 267.

306. Holsinger, *History of the Tunkers*, 121.

307. Ibid.

308. *Chronicon Ephratense; A History of the Community of Seventh Day Baptists at Ephrata, Lancaster County, Penn'a*, trans. J. Max Hark (Lancaster, Pa.: S. H. Zahm & Co., 1889), 249.

309. Durnbaugh, *European Origins*, 145.

310. Willoughby, *Counting the Cost*, 102.

311. *Imperial Solicitor to Frederick Christian Lade, May 13, 1720*, in Durnbaugh, *European Origins*, 290.

312. *Frederick Christian Lade to Imperial Solicitor, June 24, 1720*, in Durnbaugh, *European Origins*, 291.

313. William Penn, *Letter to Those Already Residing in Pennsylvania*, 1681.

314. William Penn, *Charter of Privileges Granted by William Penn, esq. to the Inhabitants of Pennsylvania and Territories, Article 1*, adopted October 28, 1701.

Notes for Chapter 14

315. *Chronicon Ephratense*, 15.

316. Holsinger, *History of the Tunkers*, 125.

317. *Chronicon Ephratense*, 22.

318. Ibid., 23.

319. Brumbaugh, *A History of the Brethren*, 289, 298.

320. *Chronicon Ephratense*, 25.

321. Ibid., 43.

322. Ibid.

323. Ibid., 48.

324. Ibid., 26.

325. Brumbaugh, *A History of the Brethren*, 299.

326. *Chronicon Ephratense*, 49-50.

327. Morgan Edwards, *Materials Towards a History of the Baptists in Pennsylvania both British and German* (Philadelphia: Joseph Crukshank and Isaac Collins, 1770), 68-90.

328. Gillin, *The Dunkers*, 108 and Bowman, *Brethren Society*, 74.

329. *Minutes of the Provincial Council of Pennsylvania from the Organization to the Termination of the Proprietary Government* (Philadelphia: Jo. Severns & Co., 1852), 283.

330. Durnbaugh, *Brethren in Colonial America*, 278-279.

331. The eleven groups, according to Zinzendorf's biographer, August Gottlieb Spangenberg (1704-1792), were Lutherans, Reformed, Quakers, Mennonites, Dunkers (Brethren), Sabbatarians (Ephrata), Schwenkfelders, Inspirationists, Separatists, hermits, and New Born. Durnbaugh, *Brethren in Colonial America*, 280-281.

332. Ibid., 284.

333. Brumbaugh, *A History of the Brethren*, 483-484.

334. These three were the Mennonites, Schwenkfelders, and Siebentagers (Sabbitarians). Ibid., 488.

335. Durnbaugh, *Brethren in Colonial America*, 287.

336. Ibid., 428-429.

Notes for Chapter 15

337. Edwards, *History of the Baptists in Pennsylvania*, iv.

338. *Constitution of Pennsylvania*. September 28, 1776.

339. Ibid., *Section 45*.

340. James T. Mitchell and Henry Flanders, *The Statutes at Large of Pennsylvania from 1682 to 1801, Volume IX* (State Printer of Pennsylvania: Wm. Stanley Ray, 1903), 111-112.

341. Ibid., 112-113.

342. Ibid., 113.

343. Ibid., 110.

344. Ibid., 111.

345. Brumbaugh, *A History of the Brethren*, 418.

346. Annual Meeting 1778, Art. 1. *Classified Minutes of the Annual Meetings of the Brethren* (Mt. Morris, Ill. and Huntingdon, Pa.: The Brethren's Publishing Co., 1886), 269.

347. Annual Meeting 1779, Art. 1. Ibid., 270.

348. Brumbaugh, *A History of the Brethren*, 414.

349. Ibid., 419.

350. Annual Meeting 1781, Art. 1. *Classified Minutes*, 282.

351. Annual Meeting 1785, Art. 2 and 1817, Art. 5. *Classified Minutes*, 277.

352. Annual Meeting 1813, Art. 2. *Classified Minutes*, 266.

353. Peter Bowman, *A Testimony on Baptism*, in Roger E. Sappington, ed., *The Brethren in a New Nation* (Elgin, Ill.: The Brethren Press, 1976), 133-134.

354. Peter Nead, *Theological Writings on Various Subjects or a Vindication of Primitive Christianity* (Dayton: New Edition, 1866), 353-354.

355. Ibid., 354.

Notes for Chapter 16

356. Brumbaugh, *A History of the Brethren*, 528.

357. *The Brethren Encyclopedia*, 1413 -1415.

358. Ibid.

359. Brumbaugh, *A History of the Brethren*, 530.

360. Otho Winger, *History and Doctrines of the Church of the Brethren*, (Elgin, Ill.: Brethren Publishing House, 1920), 95.

361. Holsinger, *History of the Tunkers*, 763.

362. Henry Kurtz, *The Brethren's Encyclopedia: Containing the United Counsels and Conclusions of the Brethren at Their Annual Meetings* (Columbiana, Ohio: By the author, 1867), 10.

363. Winger, *History and Doctrines of the Church of the Brethren*, 193.

364. Brumbaugh, *A History of the Brethren*, 479.

365. Annual Meeting 1837, Art. 3. Kurtz, *The Brethren's Encyclopedia*, 12. Also, Annual Meeting, 1848, Art. 29. *Classified Minutes*, 9.

366. *Classified Minutes*, v-vi.
367. Kurtz, *The Brethren's Encylcopedia*, v-vi.
368. Ibid., vi.
369. Annual Meeting 1805, Art. 2. *Classified Minutes*, 28.
370. Annual Meeting 1848, Art. 17. *Classified Minutes*, 31.
371. Annual Meeting 1850, Art. 28. *Classified Minutes* , 54.
372. Ibid., v.
373. Bowman, *Brethren Society*, 96.
374. Annual Meeting 1831, Art. 1. Kurtz, *The Brethren's Encyclopedia*, 87.
375. Annual Meeting 1836, Art. 6. Kurtz, 154.
376. Holsinger, *History of the Tunkers*, 470.
377. Ibid., 416.
378. Annual Meeting 1852, Art. 8. *Classified Minutes*, 301.
379. Annual Meeting 1860, Art. 1. *Classified Minutes*, 302-304.
380. Ibid., 304.

Notes for Chapter 17

381. Benjamin Funk, *The Life and Labors of Elder John Kline the Missionary Martyr* (Elgin, Ill.: Brethren Publishing House, 1900), 438.
382. *Classified Minutes*, 384-385, 398.
383. Annual Meeting 1782, Art. 1. *Classified Minutes* , 372-373.
384. Annual Meeting 1797, Art. 1. *Classified Minutes* , 373.
385. Annual Meeting 1854, Art. 1. *Classified Minutes*, 376.
386. Annual Meeting 1863, Art. 5. *Classified Minutes*, 376-377.
387. Annual Meeting 1864, Art. 35. *Classified Minutes*, 281.
388. Annual Meeting 1863, Art. 17. *Classified Minutes*, 283.
389. Funk, *Elder John Kline*, 448-453.
390. Ibid., 461-462.
391. Sappington, *The Brethren in a New Nation*, 394.
392. *The Brethren's Reason for Producing and Adopting the Resolutions of August 24, 1881*, in Holsinger, *History of the Tunkers*, 416.
393. Stoffer, *Background and Development*, 142.
394. *Miami Valley Elders' Petition*, November 25, 1879, in Holsinger, *History of the Tunkers*, 436.
395. Ibid., 437. "The single mode of feet-washing" referred to the practice of one person washing and wiping the feet of another. The Old Orders were convinced that the apostolic mode which had been practiced among the Brethren from the beginning was the double mode in which one person washed and a second person wiped.
396. Ibid., 440.
397. *Report of Standing Committee to 1880 Annual Meeting*, Ibid., 442.
398. *The Brethren's Reason*, in Roger E. Sappington, ed., *The Brethren in Industrial America* (Elgin, Ill.: Brethren Press, 1985), 377.
399. Ibid.
400. Holsinger, *History of the Tunkers*, 448.
401. *The Brethren's Reason*, 383.
402. Ibid., 384.

403. Ibid., 385.

404. Ibid., 388.

405. Holsinger, *History of the Tunkers*, 472.

406. Annual Meeting 1865, Art. 51. *Classified Minutes*, 324.

407. Holsinger, *History of the Tunkers*, 477.

408. Ibid., 473.

409. Ibid., 475.

410. Annual Meeting 1870, Art. 7. *Classified Minutes*, 357-358.

411. Annual Meeting 1873, Art. 8. *Classified Minutes*, 358-359.

412. Holsinger, *History of the Tunkers*, 484.

413. Annual Meeting 1879, Art. 16. *Classified Minutes*, 325-326.

414. Holsinger, *History of the Tunkers*, 495.

415. Annual Meeting 1881, Art. 4. *Classified Minutes*, 367.

416. Ibid., 369.

417. Annual Meeting 1882, Art. 32. *Classified Minutes*, 372.

418. Holsinger, *History of the Tunkers*, 526.

419. Ibid., 527.

420. Ibid., 528.

421. Ibid., 529.

Notes for Chapter 18

422. Annual Meeting 1882, Art. 5. *Classified Minutes*, 31.

423. *Declaration of Principles Adopted by the Progressive Convention of the Tunker Church, June 29-30, 1882*, in Holsinger, *History of the Tunkers*, 534.

424. *Proceedings of the Dayton Convention, June 6, 1883.* Ibid., 541.

425. Bowman, *Brethren Society*, 130.

426. *Declaration of Principles,* in Holsinger, *History of the Tunkers*, 536.

427. *Report of Progressive Convention, June 29-30, 1882,* in Ronk, *History of the Brethren Church*, 152.

428. Henry R. Holsinger and Stephen Bashor, "Progressive Unity – Our Principles Defined," *Progressive Christian* 3 (No. 37: 1881), in Ronk, *History of the Brethren Church*, 135.

429. Ibid., 136.

430. *Declaration of Principles,* in Holsinger, *History of the Tunkers*, 531-532.

431. *Proceedings of the Dayton Convention,* in Ronk, *History of the Brethren Church*, 163.

432. *Convention Proceedings* (Ashland, Ohio: Brethren Publishing House, 1887), 20.

433. Holsinger, *History of the Tunkers*, 546-547.

434. Ronk, *History of the Brethren Church*, 232.

435. *A Manual of Church Expediency for the Brethren Church,* in Ronk, *History of the Brethren Church*, 234-242.

436. Annual Meeting 1867, Art. 30. *Classified Minutes*, 306.

437. Annual Meeting 1860, Art. 1. *Classified Minutes*, 303-304.

438. Annual Meeting 1877, Art. 7. *Classified Minutes*, 312.

439. Annual Meeting 1879, Art. 3. *Classified Minutes*, 313.

440. Annual Meeting 1881, Art. 30. *Classified Minutes*, 309.

441. *Declaration of Principles,* in Holsinger, *History of the Tunkers*, 532.

442. Holsinger, *History of the Tunkers*, 545.

443. *Declaration of Principles,* in ibid., 531.

444. Albert T. Ronk, *History of the Brethren Missionary Movements* (Ashland, Ohio: Brethren Publishing Co., 1971), 33-35.

445. Homer A. Kent, Sr., *250 Years . . . Conquering Frontiers: A History of the Brethren Church* (Winona Lake, Ind.: The Brethren Missionary Herald Co., 1958), 121.

446. *Constitution of the Foreign Missionary Society of the Brethren Church, September 4, 1900,* in Ronk, *History of the Brethren Missionary Movements,* 49.

447. Benjamin Franklin, *The Autobiography of Benjamin Franklin* (Mineola, N.Y.: Dover Publications, Inc., 1996), 91.

448. R. H. Miller, *Doctrines of the Brethren Defended* (Indianapolis: Printing and Publishing House, 1876), Preface.

449. *Declaration of Principles,* 531.

450. Ibid., 532.

451. Holsinger, *History of the Tunkers*, 546.

452. Ronk, *History of the Brethren Church*, 201-203.

453. *Convention Proceedings*, 36.

454. Clara Worst Miller and E. Glenn Mason, *A Short History of Ashland College to 1953* (Ashland, Ohio: The Brethren Publishing Co., 1953), 34.

455. John Lewis Gillin, "Our Denominational Position," *The Brethren Evangelist* XXXIII (No. 34: September 30, 1911), 6.

456. Alva J. McClain, "The Background and Origin of Grace Theological Seminary," *Charis* (Grace Seminary Yearbook, 1951), 12.

Notes for Chapter 19

457. R. A. Torrey, A. C. Dixon, and others, eds., *The Fundamentals: A Testimony to the Truth* (Grand Rapids, Mich.: Baker Books, 2003), 5. The two laymen were later identified as Lyman Stewart, the founder of Biola University, and his brother Milton.

458. Conference Minutes 1915.

459. C. F. Yoder, *God's Means of Grace* (Elgin, Ill.: Brethren Publishing House, 1908), 124.

460. Ibid., 188.

461. Ibid., 296.

462. W. O. Baker, *A Treatise on Washing the Saints' Feet* (Ashland, Ohio: Brethren Publishing House, 1893), 29.

463. *A Manual of Procedure for Brethren Churches,* in Ronk, *History of the Brethren Church*, 343.

464. *The Message of the Brethren Ministry,* in Plaster, *Finding Our Focus*, 92-93.

465. Stoffer, *Background and Development*, 231.

466. Ronk, *History of the Brethren Church*, 368.

467. McClain, "The Background and Origin of Grace Theological Seminary," 12.

468. Conference Minutes, 1921, 16.

469. Ronk, *History of the Brethren Church*, 324.

470. Ibid., 390. Dispensationalism is a theological system that believes in the literal fulfillment of God's promises to both Israel and the church. For this reason, it emphasizes a premillennial view of the future in which Christ will physically return to the earth and establish His kingdom for a period of 1,000 years. Calvinism stresses the work of God in accomplishing His salvation in those whom He chooses. As a result, believers have unconditional security, the promise that they can never lose their salvation.

471. Stoffer, *Background and Development*, 185.

472. Task Force on Brethren History and Doctrine, *The Brethren: Growth in Life and Thought* (Ashland, Ohio: Board of Christian Education, The Brethren Church, 1975), 91.

473. McClain, "The Background and Origin of Grace Theological Seminary," 12.

474. Ibid., 12.

475. Ibid., 16-17.

476. Ibid., 17.

477. Ibid., 19.

478. Ibid., 20.

479. Ibid.

480. Ibid., 21.

481. Ibid.

482. Ibid.

483. Ibid.

484. Kent, *Conquering Frontiers*, 137.

485. Ronk, *History of the Brethren Church*, 413.

486. McClain, *The Brethren Evangelist* LVI (No. 37: September 29, 1934), 8.

487. McClain, "The Background and Origin of Grace Theological Seminary," 24.

488. Charles Anspach, *The Brethren Evangelist* LVII (No. 22: June 1, 1935), 6.

489. Anspach, *A Voice Speaks: Addresses and Prologues* (Mount Pleasant, Mich.: Central Michigan University, 1976), 14.

490. Ronk, *History of the Brethren Church*, 415.

491. McClain, "The Background and Origin of Grace Theological Seminary," 24.

492. McClain, *The Brethren Evangelist* LXI (No. 31: August 5, 1939), 25.

493. McClain, "The Background and Origin of Grace Theological Seminary," 24.

494. Kent, *Conquering Frontiers*, 139.

495. Anspach, *The Brethren Evangelist* LVIII (No. 25: June 27, 1936), 15.

496. *Open Letter to Professor Charles L. Anspach,* in Kent, *Conquering Frontiers*, 140-142.

497. *C. L. Anspach to Paul L. Bauman, Secretary of the Southern California Ministerial Examining Board,* in Ronk, *History of the Brethren Church*, 419.

498. Conference Minutes 1936, 9-10.

499. McClain, "The Background and Origin of Grace Theological Seminary," 26.

500. Ronk, *History of the Brethren Church*, 422.

501. "Trustee Committee Reply to Statement of Cal. 1938," in ibid., 423.

502. McClain, "The Background and Origin of Grace Theological Seminary," 30.

Notes for Chapter 20

503. McClain, "The Background and Origin of Grace Theological Seminary," 34.
504. Ronk, *History of the Brethren Church*, 390.
505. Ibid., 416-417.
506. Conference Minutes 1938, 20.
507. R. Paul Miller, *The Brethren Evangelist* LX (No. 34: August 20, 1938), 3.
508. Kent, *Conquering Frontiers*, 158.
509. Charles Mayes, *The Brethren Evangelist* LX (No. 39: October 1, 1938), 5.
510. Ronk, *History of the Brethren Church*, 429.
511. Bauman, *The Brethren Evangelist* LXI (No. 1: January 7, 1939), 4.
512. Hoyt, *The Brethren Evangelist* LXI (No. 14: April 8, 1939), 14.
513. George T. Ronk, "The Antinomian Controversy in the Brethren Church," *The Brethren Evangelist* LXI (No. 15: April 15, 1939), 10. The term antinomian literally means "one who is against law."
514. Conference Minutes 1939, 8.
515. McClain, "The Background and Origin of Grace Theological Seminary," 35.
516. Mayes, *The Brethren Evangelist* LXI (No. 35: September 9, 1939), 3.
517. McClain, "An Analysis of the Dayton Decision," *Brethren Missionary Herald* (March 8, 1941), 2.
518. Kent, *Conquering Frontiers*, 170.
519. Stoffer, *Background and Development*, 232.
520. Kent, *Conquering Frontiers*, 172.
521. McClain, *The Brethren Evangelist* LVI (No. 37: September 29, 1934), 2.
522. Ibid.
523. McClain, "The Background and Origin of Grace Theological Seminary," 29.
524. Ibid., 33.
525. *Covenant of Faith of Grace Seminary* 1938.
526. Hoyt, *All Things Whatsoever I have Commanded You*, 10.
527. Nead, *Theological Writings*, 64.
528. Kent, *Conquering Frontiers*, 186-189.
529. Ibid., 189-192.
530. McClain, "The Background and Origin of Grace Theological Seminary," 32. By McClain's reckoning, all but two students made the change from Ashland to Grace.
531. McClain, "A Comparative Study in Statistics," *Brethren Missionary Herald* (January 23, 1954), 52.
532. *The Brethren Encyclopedia*, 1466.
533. Kent, *Conquering Frontiers*, 173.
534. Ibid., 178-183.
535. Gillin, *The Dunkers*, 51.
536. Robert G. Clouse, "The Grace Brethren," in Donald F. Durnbaugh, ed., *Meet the Brethren* (Elgin, Ill.: The Brethren Press for the Brethren Encyclopedia, 1984), 109.
537. Herman A. Hoyt, *This Do in Remembrance of Me* (Winona Lake, Ind.: Grace Theological Seminary, 1947), 7.
538. Bauman, *The Faith Once for All Delivered unto the Saints*, 53.
539. Ibid., 82.

540. Ronald T. Clutter, "The Development of Grace Theological Seminary and the Division of the Brethren Church," *Grace Theological Journal* 10 (No. 1: Spring 1989), 65-66.
541. Plaster, *Finding our Focus*, 152.
542. Hoyt, *This Do in Remembrance of Me*, 46.
543. Hoyt, Ibid., 57.

Notes for Chapter 21

544. Gillin, *The Dunkers*, 63.
545. Ibid., 132.
546. *Conference Minutes, Brethren Annual* 1960, 20.
547. Ibid.
548. *District Court of the State of Iowa, in and for Decatur County,* January 28, 1957, in Kent, *Conquering Frontiers*, 217.
549. Ibid., 226-227.
550. McClain, *Letter to Pastors in the Brethren Church,* June 25, 1959. A copy of the letter may be found in the Grace Seminary Archives, Winona Lake, Ind..
551. *Conference Minutes, Brethren Annual* 1960, 21.
552. McClain, "Letter to Pastors in the Brethren Church."
553. James Sweeton, *Trine Immersion in the Light of Scripture and Church History* (Winona Lake, Ind.: BMH Books, 1979), 39.
554. *Conference Minutes, Brethren Annual* 1963, 26.
555. Plaster, *Finding our Focus*, 151.
556. Annual Meeting 1804, Art. 7. *Classified Minutes*, 158.
557. Annual Meeting 1821, Art. 6. Ibid.
558. Annual Meeting 1834, Art. 4. Ibid., 159.
559. *Conference Minutes, Brethren Annual* 1964, 23.
560. *Statement of Faith of the National Fellowship of Brethren Churches*, Article 9.
561. David Hocking, "The Time is Now!" *Brethren Missionary Herald* 41 (April 1979), 32.
562. *Conference Minutes, Brethren Annual* 1981, 15-16.
563. *Conference Minutes, Brethren Annual* 1978, 5.
564. Plaster, *Finding our Focus*, 161.
565. *Conference Minutes, Brethren Annual* 1981, 16.
566. *Conference Minutes, Brethren Annual* 1982, 9.
567. *Howard Mayes to David Plaster,* July 1, 1982. Files of the Two-Year Study Committee.
568. *Bob Thompson to Knute Larson,* December 21, 1982. Ibid.
569. *Conference Minutes, Brethren Annual* 1984, 26.
570. Plaster, "Minutes of the Two-Year Study Committee, May 24, 1982," in Files of the Two-Year Study Committee.
571. *Tom Julien to Luke Kauffman*, January 18, 1983. Files of the Two-Year Study Committee.
572. Plaster, *Finding our Focus*, 166-167.
573. James L. Boyer, "Brethren Baptism Notes" (Winona Lake, Ind.: Conservative Grace Brethren Association, 1991), 11.
574. *Conference Minutes, Brethren Annual* 1990, 24.

575. Boyer, "Brethren Baptism Notes," 23.
576. Ibid., 26.
577. Plaster, *Finding our Focus*, 167.
578. Ibid., 167-168.
579. Charles Turner, "Projections for 1992 National Conference: An Interview with Jim Custer," *Brethren Missionary Herald* 54 (May 15, 1992), 6.
580. *Conference Minutes, Brethren Annual* 1993, 9.
581. Plaster, *Finding our Focus*, 169.
582. *Conference Minutes, Brethren Annual* 1993, 23.
583. "C.G.B.A.'s Response to Decisions at National Conference," *Brethren Missionary Herald* 54 (September 15, 1992), 15. Gary Crandall, pastor of the San Jose, California, church, read the statement following a report that Fellowship Council had denied the Conservative Grace Brethren Association's request to be accepted as a cooperating organization to the Conference.
584. *Conference Minutes, Brethren Annual* 1993, 15.
585. Plaster, *Finding our Focus*, 171.
586. Ibid., 159 and 170.
587. Robert G. Clouse, "Brethren and Modernity: Change and Development in the Progressive/Grace Church," *Brethren Life and Thought* 33 (Summer 1988), 205.
588. Ibid., 216.

Notes for Chapter 22

589. Plaster, *Finding our Focus*, 173.
590. Ibid.
591. Tom Julien, "Seeds of Springtime," *Brethren Missionary Herald* 55 (March 15, 1993), 9.
592. McClain, *Brethren Missionary Herald* 2 (January 6, 1940), 2.
593. Plaster, *Finding our Focus*, 174.
594. *BMH Mission Statement.* Adopted 2002.
595. Julien, "Seeds of Springtime," 9.
596. *Constitution for the Fellowship of Grace Brethren Churches*, Article III, Section One. Adopted by Conference, July 1997.
597. Ibid., Article III, Section Two.
598. Ibid., Article XII, Section Two.
599. Ibid., Article III, Section Two.

Notes for Chapter 23

600. Mack, *Basic Questions*, 38-39.
601. Alva J. McClain, *Law and Grace* (Winona Lake, Ind.: BMH Books, 1954), 53.

Selected Bibliography

Anspach, Charles. 1976. *A Voice Speaks: Addresses and Prologues.* Mount Pleasant, Mich.: Central Michigan University.

Arndt, Johann. 1979 [1606]. *True Christianity.* Translated by Peter C. Erb. New York: Paulist Press.

Averbeck, Richard E. 1981. "The Focus of Baptism in the New Testament." *Grace Theological Journal* 2, Issue 2: 265-301.

Baker, W. O. 1893. *A Treatise on Washing the Saints' Feet.* Ashland, Ohio: Brethren Publishing House.

Bauman, L. S. 1977. *The Faith Once for All Delivered unto the Saints.* Winona Lake, Ind.: BMH Books.

Beer, Joseph W. 1874. *The Jewish Passover and the Lord's Supper.* Lancaster, Pa.: Inquirer Printing and Publishing Company.

Bittinger, Emmert F. 1983. *Heritage and Promise: Perspectives on the Church of the Brethren.* Elgin, Ill.: Brethren Press.

Bowman, Carl F. 1995. *Brethren Society: The Cultural Transformation of a "Peculiar People."* Baltimore: The Johns Hopkins University Press.

Boyer, James L. 1991. *Brethren Baptism Notes.* Winona Lake Ind.: Conservative Grace Brethren Association.

The Brethren Encyclopedia. 3 vols. [1983]. Philadelphia and Oak Brook, Ill.: The Brethren Encyclopedia, Inc.

Broadbent, E. H. 1999. *The Pilgrim Church.* Grand Rapids: Gospel Folio Press.

Brown, Dale W. 1996. *Understanding Pietism.* Grantham, Pa.: Evangel House Publishing.

Bruce, F. F. 1988. *The Book of Acts.* Grand Rapids: William B. Eerdmans Publishing Company.

Brumbaugh, Martin G. 1899. *A History of the German Baptist Brethren in Europe and America.* Mount Morris, Ill.: Brethren Publishing House.

Chronicon Ephratense: A History of the Community of Seventh Day Baptists at Ephrata, Lancaster County, Penn'a. 1889. Translated by J. Max Hark. Lancaster, Pa.: S. H. Zahm & Co.

Classified Minutes of the Annual Meetings of the Brethren. 1886. Mt. Morris, Ill. and Huntingdon, Pa.: The Brethren's Publishing Company.

Clutter, Ronald T. 1989. "The Development of Grace Theological Seminary and the Division of the Brethren Church." *Grace Theological Journal* 10 (No. 1: Spring).

Convention Proceedings. 1887. Ashland, Ohio: Brethren Publishing House.

Durnbaugh, Donald F., ed. 1958. *European Origins of the Brethren*. Elgin, Ill.: The Brethren Press.

_____. ed. 1967. *The Brethren in Colonial America*. Elgin, Ill.: The Brethren Press.

_____. 1968. *The Believers' Church: The History and Character of Radical Protestantism*. New York: The Macmillan Company.

_____. ed. 1984. *Meet the Brethren*. Elgin, Ill.: The Brethren Press for the Brethren Encyclopedia.

_____. 1992. *Brethren Beginnings: The Origin of the Church of the Brethren in Early Eighteenth-Century Europe*. Philadelphia: The Brethren Encyclopedia, Inc.

Eberly, William R., ed. 1991. *The Complete Writings of Alexander Mack*. Winona Lake, Ind.: BMH Books.

Edwards, Morgan. 1770. *Materials towards a History of the Baptists in Pennsylvania both British and German*. Philadelphia: Joseph Crukshank and Isaac Collins.

Estep, William R. 1996. *The Anabaptist Story: An Introduction to Sixteenth Century Anabaptism*. Grand Rapids: William B. Eerdmans Publishing Company.

Flory, John S. 1908. *Literary activity of the German Baptist Brethren in the Eighteenth Century*. Elgin, Ill.: Brethren Publishing House.

Francke, August. 1823. *A Guide to the Reading and Study of the Holy Scriptures*. Philadelphia: Hogan.

Franklin, Benjamin. 1996. *The Autobiography of Benjamin Franklin*. Mineola, N.Y.: Dover Publications, Inc.

Funk, Benjamin. 1900. *The Life and Labors of Elder John Kline the Missionary Martyr*. Elgin, Ill.: Brethren Publishing House.

Gillin, John Lewis. 1906. *The Dunkers: A Sociological Interpretation*. New York: AMS Press Inc.

_____. 1911. "Our Denominational Position." *The Brethren Evangelist* XXXIII (No. 34: September 30).

Gonzalez, Justo. 1984. *The Story of Christianity: Volume 1, the Early Church to the Dawn of the Reformation*. San Francisco: Harper & Row.

_____. 1984. *The Story of Christianity: Volume 2, the Reformation to the Present Day*. San Francisco: Harper & Row.

Harrison, Everett F. 1975. *Acts: The Expanding Church*. Chicago: Moody Press.

Holsinger, Henry R. 1901. *History of the Tunkers and the Brethren Church*. Oakland: Pacific Press Publishing Company.

Hoyt, Herman A. 1947. *This Do in Remembrance of Me*. Winona Lake, Ind.: Grace Theological Seminary.

_____. 1948. *All Things Whatsoever I have Commanded You*. Winona Lake, Ind.: Grace Theological Seminary.

Julien, Thomas. 1985. "Brethrenism and Creeds." *Grace Theological Journal* 6 (Fall): 373-381.

Keener, Craig S. 1993. *The IVP Bible Background Commentary: New Testament*. Downers Grove, Ill.: InterVarsity Press.

Kent, Homer A., Jr. 1972. *Jerusalem to Rome: Studies in Acts*. Winona Lake, Ind.: BMH Books.

_____. 1981. *Studies in the Gospel of Mark*. Winona Lake, Ind.: BMH Books.

Kent, Homer A., Sr. 1958. *250 years . . . Conquering Frontiers: A History of the Brethren Church*. Winona Lake, Ind.: The Brethren Missionary Herald Company.

Kurtz, Henry. 1867. *The Brethren's Encyclopedia: Containing the United Counsels and Conclusions of the Brethren at Their Annual Meetings*. Columbiana, Ohio: By the author.

Longenecker, Stephen L., ed. *The Dilemna of Anabaptist Piety*. Bridgewater, Va.: Penobscot Press.

Mack, Alexander. 1888. *A Plain View of the Rites and Ordinances of the House of God*. Mount Morris, Ill.: The Brethren's Publishing Company.

Mallott, Floyd E. 1954. *Studies in Brethren History*. Elgin, Ill.: Brethren Publishing House.

Marshall, I. Howard. 1982. *The Acts of the Apostles*. Grand Rapids: Wm. B. Eerdmans Publishing Company.

McClain, Alva J. 1951. "The Background and Origin of Grace Theological Seminary." *Charis* (Grace Seminary Yearbook).

_____. 1954. *Law and Grace*. Winona Lake, Ind.: BMH Books.

Miller, Clara Worst and E. Glenn Mason. 1953. *A Short History of Ashland College to 1953*. Ashland, Ohio: The Brethren Publishing Company.

Miller, R. H. 1876. *Doctrines of the Brethren Defended*. Indianapolis: Printing and Publishing House.

Minutes of the Provincial Council of Pennsylvania from the Organization to the Termination of the Proprietary Government. 1852. Philadelphia: Jo. Severns & Co.

Mitchell, James T. and Henry Flanders. 1903. *The Statutes at Large of Pennsylvania from 1682 to 1901, Volume IX*. State Printer of Pennsylvania: Wm. Stanley Ray.

Moore, J. H. 1915. *The New Testament Doctrines*. Elgin, Ill.: Brethren Publishing House.

Nead, Peter. 1866. *Theological Writings on Various Subjects or a Vindication of Primitive Christianity*. Dayton: New Edition.

Plaster, David R. 2003. *Finding our Focus: A History of the Grace Brethren Church*. Winona Lake, Ind.: BMH Books.

Quinter, James. 1886. *A Vindication of Trine Immersion as the Apostolic Form of Christian Baptism*. Huntingdon, Pa.: The Brethren's Publishing Company.

Rempel, John D. 1993. *The Lord's Supper in Anabaptism*. Scottdale, Pa.: Herald Press.

Ronk, Albert T. 1968. *History of the Brethren Church: Its Life, Thought, Mission*. Ashland, Ohio: Brethren Publishing Company.

_____. 1971. *History of the Brethren Missionary Movements*. Ashland, Ohio: Brethren Publishing Company.

Ryken, Leland, James C. Wilhoit, and Tremper Longman III, eds. 1998. *Dictionary of Biblical Imagery*. Downers Grove, Ill.: InterVarsity Press.

Sappington, Roger E., ed. 1976. *The Brethren in a New Nation*. Elgin, Ill.: The Brethren Press.

_____. ed. 1985. *The Brethren in Industrial America*. Elgin, Ill.: Brethren Press.

Schaff, Philip. 1979. *History of the Christian Church: Volume III, Nicene and Post-Nicene Christianity*. Grand Rapids: Wm. B. Eerdmans Publishing Company.

_____. 1979. *History of the Christian Church: Volume VII, Modern Christianity: The German Reformation*. Grand Rapids: Wm. B. Eerdmans Publishing Company.

_____. 1979. *History of the Christian Church: Volume VIII, Modern Christianity: The Swiss Reformation*. Grand Rapids: Wm. B. Eerdmans Publishing Company.

Shelley, Bruce L. 1995. *Church History in Plain Language*. Dallas: Word Publishing.

Shultz, Joseph R. 1966. *The Soul of the Symbols: A Theological Study of Holy Communion*. Grand Rapids: William B. Eerdmans Publishing Company.

Shultz, Lawrence W. 1977. *Schwarzenau Yesterday and Today: Where the Brethren Church Began in Europe*. Milford, Ind.: Lawrence W. Shultz.

Spener, Philip Jacob. 2002 [1675]. *Pia Desideria*. Translated by Theodore G. Tappert. Eugene. Ore.: Wipf and Stock Publishers.

Stoffer, Dale R. 1989. *Background and Development of Brethren Doctrines 1650-1987*. Philadelphia: The Brethren Encyclopedia, Inc.

_____. ed. 1997. *The Lord's Supper: Believers Church Perspectives*. Scottdale, Pa.: Herald Press.

_____. 2000. "The Brethren, Creeds, and the Heidelberg Catechism." *Old Order Notes* 22 (Fall-Winter): 7-20.

Strege, Merle D. 1986. *Baptism & Church: A believers' Church Vision.* Grand Rapids: Sagamore Books.

Sweeton, James. 1979. *Trine Immersion in the Light of Scripture and Church History.* Winona Lake, Ind.: BMH Books.

Task Force on Brethren History and Doctrine. 1975. *The Brethren: Growth in Life and Thought.* Ashland, Ohio: Board of Christian Education.

Tasker, R. V. G. 1981. *The Gospel According to Matthew.* Grand Rapids: Wm. B. Eerdmans Publishing Company.

Torrey, R. A., A. C. Dixon, and others, eds. 2003. *The Fundamentals: A Testimony to the Truth.* Grand Rapids: Baker Books.

Van Braght, Thieleman J. 2004 [1660]. *Martyrs Mirror.* Translated by Joseph F. Sohm. Scottdale, Pa.: Herald Press.

Willoughby, William G. 1979. *Counting the Cost: The Life of Alexander Mack.* Elgin, Ill.: The Brethren Press.

_____. 1999. *The Beliefs of the Early Brethren 1706-1735.* Philadelphia: The Brethren Encyclopedia, Inc.

Winger, Otho. 1919. *History and Doctrines of the Church of the Brethren.* Elgin, Ill.: Brethren Publishing House.

Yoder, C. F. 1908. *God's Means of Grace.* Elgin, Ill.: Brethren Publishing House.